INSTANT CITY

INSTANT **CITY**

LIFE AND DEATH IN KARACHI

STEVE INSKEEP

THE PENGUIN PRESS | *New York* | *2011*

THE PENGUIN PRESS
Published by the Penguin Group
Penguin Group (USA) Inc., 375 Hudson Street, New York, New York 10014, U.S.A. • Penguin Group (Canada),
90 Eglinton Avenue East, Suite 700, Toronto, Ontario, Canada M4P 2Y3 (a division of Pearson Penguin Canada
Inc.) • Penguin Books Ltd, 80 Strand, London WC2R 0RL, England • Penguin Ireland, 25 St. Stephen's Green, Dublin 2,
Ireland (a division of Penguin Books Ltd) • Penguin Books Australia Ltd, 250 Camberwell Road, Camberwell, Victoria
3124, Australia (a division of Pearson Australia Group Pty Ltd) • Penguin Books India Pvt Ltd, 11 Community Centre,
Panchsheel Park, New Delhi – 110 017, India • Penguin Group (NZ), 67 Apollo Drive, Rosedale, Auckland 0632,
New Zealand (a division of Pearson New Zealand Ltd) • Penguin Books (South Africa) (Pty) Ltd, 24 Sturdee Avenue,
Rosebank, Johannesburg 2196, South Africa

Penguin Books Ltd, Registered Offices: 80 Strand, London WC2R 0RL, England

First published in 2011 by The Penguin Press, a member of Penguin Group (USA) Inc.

Photographs by the author unless otherwise credited.

LIBRARY OF CONGRESS CATALOGING IN PUBLICATION DATA

Inskeep, Steve.
  Instant city : life and death in Karachi / Steve Inskeep.
    p. cm.
  Includes bibliographical references and index.
  ISBN 978-1-59420-315-2
  1. Karachi (Pakistan)—Description and travel.   2. Karachi (Pakistan)—Social conditions.   3. Urbanization—
Pakistan—Karachi.   4. Bombings—Pakistan—Karachi.   I. Title.
  DS392.2.K3I56 2011
  954.91'83—dc23   2011020673

Printed in the United States of America

10 9 8 7 6 5 4 3 2 1

DESIGNED BY NICOLE LAROCHE

FOR CAROLEE,

who put up with the author and his absences

CONTENTS

A NOTE ON SPELLING

English transliterations of South Asian names evolve. The province that includes Karachi, for example, was Sind in 1947 and is Sindh today. While I have used modern spellings, any quoted material preserves the spelling from the original source.

Many boys in Karachi stand in traffic holding birds. The birds hop up and down in little nets. The boys hop between cars, offering the birds for sale. If a driver is having a hard day, or a hard life, and wants to do a good deed to gain the favor of God, he rolls down the window to pass a boy a few bills. Having collected this ransom, the boy sets a captive bird free.

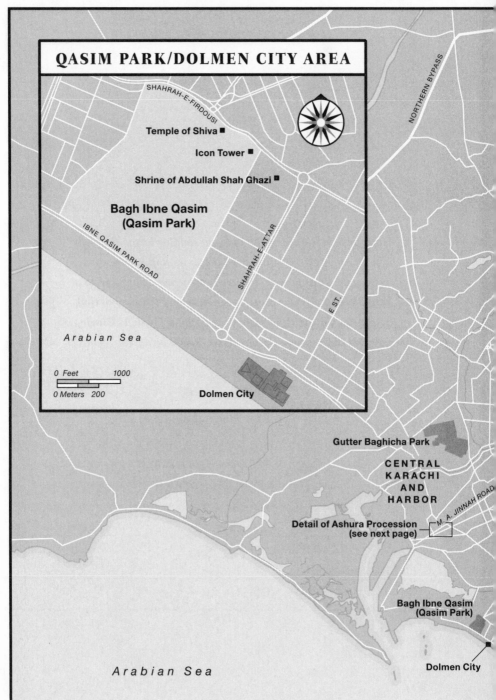

© 2011 Jeffrey L. Ward

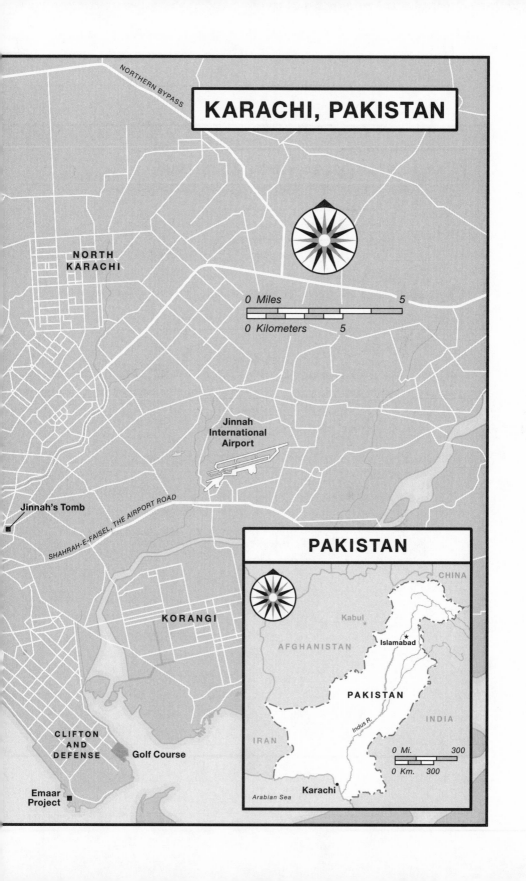

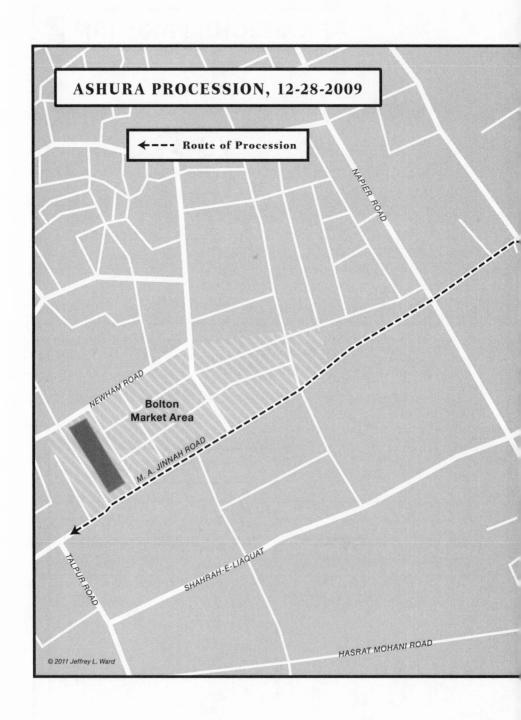

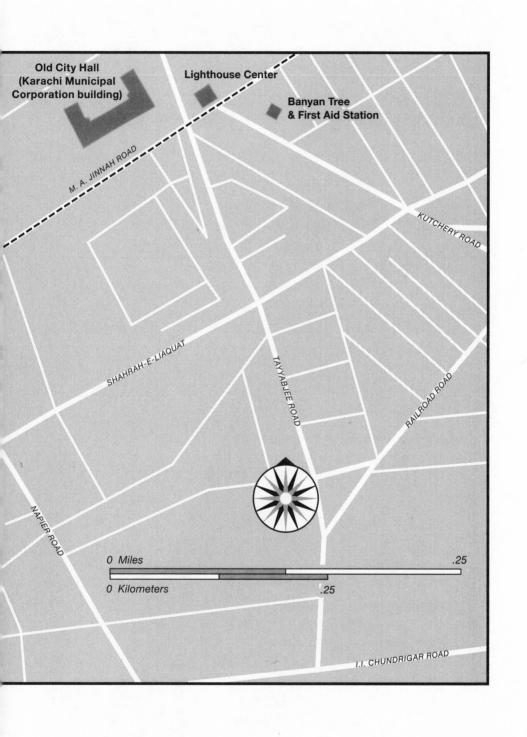

NORTH OF NORTH KARACHI

K arachi as we know it appeared in a blink.
 Nineteenth-century maps show a dot labeled Karachi, or "Kurrachee."
But this place was a tiny fraction of the city that exists today.

At the end of World War II, Karachi's population was around four hundred thousand.

Today it's at least thirteen million, one of the larger cities in the world.

Once I saw this giant metropolis from the roof of the old city hall. The building is an arch-windowed, rambling pile of reddish stone, which dates to the era when the British controlled Karachi as part of their Indian empire. Its design blends the cultures of rulers and ruled. The businesslike lower floors could be facing some European square, but on the roof I was standing amid a series of South Asian onion-shaped domes. A flock of birds settled on the dome to my right, clustering up near the point.

A city employee beckoned me to a door. It led us into the clock tower. We barely had room to step inside, because the floor was covered with thousands of municipal documents—building designs, memos on land use, and maps from the previous century. Past administrations had filed the old papers by dumping them in a pile so enormous that it interfered with the dangling weights that drove the clock.

Stepping over dusty pages at the edge of the pile, we climbed the stairs that circled the clockworks and emerged on a balcony below a clock face. Karachi lay below us like an unfolded map. Motorcycles whined on the street below. One of the office buildings to my right was covered in checkerboard squares of yellow and black.

Above central Karachi.

To my left, busy streets stretched away until they vanished in the haze. The low buildings that lined those streets were shades of khaki and gray, their colors washed out by pollution and the sun.

Eight miles away, I knew, the broad streets cut through North Karachi, which was built in the 1960s as a distant suburb. The expanding city promptly filled the intervening space.

Then it continued beyond.

Today many people live in New Karachi, a sprawling area to the north of North Karachi. Others live miles *farther* north, in areas even newer than New Karachi.

What spread out before me was an instant city: a metropolis that has grown so rapidly that a returning visitor from a few decades ago would scarcely recognize it. The instant city retains some of its original character and architecture, like Karachi's city hall, but has expanded so much that the new overshadows the old.

For most of history, the overwhelming majority of the world's people lived in the countryside. The global population remained heavily rural even after American and European cities industrialized and grew in the nineteenth and early twentieth centuries. Now the balance has shifted within the span of a single life. Since the aftermath of World War II, the urban population has grown by close to three billion people. Urban dwellers became a majority of the global population around 2008, and many urban areas are still growing.

This trend has produced the instant city, which I define as a metropolitan area that's grown since 1945 at a substantially higher rate than the population of the country to which it belongs. In the United States the population has doubled, but Los Angeles and its suburbs more than tripled. Houston has expanded more than sixfold, and its exuberant growth is modest compared with the developing world. Istanbul is about ten times its previous size. Ürümqi, a business hub for western China, is about twenty-three times more populous than the estimate for 1950. And then there's Karachi. Conservative estimates suggest that it's *at least thirty times larger than in 1945*—meaning that there are at least thirty residents today for every one at the war's end.

This kind of growth reflects more than natural increase, the number of births over deaths. It's true that the global population ballooned in recent decades, an epic trend that contributes massively to the expansion of cities like Karachi. But that's not the whole story. The city has grown too quickly for that. Modern cities also add population by sprawling into rural areas, which is part of what I was seeing from the clock tower: Karachi swallowed hundreds of villages that used to be miles out in the countryside. But even this cannot fully explain the instant city.

Something more is happening: the city is attracting migrants. People arrive from rural areas or from other countries. They work in new industries and build new homes. They bring diverse customs, languages, or religious practices, and they make the older inhabitants tense. Lifelong residents and newcomers alike jostle for power and resources in a swiftly evolving landscape that disorients them all.

In recent decades, the most significant movements to cities have come in Africa and Asia. Karachi has been a destination for some of the most dramatic migrations of all.

No one metropolis could capture the full variety of the world's growing cities, but Karachi is representative in several ways. It's on the Asian coastline, where massive urban growth is under way. Its modern foundations were laid during the age of European colonialism. Its great expansion coincided with the postwar collapse of empire, when industrialization attracted people to the city—as did the desperation of people seeking shelter from political or economic catastrophes.

And it's surprising to learn how often Karachi's course has been influenced by trends, ideas, or investment from other cities. It's a listening post where we can take in a global conversation.

Within this one metropolis, we find a range of possible options for the future of the instant city. Traveling across the landscape visible from the city hall balcony, we can encounter anything from shining glass towers to chaotic violence. Lately, Karachi has seen a little more glass, and a lot more violence. Migrants have come from all over Pakistan, concentrating the energies and sorrows of an entire troubled nation in one place under the sun.

What follows is the story of a single day in Karachi's life. It was a date that almost everyone in Karachi remembered: many vividly recalled where they were and what they were doing. I set out to learn the events of that day, the history that led up to it, and the aftershocks and consequences that followed. It's a slice of the urban world we've all been building.

From the clock tower, I saw the place where the story begins. It's just down the street from the old city hall: a white marker, next to the faded paint of a crosswalk. The marker was recently made. It's a memorial stone.

PART ONE

JINNAH ROAD

1 | **PROMENADE**

A short walk from the old city hall, beside the faded crosswalk and the memorial stone, a banyan tree spreads its branches over a patch of dirt. The dirt fills a triangle where two streets intersect. Somebody must have planned a park there long ago, judging by the battered iron fence, but street hawkers occupy the space today. They sell shoes, spread on wooden carts or hung from a rack like prize fish. Sometimes a man sits with his back to the fence, mending a castaway shoe he's plucked from a pile on the ground.

The vendors work at one of the city's more colorful corners. Shops on all sides sell curtains, clothes, and ceiling fans. A restaurant facing the banyan tree serves *biryani*, a spiced rice dish commonly cooked with chunks of meat, stirred in a pot by the entrance. The owners call their restaurant the Delhi Darbar, in honor of their ancestors from nearby India. When I have eaten there the manager has waved me toward a table at the back, near the wall fan, but I have preferred the table at the front, where I can see outside past the cooking pots, looking back toward one of the onion domes atop the old city hall.

Anyone who looks closely at city hall will notice that city hall is looking back. A security camera hangs on the corner of the building.

It was aimed down here toward the banyan tree on December 28, 2009.

On that day an annual procession was scheduled to move through Karachi. It was a religious march, affirming an historic faith: Muslims from the Shia sect were mourning the killing of the Prophet Mohammed's grandson more than thirteen hundred years ago. But the procession also reflected the present. It put the whole community on display, much like parades in America. Although Shias are a minority in Pakistan, the shops along the route were closed that

The KMC Building, or old city hall, completed in the 1930s.

day, a national holiday known as Ashura. People climbed on their rooftops to watch, and some of the city's majority Sunni Muslims always held their own march following the Shias. Pakistan Boy Scouts led the way—local youths who were part of the same worldwide movement as the Boy Scouts of America. Politicians and celebrities showed up, while police and paramilitary forces provided security.

The procession route led past the banyan tree, where on that morning the shoe vendors were temporarily replaced by Boy Scouts running a first-aid station. An ambulance was parked a few feet away.

THE PROCESSION COULD almost have been designed to offer a tour of the changing city. The marchers planned to begin near the great white dome of the tomb of Pakistan's founder, Muhammad Ali Jinnah, who grew up in Karachi. They would pass near Empress Market, its stone tower built to honor the nineteenth-century empress of India, also known as Britain's Queen Victoria; today the market is notable for rows of caged birds for sale in the back, as well as the acrid smell of hashish that men smoke in dim corners. Surrounding

M. A. Jinnah Road. The park with the banyan tree is on the right.

streets form the heart of an area called Saddar, once a great cultural district including nightclubs and bars, now shabby but dotted with billboards featuring Bollywood movie stars. Farther along, past the banyan tree, rose the red-brick minarets of a mosque called the Memon Masjid, and the spire of a Hindu temple. The route ended in one of the oldest sections of Karachi, several blocks from the waterfront where ships regularly glide into the harbor and the city's elites enter children in rowing competitions at the Karachi Boat Club.

Each of these landmarks hints at the city's past and present. The harbor and the old signs of empire remind us how Karachi has been shaped by different forms of globalization. Other landmarks might puzzle a newcomer. What caused all those old bars and nightclubs to close? And why, in a city that's overwhelmingly Muslim, would a Hindu temple occupy such a prominent place near the old city hall? The answers to these questions are revealing, as we will see, and also relevant to the fate of the Shia procession.

The Boat Club is the most revealing landmark of all. Club members meet for dinner on a terrace by the water, men in suits and ties, beautiful women draped in brilliantly colored cloth. Everything about their surroundings—tables overlooking a placid channel off the harbor, a perfectly tended garden, uniformed waiters delivering deliciously cooked fish—serves as a reminder of Karachi's wealth. Those who imagine masses of poor people in a metropolis like Karachi have an image that is accurate, but incomplete: the laboring poor can make a fortune, even if they make it for somebody else. The marchers on December 28 were walking through the economic heart of one of the world's most populous nations, home to textile mills and a vast steel mill. Part of the procession route ran parallel to the financial district, within sight of office towers and the red neon sign of the Karachi Stock Exchange. Nearby are the offices of several media empires, with newspapers and television channels serving the entire country, in English, Urdu, and several regional tongues. Karachi's seaport is a gateway to Central Asia, one of the few harbors within range of Afghanistan and other fabled lands over the mountains to the north. At waterfront piers, truckers load supplies for shipment to American forces fighting in Afghanistan. Other shipments move contraband: drugs, weapons, fugitives. And for almost any business transaction there may be a port official, policeman, or politician who quietly extracts a share of the profits in exchange for his invaluable cooperation. Measured by their income, education, and health, Karachi residents are living better than people almost anywhere else in Pakistan.

Of course, prosperity is not spread evenly. In poorer neighborhoods, some within a few blocks of the procession route, textile workers commonly bring home the equivalent of a few dollars per day. Many people have no jobs at all. And millions live with the consequences as well as the benefits of Karachi's economic activity. Pedestrians dodge streams of reddish liquid in the streets, said to be pollution from tanneries. The crowded neighborhood called Machar Colony is bisected by an open sewer the size of a river, its surface clogged with so many plastic bags and other debris that it almost seems possible to walk across the water. The sewage flows untreated into the same coastal waters where Karachi fishermen cast their nets.

"We're not a poor country," a Pakistani businessman once told me over dinner at the Boat Club. "We're a poorly *managed* country." To find evidence of this we need go no farther than the nearest electric light. Karachi, like all of Pakistan, has so badly outgrown its electricity supply that the power must be cut off for hours every day; this suggests the struggle for basic resources that threatens the future of many an instant city. To spend time in Karachi is to know the change in a room when its ceiling fan slows down and stops—and you feel it instantly, because the local weather combines the withering heat of the desert with the humidity of a swamp. Then again, the daily blackouts also demonstrate people's adaptability. They ignore the heat, or cover their windows to keep out the sun, or just wait. And Karachi rewards their patience. The temperature drops when the sun sinks low, and a cool ocean breeze blows on soaked shirts. By evening boys are playing cricket in the street, bouncing the ball off the asphalt in total disregard of traffic, while lovers discreetly encounter each other in the lengthening shadows of the park surrounding the tomb of Pakistan's founder. City life expands as the mercury contracts: ten o'clock, or even midnight, is not too late for friends who can afford it to meet for dinner at a rooftop barbecue restaurant.

If only it were so easy to find relief from the violence that stalks the city. Much of the world knows Karachi as the scene of the videotaped murder of the journalist Daniel Pearl in 2002, but Karachi residents are intimately familiar with many other killings—1,747, by one count, in the year 2009. Karachi is hardly the deadliest city in the world, but it's notable for spasms of political killings that can shut down parts of the city for days. Gunmen on motorcycles commonly weave through traffic, shoot a man in the head, and roar away. Armies of security guards watch over the wealthy and powerful, but when people move about the city they have reason to wonder if they will return home alive.

Everything that makes this instant city vibrant can also make it violent. Its swift and disorderly growth creates room for corruption and organized crime. Ethnic groups migrate here from different places, speak different languages, and coalesce into rival political parties that battle over money, power, and real estate. It's notable that most of Karachi's violence is *not* blamed on Islamist extremist groups. But extremists have established a presence in Karachi, attracted by many of the same factors that make the city rich. Karachi's commercial connections with northern Pakistan and Afghanistan also link the city to the region's wars. Migrants move south from the war zones seeking work, making it easy for militants to blend in with them. Taliban fighters are believed to visit Karachi when they need places to hide. In the years before al Qaeda founder Osama bin Laden was found and killed in northern Pakistan in 2011, several of his associates were based in Karachi or arrested there; al Qaeda used the city as a receiving station for militant recruits and a base for attacks outside Pakistan. This should be no surprise; the international airport and financial system offer links to the outside world, while some universities and religious schools have become centers of Islamist political thought. If militants merely hid in the mountains, they would only be a local threat, but like so many people, they have seized the global opportunities of the instant city.

Karachi residents used to speak of their city as a back office for militants, who unfortunately made use of the metropolis but fortunately did not attack it. To believe this comforting thought, however, people had to overlook a variety of extremist attacks within Karachi itself. On December 26, 2009, an explosion injured people at a Shia religious procession. The next day an explosion struck another procession. They were small explosions, killing no one, but the city was on alert as marchers formed the procession on December 28.

THE AMBULANCE PARKED by the banyan tree had a word in red on the side, in English and Urdu: "Edhi."

Identical ambulances were parked some distance down the street, in front of a shabby suite of offices. Telephone and electrical wires spread like vines over the office walls; men studied newspapers and waited by the phone in case anyone should dial an emergency number. This was a station of the Edhi ambulance service, which for more than half a century has served the sick and the poor.

Faisal Edhi, son of the old man who founded the service, sometimes settled behind a desk in these rooms, but Faisal would have little use for a desk on the day of the Shia procession. He would be out riding ambulances, as he commonly did, coordinating the response should anyone need medical attention. Faisal, a thin man in his late thirties, was easily recognizable with his black-framed glasses and close-cropped beard. He had a trait that I found often in Karachi: he laughed when talking about disasters. He needed this trait, because when he heard reports of gunfire, his job was to take the wheel of an ambulance and drive toward it.

Faisal hadn't always lived this life. In his late teens he moved from Karachi to New York City. He slept in other people's apartments and got a job. He stood in traffic in Brooklyn, hawking the newspaper *Newsday*.

By moving to New York, Faisal put some distance between himself and his dominating father, but in one of our conversations he told me he always knew that duty would call him back to the family business. His father, Abdul Sattar Edhi, was renowned in Pakistan and abroad. The Edhi ambulance fleet provided cheap service—and it *had* to be cheap, since very few people had health insurance in Pakistan. An Edhi ambulance was a simple white van with one driver, two gurneys, and not much medical equipment; its virtue was not its level of sophistication, but that it showed up. Edhi drivers were poor men who were given a little training, paid a modest wage, and sent out to respond to almost anything that went wrong in Karachi. More than Karachi—the service had spread outside the city to other parts of Pakistan.

In his eighties, the elder Edhi still ran the service. Wearing black clothes, a white beard, and a wry expression, he suffered from many ailments but still looked spry when climbing a flight of stairs. And the ambulances were only the most visible part of his dominion. The family ran two blood banks and a home for poor children and runaways. Edhi offices were equipped with cradles, where unwed mothers could give up their babies for adoption. Edhi operated a graveyard in a distant sector of the city; it was said that he had personally washed thousands of bodies in preparation for burial. And sometimes he still climbed into an ambulance to catch a ride to a crime scene.

The old man was one of the migrants who turned Karachi into an instant city. He'd arrived with his parents in 1947 and went to work as a street peddler. He was part of a mass move to Karachi, which more than doubled the population within a few years. The growth never stopped. And so Abdul Sattar Edhi had witnessed the creation of one of the larger cities in human history. It happened within the span of his life. He also had a front-row seat, or more precisely the front seat of an ambulance, to witness the violence that had grown along with the city.

Edhi thrived in this environment—he once described himself as being "obsessed with self-imposed discomfort"—and built a service meant to alleviate his city's sorrows. His ambulence service would be filling a critical role on December 28. Thousands of people gathered that day at the start of the procession route, intending to promenade for miles through the dilapidated grandeur of the old downtown. They were marching in the direction of the banyan tree.

It grew in an area called the Lighthouse Bazaar.

2 | LIGHTHOUSE

The Lighthouse Bazaar takes its name from a building across the street from the banyan tree. It's five stories high—ground plus four, as locals phrase it, stores and law offices and apartments. Its flat white façade has an air conditioner here and there on a windowsill. The ground-floor storekeepers improvise awnings to keep the intense sunlight out of their shops, red and gray squares of cloth that give the building the look of a man dressed in rags. But when Karachi residents pass this property, they remember its colorful history.

Many years ago, movie billboards obscured the façade, and the building was the Lighthouse Cinema.

By chance I met the man who had grown up as the prince of that cinema. His name was Sharfuddin Memon, and he was a Karachi businessman. When he was young his father owned the theater, which offered movies from England, Hollywood, and Bombay. Memon especially remembered a 1969 American western he'd seen as a boy. It was called *Mackenna's Gold*—Omar Sharif and Gregory Peck in a tale of men corrupted by their lust for wealth.

Memon grew up to become an engineer and the owner of a construction company. He moved to America for a time, and encouraged Americans to call him "Bobby" when they couldn't get their tongues around his first name. Then Bobby Memon returned home, where he controlled several pieces of Karachi real estate, including a KFC restaurant by the beach.

He also owned the Lighthouse Cinema, though it was not a theater anymore. Pakistan's domestic film industry had collapsed, and though Hollywood and Bollywood movies drew interest, people often watched at home. Young

The Lighthouse Centre, left, across M. A. Jinnah Road from the banyan tree.

couples had trouble going on dates to a theater, where they might be harassed by religious conservatives. ("You need someplace to sit with a boy, and don't imagine we didn't think about that," a young woman who'd grown up in Karachi once told me.) Memon reconstructed the building as retail and office space that he called the Lighthouse Centre. It was still, he said, "a landmark of the city." Tenants could watch the swirl of life around the banyan tree below.

The Lighthouse offered a perfect view of the processions that moved down the street on holidays. One of the largest was the Shia procession on Ashura—or the tenth day of the month of Muharram on the Islamic calendar. "I am not a Shia," Bobby Memon told me when we met for tea in early 2010, "but as kids, I remember we used to go on the rooftop. My friends and family used to stand up there and watch the procession. It's a day of mourning, but . . ." He trailed off, not wanting to sound disrespectful, but speaking of Ashura the way Americans might speak of Memorial Day—as a day off.

Memon had glasses and a well-tended beard. He wore a dark suit, and exposed a cuff link when he reached for his cup. He was a civic leader now, and when the Ashura procession came on December 28, 2009, he had no need to climb the stairs of the Lighthouse. He took a more sophisticated vantage point. He drove to the Civic Centre, a gray slab of an office building miles away. This was the new city hall, the headquarters of metropolitan Karachi's mayor.

Memon gained admittance to a wood-paneled, glass-partitioned room. Fifteen video screens covered a wall. Police flipped from channel to channel, monitoring scores of security cameras that overlooked streets and intersections across the city.

Memon rated a place in the room because he held a special position, as head of the Citizens' Police Liaison Committee. Organized in response to the kidnappings of businessmen—an alarmingly common crime that police rarely solved on their own—this business group was now a permanent part of the local law enforcement structure, with offices on the grounds of the provincial Governor's House, the ability to trace phone calls, and even the power to make arrests. So Memon came to the Civic Centre with other officials and watched the wall of video screens. "It's like a small country," he marveled later, as he considered the diverse and expanding city visible in camera after camera.

As Memon knew, the video room was sponsored by the mayor, Mustafa Kamal, who had built his reputation on such improvements. Just thirty-four when he was elected in 2005, the mayor, or *nazim* of the City District Government of Karachi, as he was called in the local government system of the moment, was a hyperkinetic man who swept through the city overseeing the construction of highway overpasses and water lines. He had the security cameras installed despite the skepticism of the police, who did not operate under his authority. Kamal considered it a matter of ceaseless irritation that the police answered to the provincial government, which was in the hands of a rival political party—and it was a blood rival, the Pakistan People's Party of the famous Bhutto family. When Kamal showed visitors his roomful of screens, he cheerfully instructed a camera operator to play a video recorded sometime earlier showing police officers collecting money from the driver of a stopped car.

Despite such embarrassments, or because of them, the police sent men to sit in the black swivel chairs and monitor conditions around the city. On the day of the Ashura procession, the city police chief and other officials came to the room, the best place to watch a procession that would travel for miles. The many video feeds available included those from the cameras attached to the old city hall, locally known as the KMC Building. The initials stood for the Karachi Municipal Corporation, the city government's discontinued name that still showed up in occasional news headlines, whenever some former KMC official was charged in a long-ago case of corruption.

I MET ANOTHER MAN who remembered watching video screens on December 28: Abbas Kumeli, former Pakistani senator and a spokesman for the Shia Muslim community.

Kumeli lived in a corner house. It pushed up to the edge of the sidewalk, leaving little room for his armed guards. After confirming that I had an appointment, the guards sent me through the gate and upstairs, where Kumeli welcomed me into a comfortably cluttered living room. Every flat space was covered by papers or framed photos. Kumeli dominated the room, an imposing and bespectacled man of sixty-four. He'd been watching television when I arrived, but a moment later the set snapped off as the neighborhood plunged into the latest of Karachi's daily blackouts. We settled on couches and talked by the light from a half-open balcony door.

He spoke in the slow and precise English he had refined at St. Patrick's Catholic high school, which had educated Karachi's elites since 1861. (The boys' school claimed Pakistani presidents, prime ministers, and a military coup leader among its graduates.) Kumeli spoke for a community that had become insular and suspicious, and with reason. One of the first stories I covered as a reporter in Karachi involved the Shia community: in 2002, men on motorcycles were following Shia professionals and community leaders—doctors, lawyers, engineers—and shooting them in the head. The killings had become normal. They happened all the time. Presumably the culprits were Sunni extremist groups who considered Shias to be apostates.

The Shias had their own militants. In 2006 a gathering of Sunnis was bombed in Nishtar Park, around the corner from Abbas Kumeli's home.

As accustomed as he was to sectarian violence, Kumeli sensed something different in December 2009. "There's a lot of terrorism in this country," he told me, "but not on the days of mourning." The annual Ashura procession had normally been left alone, but this year, "the government itself was receiving threats, and was expressing its suspicions."

Shortly before the procession, Pakistan's interior minister visited Karachi.

"He met with me in this room where we are sitting," Kumeli said. The interior minister brought along the governor of Sindh, the province of which Karachi is the capital; each man represented a leading political party—one came from the mayor's party, known as the MQM, and the other from the rival People's Party. Both parties had joined an uneasy coalition that was attempting to share power in the province as well as the national government. And today these two officials were delivering a carefully calibrated message to Shia leaders around the city. "They were saying that they had made foolproof security arrangements, and also expressing the satisfaction they were hopeful that no such thing would take place.

"But they were expressing their fears as well."

The visitors didn't say exactly why they were afraid, but the list of plausible suspects was well known, starting with Sunni extremist groups that targeted Shias. Then there were Taliban insurgents, who were bombing Pakistani cities that year in response to an army offensive against their mountain sanctuaries. Karachi politicians who showed up for the parade could become targets for enemies or rivals. And as Kumeli mulled the possibility of attack, he learned of the explosions at two smaller Shia processions on the two days before the climactic march. The blasts increased the tension, even though police blamed one of the explosions on gas from an open sewer line.

On the morning of Ashura, December 28, Kumeli woke and went to Nishtar Park around the corner from his house. Today it was the Shias' turn to fill this broad expanse of earth. Security guards had set up a network of closed-circuit cameras to oversee the checkpoints leading into the heavily guarded area, and in a room near the park, Kumeli studied the TV monitors, one angle and then another. He saw nothing unusual. Men were waving security wands at the masses lining up to enter Nishtar Park that morning. They would attend a *majlis*, or meeting, before walking to the procession route that began nearby. Police had already performed a security sweep and cordoned off the route, leaving only two entrances near the beginning and a single exit several miles away at the end. Thousands of police guarded the streets leading to the perimeter. They were backed up by the Rangers, paramilitary gunmen who provided muscle when the police were not enough, urban warriors in T-shirts and camouflage pants, who rolled through the streets in pickup trucks. Each truck had a man balanced on the truck bed as it moved, holding a machine gun that was aimed forward over the cab.

THE SHIA RITUAL that Kumeli oversaw that day frequently baffled outsiders, although its emotional contours could feel familiar to Christians, who at Easter celebrate a story of both death and resurrection.

For Shias, the Ashura procession was both an occasion for sadness and an affirmation of their faith. The procession marked the long-ago death of the Prophet's grandson Hussein in what is now Iraq. It was said that Hussein had only a relative handful of followers when he threw his outnumbered band into a hopeless battle against his rivals at the city of Karbala. The story of his sacrifice, passed down through generations, steeled Shias to endure suffering and fight for lost causes. They believed that Hussein had been deprived of his place as the rightful leader of the Muslim world, and it was entirely consistent with the traditions of their faith that after the passage of more than a millennium they refused to accept this injustice, and even blamed themselves: how could they have failed to sustain Hussein in his time of need? Some of the mourners scourged themselves, performing acts of ritual grief—many would say it was genuine grief—over Hussein's death. Some slashed their own backs with specially made blades on the ends of chains. Others cut their foreheads with knives. Some needed stitches afterward.

Most Shias did not go to such extremes, but did display their devotion by marching for miles through the city—and they were moving now, many holding banners in front of them as they streamed out of Nishtar Park and onto the secured route. They were passing the white dome of the tomb of Muhammad Ali Jinnah. Later in their procession they would walk for miles down a street named after the founder of the nation, M. A. Jinnah Road, which led past the banyan tree.

The marchers soon left the view of the closed-circuit cameras that Abbas Kumeli was watching. They moved forward under the eyes of the citywide video network set up by the government of Karachi. This was what Bobby Memon saw as he looked over policemen's shoulders at the Civic Centre.

If, by chance, someone noticed a video feed from one of the outlying streets, he might have caught a glimpse of a bearded man in a hurry. He was racing to catch up with the procession. The hurrying man was a devoted Shia, so much so that his very devotion made him late. His name was Syed Mohammad

Raza Zaidi—the name "syed" was an honorific, indicating that he claimed descent from the Prophet Mohammed.

Zaidi woke that morning at home in a distant Shia neighborhood, far enough away that when I stood in the clock tower of the old city hall and looked out over Karachi, his neighborhood, called Sau Quarter, was one of those that was invisible out in the haze. It had been built in the 1960s, when the city was exploding outward to the north and the east. Zaidi faced a long journey across town, and much to do before he could start.

He was a fortyish man with a graying beard, two children, and a lifelong interest in his religion. As a younger man he traveled to Iran, an overwhelmingly Shia country, where he studied at the religious center of Qom and visited the sprawling domed shrine of a saint in the city of Mashhad. On returning to Karachi the young man followed a more earthly pursuit: he drove a rickshaw, one of the three-wheeled Chinese-made motor taxis that were ubiquitous across the city. He earned enough money to buy several rickshaws, but his youthful interest in Islam returned. When he was chosen as trustee and caretaker of the Shia religious meeting hall, or *imambargah,* down the street from the family home, he sold the rickshaws and devoted himself full-time to this new occupation. It was an unpaid position, but Zaidi could afford the sacrifice because he lived as part of a joint family—he was one of several sons who had brought their wives home to live in their father's increasingly crowded house, while the daughters were married off and sent elsewhere.

The position as caretaker included a variety of odd jobs. It was Zaidi who tended the tightly trimmed lawn outside the *imambargah.* And on December 28, 2009, Zaidi took on a duty that made him miss the start of the procession.

He helped to provide security for a smaller neighborhood procession that morning, waving a metal-detecting wand at the marchers who entered the route. By the time he finished, the major procession was already moving through the central city. Zaidi would have been forgiven if he missed it—other members of his family did, finding the neighborhood procession to be enough devotion for one day. But as the trustee of a prominent place of worship, he was of no mind to stay home. Nor was he content to start the procession late and trail along at the end. He wanted to walk near the front. Racing across town, he caught up to the marchers, angling to reach the head of the procession just before the banyan tree at the Lighthouse Centre. There was no authorized entrance there—policemen barred his way—but Zaidi managed to talk his way past them.

By the time he emerged on the broad expanse of Jinnah Road, Zaidi was wearing a coffin sheet draped over his shoulders—the same kind of white cloth in which Muslims were commonly buried. The coffin sheet was painted with a slogan, "Mourning or Martyrdom."

Later, I asked Zaidi's family what he meant by that slogan. They explained that many marchers carried sheets with the same words. Zaidi was saying to the world: You would have to kill me to keep me from walking in this procession.

March or die.

THE SHIAS' BLOODY RITUALS contributed to prejudice against them. Some Sunni Muslims spoke of the rituals with revulsion, and their distaste added to the tensions built into the holiday itself. The Ashura ritual recalled the start of the schism between the sects: Shias supported the claim of the martyred Hussein to rule the Muslim world, while Sunnis did not. Over the centuries since then, religious scholars and political leaders sometimes narrowed the sectarian divide, and sometimes widened it. In Pakistan, several minority Shias had actually governed the country since its independence in 1947, starting with the national founder Muhammad Ali Jinnah. The trouble was that fundamentalist movements had gained strength in recent decades, calling more attention to religious distinctions and leaving less room for tolerance. Pakistan became a battleground for influence between Sunni-dominated Saudi Arabia and Shia-dominated Iran. By the 1980s, anti-Shia extremists were drawing on some of the most intolerant traditions of Sunni thought. They found recruits and sympathizers in a country that contained its share of casual bigotry; years ago I went on a long drive with a colleague in northern Pakistan, utterly decent and kind in every other respect, who started on the subject of Shias and seemed unable to stop, complaining of their rituals, their bathing habits, their dishonesty, their lack of intelligence, and other supposed Shia traits I failed to notice.

BUT THESE VIEWS never became universal. On the day of the Ashura procession in 2009, many Karachi residents of other sects and faiths volunteered their time to ensure the safety and comfort of the Shias as they marched. And chief among these were scores of young men who turned up now and again in the city's security videos, often wearing distinctive khaki uniforms. They were Pakistan Boy Scouts, including Sunni Muslims, Hindus, even Christians.

The Scouts were a familiar presence in Karachi. They had been for generations. A British general had begun the worldwide Scouting movement in 1908, and it spread across much of the British Empire at the same time it was spreading to America. In the 1920s, a Hindu businessman paid for the Karachi Boy Scouts' handsome stone headquarters. In 1947, the founder of the nation, Jinnah himself, accepted the designation of Pakistan's chief Scout, a title that passed to his successors. The current chief Scout was President Asif Ali Zardari, whose mustached image graced the inside of the Karachi headquarters right next to Jinnah's portrait, and who would, early in the following year, issue a statement urging young Scouts to help battle terrorism.

While American Scouts are associated in the public mind with suburban kids and thin mint cookies, Pakistani Scouts live closer to the edge. "America is a developed country, and we are a backward country," said Najeeb Ilyas, a Scout leader who met me once at the old Scout headquarters. "In Pakistan, mostly poor boys become Scouts." Ilyas spoke in a high, scratchy, expressive voice. He had close-cropped hair, a short gray beard, and a calm expression. There was no shortage of poor boys (as well as poor girls, though the Girl Scouts were not assigned duties in the Ashura procession). The organization claimed sev-

Pakistani Boy Scouts.

enty thousand members in Karachi, including Ilyas's three sons, who put on uniforms accented by multicolored neckerchiefs and by little green-and-white Pakistani flags stitched on the right breast. The family lived in Lyari, an old and crowded section of the city that was equally famous for its progressive politics and the gun battles of its criminal gangs. Ilyas believed that Scouting kept his kids away from trouble.

Sometimes the city boys traveled to Pakistan's northern reaches for the classic Scouting experience, a camping trip in the mountains around the Swat Valley, although in recent years the trips had to be canceled. Too many mountains were filled with Pakistani troops chasing the Taliban. But the Scouts still performed community service in Karachi on days like Ashura. Shia Scouts marched at the front of the procession or helped with security. Scouts of other sects or faiths were at first-aid stations along the route, where Najeeb Ilyas was in charge. His sons joined him at the station across from the Lighthouse Centre, on the patch of land by the banyan tree, within range of the camera on the corner of the old city hall. His youngest son, Ghulam, was twelve, a tiny boy with a strong and steady gaze.

For the Scouts at the Lighthouse, the first sign of the approaching marchers was the arrival of the little white vans of the Edhi ambulance service. Any mourners who were overcome by exhaustion or injured themselves on the route were helped into Edhi ambulances for a ride ahead to the first-aid station. There, some would get basic treatment, while those who needed more would be carried on to a hospital.

The first-aid station was filling with bleeding men by the time the procession came into view. Shia Scouts, dozens in a row as wide as Jinnah Road itself, held a rope to keep the rank straight and the marchers behind them. Flag-bearers held up banners in red, black, and green, decorated with religious inscriptions and images of minarets. Behind the flags a mass of humanity moved forward in good order, many singing or chanting traditional slogans bemoaning the long-ago loss of the martyred Hussein.

That mass included Mohammad Raza Zaidi, the caretaker of the *imambar-gah*, walking with his coffin sheet over his shoulders and at last in the position where he wanted to be. Sometime after four o'clock in the afternoon he telephoned his family with his good news. I am near the front, he announced over the phone, I am walking just behind the banners. Just up ahead of him and a little to the right rose the white façade of the Lighthouse Centre. To the left was a small opening in the wall of buildings along Jinnah Road—the little triangle of earth with the first-aid station and the tree.

Some of the Scouts were relieved when they saw the marchers approaching safely, since they had forebodings about the day. They moved up to the side of the road to watch the mourners pass. Scout leader Najeeb Ilyas turned to his sons and the other boys by the roadside. "Start passing out the sweet water," he called out.

A few meters away from Najeeb, a metal box stood next to a light pole. It was a box of considerable size, more than six feet high on metal legs, with a sloping metal roof. If anyone should come across a damaged Koran, or discarded paper with a Koranic inscription, people were supposed to drop it through a slot in the box so that no one would throw the holy words in the garbage or trample them underfoot. The box stood near the banyan tree, and it was inside that box of wayward scripture that someone had planted a bomb.

THE CITY SURVEILLANCE video includes no sound.

The camera looks silently down on Jinnah Road from the old city hall. The banyan tree is visible in its little triangular park, across the street and maybe a hundred yards away.

The video recording shows the mourners coming into sight, walking toward the camera. The lead ranks, including the Shia scouts, have just passed the tree, which is visible behind them. They calmly pass in front of the blue-and-white sign for the Subhanallah Bakery.

Then the explosion rips into the body of the crowd. Within two seconds, thick gray smoke has risen as high as a five-story building. The flags and banners at the front of the parade sag as their bearers stagger or fall. People in front of the flags, those with room to run, scurry forward in search of cover. Behind the flags the rest of the marchers, those who survived, are stuck in the shrapnel and smoke.

Survivors affirmed later that there were two explosions. The first was sharp and small, like a firecracker, coming from near a water barrel. It may have been designed to startle people, fix them in place. Then the main explosion knocked Najeeb Ilyas to the ground. He speculated later that he was shielded from the blast by the people around him. "I am an unlucky man," he told me. "If I got martyrdom on Ashura, I would be in heaven now." (I told him I was glad for his bad luck.) He rose to see the corpses of three men to his left, and the bodies of five women on the ground behind him. He saw his fifteen-year-old son Waqas, wounded and lying on the ground, and shouted for help. Another of his three sons approached, though at first, Najeeb recalled, "I didn't recognize him because of the dust and smoke." All of his sons had survived.

Behind Ilyas, at the first-aid station, a fourteen-year-old Scout named Mohammad Kumail was knocked senseless. The Scout was tall for his age, brown-skinned and studious-looking behind the rectangular frames of his glasses. He couldn't see anything after the explosion except smoke. He couldn't hear anything either. Eventually his head cleared, the cacophony of shouts and howls around him jolted his brain, and he began to look around. What stayed in the boy's memory were the body parts strewn about the first-aid station.

The epicenter, December 28, 2009. *[Asif Hassan/AFP/Getty Images]*

The explosion destroyed the Edhi ambulance that was parked beside the box, but within a few minutes more ambulances arrived; Faisal Edhi, the son of the founder of the ambulance service, arrived with them.

Even though as a younger man he'd moved to America for a time, Faisal liked his work here. He seemed energized by facing the horror of it. If he didn't do it, who would? He worked with ambulance drivers to clear away the wounded and the dead. He crossed Jinnah Road to the building next to the Lighthouse

Centre, climbed the stairs, and emerged on a balcony overlooking the scene. "One of the bodies I shifted, from about the third floor, was a half body," he remembered later.

Somewhere in the chaos of the next few hours, Faisal would find a moment to inspect Edhi ambulances that had been near the bomb, including the one that crumpled. He found the ambulances' metal skin peppered with little dents and holes. They had been sprayed with steel nuts, the kind typically screwed on the end of a bolt. More of these nuts would be found strewn about the park and on the pavement of Jinnah Road, later to be swept up as evidence by the police. Many of the nuts had also plunged into the bodies of the marchers in the procession.

More than thirty people had been killed, and hundreds wounded.

By now, photographers and video crews were moving up and down Jinnah Road. The many newspapers, news agencies, and television stations with offices in range of the banyan tree soon spread the news across the city and around the world. In recent years, Pakistani cable television news channels had multiplied even more rapidly than the population. Live coverage in Karachi prompted people across the city to begin frantic searches to learn if their loved ones were safe. They called the marchers' mobile phones, dialing again and again; sometimes an ambulance driver would answer, saying: This phone's owner is dead.

The family of Mohammad Raza Zaidi, the caretaker of the Shia religious hall, received no such confirmation. They dialed and dialed the phone from which he had called them near the head of the procession. Nobody answered.

As the afternoon became evening, members of the family traveled into the central city from their house in Sau Quarter. They began searching the hospitals, and kept searching until they found his body. In accordance with tradition he was buried that night, along with the torn remains of the coffin sheet he carried to his death. He was buried on the grounds of the Shia meeting hall where he was trustee and caretaker, at the edge of the green lawn he tended.

3 | NATIONAL ARMS

We have only begun to recount the multiple events of December 28, but the Ashura bombing alone demands some explanation. Authorities made their first efforts to assign some meaning to the blast well before the day reached its disastrous conclusion. Early media reports quoted government officials who blamed a "suicide bomber." Pakistan's interior minister Rehman Malik said the bomber had links to two militant groups, including Pakistan's version of the Taliban. The Taliban soon claimed responsibility, also describing it as a suicide attack. Evidence, however, began pointing in another direction. Federal investigators studied steel nuts that were strewn on the road, the same ones Faisal Edhi had noticed, and the nuts made them doubt that a suicide bomber was responsible. Hundreds of nuts were too heavy to carry as shrapnel. When choosing a final wardrobe, investigators believed, the discriminating suicide bomber would prefer lightweight ball bearings.

Karachi police gained more analysis in the days that followed, when a businessman came to see them. He brought along a computer scientist, a Fulbright scholar back from getting his doctorate in the United States, where he had studied the computer reconstruction of suicide bombings. After the police took the scholar to study the corner by the banyan tree, the young man said the "casualty pattern" didn't fit with a suicide attack. Even more proof came in the form of torn metal fragments. They originated from the box of Koranic scripture. Video images from before the blast showed an Edhi ambulance parked beside the box. Images taken afterward showed the ambulance crumpled like an aluminum can, but still parked in place. The box was gone, blown apart, with pieces flung outward in all directions. The explosion could only have come from inside it, likely detonated by remote control.

A dead boy who had been mistakenly described as a suicide bomber was identified as a Boy Scout.

Police eventually dismissed the Taliban as suspects, instead linking the attack to a little-known Pakistani militant group with ties to al Qaeda. We will see as our story unfolds that this militant group was originally organized to punish Pakistan's government for cooperating with the United States in hunting down militants. So if the police were correct, we can read the attack as one bloody episode in al Qaeda's long war with the West.

But on another level, the Ashura bombing had little to do with the West. No Americans were targeted. The bombers did not even directly strike America's allies in the Pakistani government, instead wiping out common citizens on the street. People in the United States barely noticed the attack, which received only brief coverage in the midst of the American holiday season. (Americans were far more concerned about the so-called underwear bomber who'd been caught with explosives in his pants on a U.S.-bound plane that Christmas.) The Ashura bombing was instead an atrocity staged for a local audience, in which attackers and victims alike were Muslims. We may better understand it as part of a long battle within Islam, as well as a struggle for power in Pakistan. The details of the attack—the targeting of a vulnerable minority, the state's failure to provide effective security, and explosives placed with awful symbolism in a box of damaged Korans—reflected disturbing trends through much of the modern Muslim world. They also reflected Pakistan's own peculiar problems. In this expressly Islamic state, well over 90 percent of the populace shares the same basic faith, yet throughout Pakistan's history, as we will see, that surface unity has masked great diversity and deep divisions. The divisions are especially evident in Karachi, which after receiving migrants from many places is Pakistan's most diverse city.

Karachi also faces a diversity of conflicts, which came into play after the Ashura bombing. A second event extended the day's destruction, and revealed more of the competing pressures that shape the instant city. Rival politicians, businessmen, soldiers, and thugs jostle for power and land. Religion, while often invoked, is just one of several social divides; people are at least as likely to be split by their class, the location of their ancestral village, or the language they speak at home. Few people trust the government to mediate their differences. All these conflicts combine and intensify one another, like pouring chemicals on a building that's already on fire, creating unpredictable conflagra-tions that define life and death in Karachi.

A conflagration on December 28 left scars that were visible for months afterward along Jinnah Road. When I moved along that road from the banyan tree in 2010, one of the first buildings I came to was the old city hall. At the curb behind it I discovered a line of pickup trucks belonging to the city fumigation service. Each truck bed carried insecticide-spraying machinery. The windows of each truck's cab were broken, and the insides blackened by fire.

"Eighteen," a security guard said when he noticed me counting trucks. "There are eighteen of them."

Farther down Jinnah Road I found long stone buildings, three and four stories high. This was a wholesale district. Anything from clothes and chairs to appliances and balloons was sold in hundreds of shops along Jinnah Road. But I saw gaps in the otherwise crowded landscape. Daylight showed through the archways on the façades of a row of stone buildings. Through the doorways I saw a field of rubble. The buildings behind the façades were gone.

Next to the rubble was a piece of corner real estate that I knew had held a market not long ago. Now it was a parking area covered with motorcycles.

I turned onto a narrow side street, which led into an even narrower street, where the buildings offered shade and shelter from the brutality of the sun. Here I encountered a shopkeeper named Khalid Rashid. He wore the Pakistani cloth-ing known as a *shalwar kameez,* a long loose shirt over baggy pants, with white fabric as sweat-stained as my own shirt. Rashid had bags under his steady dark eyes. His mustache curved upward in a smile. Though we'd never met, he sent someone running for a cold drink and welcomed me into his plastics shop. He sold simple items like stools; we spoke while sitting on two of them. But he had very little inventory that day.

Rashid was just beginning to repair the place, where he'd done business from 1971 until December 28, 2009, when the shop burned during a massive episode of arson.

THE FIRES SPREAD along the route we have just traced, beginning at the ban-yan tree.

Minutes after the Ashura blast, people began breaking into the closed stores in the Lighthouse Bazaar. They pried open the corrugated metal gate to a store selling bolts of cloth and shiny men's suits. The shop reached far back into the building; the men set it all on fire. Other shops were torched the same way. Some people crossed the street from the bazaar to the old city hall. They smashed the windows of the city fumigation trucks parked by the building and torched them one after another. Soon the flames reached a portion of the building itself. Fire trucks began arriving within minutes, but the crews were quickly driven away by the enraged survivors.

"There was fire all around," remembered Faisal Edhi of the ambulance service. "I was there about one and a half hours. We were asking the fire brigade to fight against the fire, but they were not present there, they were afraid to come." They only came later, and "the markets were burned by that time."

The thousands of police and paramilitary troops along the route made little effort to control the situation, choosing instead to make a tactical retreat.

In the video room at the Civic Centre, Bobby Memon and the police officials saw the chaos unfolding and made no effective response. In Memon's view, it was a simple lack of coordination. "We always talk about that in a city like Karachi, there should be a central command system; they should have a camera working; and that should be linked to the barricade—should be linked to the ambulances—linked to the hospitals. And that's only where you can respond to a crisis situation," he said. Any police officer watching those screens "was just in there watching. If something happened, what were they going to do?"

Other accounts suggested that the chain of command worked only too well—and that it restrained the police from acting. A Pakistani newspaper, the *News International,* reported that police requested permission to shoot the arsonists and were refused. Officials feared that if they responded to the violence with force, the situation would escalate and the whole city would explode.

During that first hour after the blast, two dozen or more men appeared on Jinnah Road. Many were about a mile ahead of where the parade had stopped—on the far side of the old city hall. Here they stood between long grand buildings of yellow stone—Gizri stone, it was called, after the location of the quarry that produced it. This was the wholesale district, known as Bolton Market.

The men broke into National Arms, a store that had sold weapons on this spot since 1948, and made off with Chinese- and Turkish-made handguns. They broke into a second gun store. Some men had torches. Soon entire buildings were in flames.

Television crews broadcast much of this live, which was how the shopkeeper

Bolton Market area.

Khalid Rashid learned of the destruction of his property. Rashid began the Ashura holiday at home. There he saw video images of the fires, and told me that "the Rangers and police were there but were saying they couldn't do anything." Like other shopkeepers, he rushed to Jinnah Road, but was blocked by the police who had cordoned off the area. Behind the police cordon, the fires were spreading.

"We said if you are unable to do something, give your weapons to us and we will defend our stores," Rashid recalled. "We tried to come, but the police turned us aside. Not until ten o'clock in the evening did we get here and see what happened with our shops."

Rashid's shop was destroyed and smoking; across the narrow street, a five-story building was burning. He told me how he watched as the fire worked its way downward from the top: "Five floors! Then it burned the fourth, then the third, step by step down to the ground." The building was full of plastic goods that burned uncontrollably.

Once the fire crews felt secure enough to operate, they moved from one burning building to another, yet the fires did not die. Mustafa Kamal, the young mayor of Karachi, moved among the firefighters, offering exhortations and encouragement. It was much too late. The fires burned all night and for

Police and paramilitary forces stayed away from the fires.
[Asif Hassan/AFP/Getty Images]

several days afterward. Hundreds of shops were destroyed. More than a dozen people were killed in the chaos on the streets.

"Who do you think did all the burning?" I asked Rashid, the plastic seller.

"I just don't understand," he replied. He reminded me that the fires in the Bolton Market only seemed to have spread to one side of Jinnah Road. "You will see that all the shops on the right side are affected. Not a single shop on the left side was burnt. Not a single shutter was broken." That was one of many observations that shopkeepers made to each other as they speculated that certain buildings or blocks might have been deliberately targeted.

A question began forming in their minds—a question without any firm foundation, but one shopkeeper after another was asking it.

Was someone trying to clear off certain properties for later use?

Their question was spreading like the fires.

FLAMES AND SMOKE still rose over Bolton Market, visible for miles through Karachi's haze, as police began to investigate. Agents from Pakistan's equivalent of the FBI arrived up the street at the Lighthouse Centre; we have already glimpsed them, peering at steel nuts and dead bodies. They were joined by the special investigations unit of the Karachi police, which handles terrorism cases.

The antiterrorism specialists who focused on the bombing case did not examine the fires at all, classifying them as, essentially, unrelated crimes. "There are two different things," said Raja Umer Khattab, a senior superintendent of police, when we talked about the case. "One is the blast, and the second is after the blast." He told me that separate investigators were assigned to the fires, and their examination produced only the arrests of a few Shia Muslims, in line with the police theory of the case: the fires were set by people in the procession who were enraged by the bombing.

This explanation appeared to satisfy almost nobody outside the police force. Abbas Kumeli, the Shia Muslim leader, argued that the theory made no sense. Granted, the Shia marchers were standing there at the Lighthouse Centre, where some of the fires took place, but the marchers were nowhere near the Bolton Market. Why had the worst fires been set there? Why would angry Shia marchers walk past a mile of buildings and leave them all untouched, then start lighting fires again?

In the absence of a convincing official explanation, people were already supplying their own.

IN SEARCH OF more information, I visited the local office of the Human Rights Commission of Pakistan. To get there I had to climb a set of concrete stairs to an open-air walkway, overlooking a courtyard. Off to my right stood the half-demolished stone façade of some nineteenth-century building from British colonial times. To my left was an apartment building, darkened by pollution but full of life. Half a dozen girls crowded onto one of the balconies, giggling as they taught each other how to put on makeup. Their laughter reverberated across the courtyard, which had been turned into a parking lot, blocked by a red-and-white gate and watched by riflemen who provided an illusion of security.

In the commission's offices, the electricity had gone out and the temperature was around 105 degrees Fahrenheit. The man I had come to see led the way to a conference table in the breeze near an open window. His name was Abdul Hai. In the days after the fires, he was part of a Human Rights Commission team that conducted its own interviews with shopkeepers and others. Their report released on January 9, 2010, included this provocative paragraph:

> After interviewing and listening [to] the sufferers point of view, the team was of the opinion that the burning and looting was pre-planned and was done by 25 to 30 persons who were fully trained and were possessing steel cutters, tools, fire arms and chemicals. It is very important to note that [the] procession of mourners after the bomb blast passed away and there was none of them at burning and looting sites.

An operation that was preplanned? It was a strong statement in an otherwise carefully worded report. A covering note minimized its key finding: "This report is a mere compilation of the views of people affected directly by the attack." Not, in other words, any sort of official conclusion.

Abdul Hai made a copy of his report on the Ashura bombing and gave me a chance to look it over. He emphasized again that the report simply passed on the claims of shopkeepers. "I have no opinion," he said, gradually becoming more vague and evasive, or so it seemed to me.

I pressed him politely. He was a professional; he knew Karachi; he had talked with victims, some of whom may have witnessed the fires; he had even issued this report. What did he *think* might have happened? Who was responsible for burning several blocks of the city?

Some kind of mafia, he said.

And who might that be?

"Ah," he said, in a tone that suggested: *Now there's the hard part.* "Everybody knows, but nobody will tell you," he said. "These mafias are all under the shelter of the police."

As I moved across the city asking questions, it sometimes seemed that Abdul Hai had it right: everybody knew, but nobody would tell. Usually, however, it seemed to be the other way around. People across the city opened their lives and their hearts to me. Many were eager to tell me what happened that day.

I just wasn't sure if anybody knew.

Pakistan is a land that embraces conspiracy theories. Of course the people of any nation, including America, can display a paranoid streak, and Pakistanis seem especially susceptible given their national history of repeated coups and covert wars. After the Ashura fires, everybody seemed to have a conspiracy theory. One came from Faisal Edhi. "I think it was a conspiracy to cause a clash between Shias and Sunnis," he told me. He believed that the burned shops belonged to Sunni Muslims, who were deliberately attacked in tandem with the bombing of the Shia procession. Maybe so, though I later met a Shia shop owner who had also lost everything.

Other theories implicated the city's two leading political parties. The major parties had armed wings as well as links to various criminals. One notion pointed to the city's ruling party, Mayor Kamal's party, the MQM. Some hypotheses said the MQM destroyed the shops of political opponents, or tried to repossess land for the city's use. No proof emerged.

Another theory blamed arsonists under the protection of the MQM's political rivals, the Bhutto family's Pakistan People's Party, or PPP. That wasn't proven either, although the police and Rangers, who failed so miserably to stop the fires, were under the authority of PPP government ministers.

When I met with Raja Umer, the police investigator, I asked about the claims of storekeepers and other witnesses, who believed that chemicals had been poured on the fires to accelerate the burning. People traded stories of arsonists wearing gloves and holding weapons. "No, no, this is wrong," said Raja Umer. "Totally wrong. People said those who were burning the shops were wearing gloves they kept with them so they would not leave fingerprints. But after investigation it was decided that there was a medical store that was broken into."

"They were wearing surgical gloves?"

"Yes," he said. And the fires burned so fiercely not because of chemical accelerants, but simply because the buildings and their contents were so flammable. "It was a chemical market, a plastic market, clothes market, so it can burn easily. There is no evidence we can get about chemicals used for burning."

Raja Umer's assurances did not prevent members of Karachi's elites from casting their own suspicions. One of the more chilling theories came from Yasmeen Lari, a woman who was well connected to Karachi's political establishment and among the city's most distinguished architects—she was known as "the first woman architect in Pakistan." She led Pakistan's Heritage Foundation, dedicated to preserving historic buildings and other artifacts; when thousands of old documents were found in that giant pile in the city hall clock tower, it was Yasmeen Lari's foundation that organized an effort to begin preserving and archiving them. She also went into action after the fires. She rushed to the ruined markets, many of which were in buildings dating back to colonial times. City officials were inclined to tear down what little of the buildings remained, but she sought to save historic façades. And this work led to her theory: she, like the shopkeepers, believed that somebody wanted the land beneath the stores.

"I've come to this conclusion," she told me, "because M. A. Jinnah Road is now prime commercial land. These buildings are three or four stories high. They were burned down to try to see if, you know, a multistory tower could be put up in their place. Because as soon as we got to the site, within a few days, although we were offering that we would try to raise money for them to restore the buildings, these owners kept on saying to me, 'Don't worry, we have no problem of money, we have people who are sitting there saying they will build it for us.' So the question is how come?" Many of the buildings were full of shopkeepers whose families rented space at exceedingly low rates, having held on to their shops for generations. It would not be unprecedented for real estate owners to seize a chance to burn out tenants. "There is a huge mafia in this city," Yasmeen Lari said, "which really wants to get this prime piece of land to build these multistory towers. I have no doubt in my mind there was a great conspiracy."

I heard an even darker version of this theory from Arif Hasan, a Karachi urban planner and architect who was writing a five-volume history of his city. Hasan was a broad-faced and solid man, whose stern expression somehow carried with it a hint of mirth. Sitting behind the white table in his home office, Hasan spoke in his quiet and precise voice. "Land mafias" had been growing in power for many years, he said, seizing real estate by any means and maximizing its value. "Our politicians became a part of it," Hasan said. At first the politicians were in control of the mafias, or imagined that they were. "But then the Bolton Market tragedy happened," he said, "and that showed our politicians that the mafia was stronger than them."

Hasan had identified something that drove a city when it grew this rapidly—drove its economy, its politics, its conversation, its dreams and its nightmares. Real estate was the heart of the instant city in the early twenty-first century. It was a swiftly growing city's true faith, a source of passion, hope, mystery, and superstition. Even if all the conspiracy theories were completely wrong (and certainly none was ever proved), the political result was the same. The abruptly vacant land took center stage in the political debate.

Even the bombing of the Shias prompted less comment than the real estate. A reporter for the *News International* wrote a few days later, "Within an hour of the Ashura blast, which tragically was quickly forgotten, the battle for prime real estate of Karachi began in earnest." Shias were always being killed in Pakistan. But real estate on Jinnah Road did not become available every day. The question of what to do with the Bolton Market land instantly became a problem for everyone, including Karachi's mayor, Mustafa Kamal. It even attracted interest and money from the United States.

When I thought about Arif Hasan's theories of the Bolton Market fires, I recalled something he'd told me a couple of years before. He compared the situation in Karachi to man's ancient lust for gold.

"Land has replaced gold," he said. "Everything that was done for gold, is now done for land."

A few months after the fires, Hasan was invited on a talk show on a local television channel and offered his views on land mafias in Karachi. Soon afterward, his telephone rang. He answered, and heard his name spoken by an unfamiliar voice.

"You don't know who I am," the caller said. "I am a well-wisher. I have enormous respect for you, you are a great asset to this country, but there are many things you don't understand. We have heard your television statements. They are factually incorrect; you have been misinformed. And we would like you to remember that although we respect you very much, we have to live in the same city."

"Is this a threat?" Hasan replied. "Are you threatening me?"

"No," the caller said. "How can we threaten you? We love you so much. We're just asking you to understand that we have to live in the same city."

Hasan said he was sorry if he caused offense. The caller bid Hasan a courteous goodbye, saying he hoped that they would meet someday.

FIRE CREWS PUT OUT the last of the flames after hundreds of shops were destroyed, but it would be harder to tamp down the political debate. The People's Party claimed the MQM had failed to properly mobilize the fire crews, which were under the control of MQM politicians. The MQM said the People's Party had failed to unleash the police. This distraction came at a moment of great tension, when the People's Party, the MQM, and other political parties were maneuvering against each other for the long-term control of Karachi. The provincial law that had created the local government was about to expire. The parties disagreed on whether and how to renew it, and their indecision raised the possibility that the mayor, the city council, and every other elected official could see their offices changed or even abolished. The moment was even more dangerous because Karachi's political parties were generally divided between ethnic groups—or more precisely language groups, because each major group had its own tongue, such as Urdu, Sindhi, Punjabi, Baloch, and Pashto, and language was the way many defined themselves. A man's political rival was also his blood enemy, implicated in ethnic warfare that had gone on for decades.

And so it should not have been surprising that, with the authorities over-whelmed, the political war of rhetoric was accompanied by a hail of bullets. The day of mayhem on December 28 would be followed by numerous days of gun battles between members of political parties across the city.

The year 2009 was an unusually deadly one for politicians and activists, hundreds of whom were killed, but the monthly pace actually increased in January 2010, according to figures compiled by the Human Rights Commission. During that month thirty-seven deaths fell under the heading of "targeted killing," which was the typical phrase for the shootings by gunmen who rolled away on motorcycles. Twenty-six more deaths were labeled "political workers killed." These figures included a political worker who was beheaded in early January. Were the killings related? Unrelated? Who really knew? Many people had theories, but few of the crimes were ever solved.

Nor would the city have much time to recover from the killings.

Forty days after the December 28 bombing and fires, a Shia procession began that was linked to the first. This march, on February 5, 2010, marked the end of the ritual period of mourning for the long-dead Hussein. Again Shias began assembling from across the city, carrying banners and coffin sheets, preparing to be summoned again to their faith by stories of sacrifice and loss; again the police and Rangers made elaborate plans and formed layers of security. Police sent out advisories to be prepared for trouble. Shopkeepers rolled down their metal gates. People waited, asking each other what would happen.

Seemin Jamali, a Karachi doctor, was inside her home that afternoon. "I was watching the television, but I heard this blast myself," she recalled. "All the win-dowpanes of our house were shaking, and there was a strange kind of vibration in our home. And I just knew that it was the sound of a blast."

Dr. Jamali looked at her husband, who was also a doctor, and they did what they always did in such circumstances. They stood up and went in to work.

For more than twenty years now she had worked at the Jinnah Postgradu-ate Medical Centre, a free public hospital in Karachi. When I met her there, Dr. Jamali wore a green *dupatta*, a scarf that Pakistani women use for modesty—

sometimes covering their hair, sometimes letting it fall around their shoulders. She wore a glittering stud in her nose. Her eyes were alert to the constant motion in the emergency department, as doctors walked among the patients on wheeled gurneys. She kept a photo of her children at the side of her desk. In a roomful of gurneys outside Dr. Jamali's office, a sign read: "CAUTION! Display of Weapons is Strictly Forbidden in the Emergency Department. By Order of Incharge." For some years now the person in charge had been Seemin Jamali herself. She was director of the emergency department.

On February 5, when she felt the explosion at her house, she went to the emergency room and waited for the ambulances to arrive. The drivers pulled up just outside the sets of glass doors that led to the reception desk, and gradually the details of the bombing filtered in: this time a motorbike with explosives on board had been placed near a busload of mourners.

"First we received the dead," Jamali told me. There had been no triage at the scene of the explosion, no effort to select the casualties who most urgently needed attention; so the first ambulances came with corpses. "Next we had the walking wounded, we had everybody coming in ambulances to the hospital, and in minutes they were given first aid." A dozen people had been killed, and dozens more wounded. They arrived attended by scores of angry and wailing relatives.

It was a heavy toll, but Dr. Jamali had seen worse. The hospital was well prepared, having received an alert from the police to expect the possibility of violence during the procession. As the gurneys rolled in, loaded with stunned and bleeding people, doctors swiftly evaluated them and made decisions. Some were sent upstairs to the operating theaters. Others went to various hospital wards, making room for those who would follow.

More ambulances arrived, and from the cab of one of them stepped Abdul Sattar Edhi, the patriarch of the Edhi ambulance service, who had come to see the tragedy for himself. The old man was unmistakable in his simple black clothes and his flowing white beard. He was no doubt wearing the wry expression that he carried even into the worst situations. Edhi once told me, "I feel happy to drive an ambulance with a dead body behind." He had, with the help of a writer, published a memoir that went on at some length about his willingness to wash dead bodies, and his distaste for those who refused to touch them—in his mind such people were hypocrites, in the same class as bigots and politicians and those who looked down on the poor.

Dr. Jamali spotted Edhi and stopped what she was doing, showing proper deference to an elder of such great stature. She took him around the emergency room where some patients were receiving initial treatment. Dr. Jamali guided the old man back through the two sets of glass doors and out to the driveway, where she bid him goodbye. She believed the he had gone away, but Edhi told me later that he took a seat inside one of the Edhi ambulances that were parked outside the entrance.

The parking area was a strip of asphalt running along the side of the build-ing. It was narrow. Little convenience stores were across the way, topped by blue Pepsi signs. So it was a constricted space, with ambulances coming and going, wheeled gurneys sitting on the sidewalk, and crowds of family mem-bers arriving to ask after injured relatives. And after seeing off Edhi here, Dr. Jamali encountered a complication. A number of prominent Shias arrived at the emergency department. "Their leaders came and said the government has announced compensation and free treatment at one of the private facili-ties," a hospital that would normally be out of reach for most of the victims. "Now, that is where the commotion started." People in the crowd began shout-ing all at once. Some wanted their relatives moved from the public hospital right away. Dr. Jamali did not think it was wise to move anyone through "all of this mob," but finally consented, and began to think of her plans to remove the wounded. She saw off a city official at the entrance, then spun around and stepped back through the glass doors. She turned her head to begin giving instructions to a member of her staff.

As Dr. Jamali spoke to her subordinate, as the crowd milled in anguish, and as Abdul Sattar Edhi rested his feet, they did not know that a motorcycle was parked and unattended near the entrance to the emergency department. It had a strange-looking object strapped behind the seat.

PART TWO

LANDMARKS

4 | JINNAH'S TOMB

What really happened on December 28, 2009?

We have already seen clues to the story, which stretches back through time. The story involves the growth and the change of the city. It begins with the man who founded Pakistan, and also made a decision that changed Karachi forever.

His name is all over Karachi like markings on a trail. It graces Muhammad Ali Jinnah Road, where the first procession was bombed, and Jinnah Postgraduate Medical Centre, where Dr. Seemin Jamali's afternoon was only going to get worse. The mayor's political party holds its rallies in a park called Jinnah Ground, and Jinnah's portrait looks down on boys at Scout headquarters. The same face stares out from every denomination of Pakistani currency used to buy goods in the Lighthouse Bazaar. His tomb rises near the start of the procession route, domed and white and attended by an honor guard.

The buildings and pictures and signs were meant to tell us something. And they do, even if it is not necessarily the message that their creators intended.

Jinnah's story helps to explain Karachi's explosive growth.

It helps to explain the bombing and fires along Jinnah Road.

It helps to explain why a hospital emergency department was seconds from disaster. His life also helps us to understand the Edhis, Dr. Jamali, and others who have fought to hold their city together. So the next several landmarks we encounter will pull us into the instant city's short but crowded past.

A few blocks from the scorched remains of the Bolton Market, I came upon a high stone house. It was a narrow building, wedged onto a corner. It was wrapped in layers of iron-railed balconies, in a manner that brought New Orleans to mind, and the balconies were wrapped in scaffolding, for the house was under renovation. Power tools whined in the hands of men inside. A supervisor said I could not possibly look around while work was under way, but a moment later his Karachi hospitality asserted itself and he led me into the building. Just don't take any pictures, he said. We climbed the stairs to a room that opened onto a balcony. Here, workers had installed recess lights and sanded the hardwood floor. The man said that this room, in the house called Wazir Mansion, was the birthplace of the founder of Pakistan.

Jinnah's exact birth date was not recorded, since many families at that time considered birthdays unimportant. In later life he gave a date for the record: December 25, 1876. The son of a Karachi merchant, Jinnah left the city for years at a time, but returned for Pakistan's independence in 1947.

He is the man on whom Pakistan built its national myth, much as early generations of Americans plastered George Washington's name on monuments, streets, and cities. Jinnah's portrait hangs in buildings all over Pakistan. When he was young he was handsome, Burt Lancaster handsome, but many portraits show him late in life, when he was sicker and thinner, though still with

Muhammad Ali Jinnah. *[William Vandivert/Getty Images]*

flinty eyes. On the hundred-rupee note Jinnah looks a bit to the side, giving the impression that he has just spotted an unexpected opportunity across the room. In other portraits he stares straight at you, his mouth pursed, his expression suggesting that whatever you just said was the stupidest remark he ever heard.

The official images of Jinnah turn him into a silent symbol that the state can manipulate as required. He's tinted purple on the fifty-rupee note, and orange on the twenty; he's gray in the grainy (and frequently soundless) film clips that play on holidays on Pakistani TV. It is easy to forget that Jinnah was a living man, with a taste for fine suits and waspish remarks. He lived in an age of titanic figures such as Gandhi, Nehru, and Churchill. Jinnah matched wits against them, and made himself part of a great global movement. He was among the men who, after the Second World War, led the nations of the colonial world to their independence.

Jinnah lived at the dawn of an international order that even today has not passed away. The war's victors created global institutions such as the United Nations and the International Monetary Fund. They cleared the way for the modern global economy, and in the process encouraged the growth of many of the world's cities. The war's victors also laid the foundations of new conflicts. Maps drawn in the postwar years defined generations of struggle—from South Asia to the Middle East, and from Korea to the heart of Europe. Jinnah became an essential player in this process when he took part in the perilous decision to divide India along religious lines. The catastrophic consequences were still evident more than sixty years later, in the Ashura bombing and its aftermath.

Jinnah was cosmopolitan. When he moved to London as young man, he briefly aspired to be an actor before settling on a career as a barrister instead. He owned a mansion in Bombay and bought a landmark stone house in Karachi. His words suggest he liked Karachi as it was in the summer of 1947, when he praised its architecture and "large open spaces" that, in contrast to more crowded cities, "give to the visitor a feeling of space and ease." He was so utterly comfortable in the urban world of 1947 that it is tempting to wonder what he would think if he could walk through Karachi today and see how much he changed it.

IT IS EVEN MORE alluring to imagine Jinnah's urban world, so near in time and yet so different. That summer of 1947 was the last moment that he could have praised his hometown's open spaces. The city was filling so rapidly that nobody could find a hotel room. Room rates climbed so high that authorities imposed price controls to stop "racketing." Those who couldn't find a room had to settle for tents outside town. A newspaper ran the headline "Swamped Over By Outsiders," and more people were arriving on boats and trains.

Thousands of newcomers were learning their new home. They caught the breeze on a stone promenade that led down toward the Arabian Sea, or visited the shrine of Abdullah Shah Ghazi, a revered descendant of the Prophet Mohammed. They could attend movies from Bombay, with billings that seemed to catch the zeitgeist: *Dunyadari* was the "modern story of a modern woman who lived & suffered for the one man who hated her the most." The Jubilee Cinema advertised plans to mark the day of all days:

JUBILEE

It's A Date!

15th August will Herald in the Independence of

Hindustan & Pakistan

With a Feast of Dance, Music, and Delicate Romance

In

JEEVAN PICTURES

ALL INDIA PREMIERE

ARSI

Moviegoers could continue on for dinner at Mishat, which was planning to open on the same day, August 15, offering the "best Indian & European dishes" at the "only ideal & exclusive restaurant in the town."

The migrants were adopting a prosperous port city with a population of around four hundred thousand. Factories turned out chemicals, paper, and glass. People drove Chrysler sedans, and could order "home delivered" British Singer roadsters from a dealer on Mahatma Gandhi Street. A radio station was just opening for business, offering local songs of Sindh, the province that includes Karachi, as well as a program of "recorded Western music" called "The Birth of the Blues." Newspapers catered to a sophisticated readership; some of the city's elite had been educated in England. Pan Am Clippers arrived several times a week from Calcutta, big four-propeller airliners stopping to refuel on their way to points west.

The main street that we know as Jinnah Road was called Bandar Road then, *bandar* being the word for "port" in the language of the ethnic Sindhis who had lived in this province for generations. Then as now, the city hall was a stone pile topped with onion-shaped domes. British officers commanded the Army

Bandar Road, the future Jinnah Road, mid-twentieth century. *[imagesofasia.com]*

of India, whose Karachi-based soldiers rested at Napier Barracks, named for the Victorian general who conquered Sindh and added it to the British Empire.

Karachi was the closest Indian port to the sea lanes leading toward England. And so for the British it was a gateway to the greatest and most outrageous of all the prizes seized in the age of colonialism: an entire subcontinent ruled from afar. The British in India traded in everything from textiles to opium. They bought cotton from the farms in the Indus River Valley above Karachi. They established courts under British law, and extracted taxes from the Indians themselves to pay for the whole enterprise. Indian soldiers fought in British armies around the world, while great figures in British history spent years in India: the Duke of Wellington, Rudyard Kipling, Winston Churchill. Indians traveled the other way to London, among them a student named Gandhi, who was a devoted subject of the British Empire before his life moved in unexpected directions.

Now the grand hallucination of British India was about to disappear—that mixture of tradition, firepower, and sheer bluff that the British called prestige, which allowed handfuls of men to rule hundreds of millions. In a few days the king's final viceroy was planning to surrender the subcontinent, bowing to decades of Indian demands for freedom. India would become a pair of self-governed states, each dominated by one of South Asia's two largest religious groups, Hindus and Muslims. Pakistan, the Muslim state, was an awkward-looking creation, cut in two pieces—one to the east and one to the west—and separated by a vast stretch of India. The western portion, focused on the valley of the Indus, included Karachi. And that explained the arrival of the migrants to Karachi: they were Muslims drawn from elsewhere in India to the new Islamic nation.

On August 7, a twin-propeller DC-3 Dakota appeared in the sky over Karachi. It came from New Delhi, bearing the most important migrant of all. Police had been warned of the plane's approach, but quickly lost control as a hundred thousand people came to meet the plane. "Surging crowds broke several rings of police cordon," a witness reported, "and mobbed the Mauripur air field when Mr. M.A. Jinnah . . . landed at 5-38 p.m." Jinnah emerged from the plane dressed in a silk *sherwani,* a long garment like a coat. His sister Fatima stood smiling beside him at the top of the airplane stairs, wearing white satin.

Jinnah would become the Muslim state's first leader by virtue of his stature in the movement for freedom—even Gandhi addressed him as the Quaid-e-Azam, which translates as Leader of the Nation or Great Leader. If Gandhi was the spiritual architect of Indian independence, Jinnah played a different and often dissenting role. He was the leader of a political party called the Muslim League, and a force for decades in the independence movement. But as freedom approached, Jinnah differed with Gandhi and others over how India should be governed once the British left. He insisted that people of his religious tradition, a minority in India, were a separate nation who deserved an equal share of political power with India's majority Hindus. Jinnah's insistence on this point was one of the factors that led to the creation of separate states.

Like Gandhi, Jinnah was a first-rate lawyer, powerfully shaped by his experience in the capital of empire. Late in life the British influence was more obvious with Jinnah, from his reverence for law and order to his wardrobe of two hundred fine English suits. He put on one of those suits soon after his arrival in Karachi, and a newsreel crew took footage of the Great Leader stepping briskly through a portico, at age seventy as erect as the military officer beside him. The old man combed his white hair straight back from his forehead in a manner that stressed the severity of his face, hollow-cheeked and narrow, fleshless and straight-lined—straight mouth, straight nose, level gaze. His blazer flapped in the breeze, revealing the waistcoat of a suit perfectly tailored to him, or at least

Jinnah and Gandhi, 1939. *[Topical Press Agency/Hulton Archive/Getty Images]*

perfectly tailored to the man he had been at one time. The cloth hung loosely around his arms and legs, suggesting a body even more skeletal than his face. He had told nobody that he suffered from tuberculosis.

Jinnah had been working out of Bombay and New Delhi, making arrangements for his new nation. Now he was returning to make his hometown the capital of Pakistan. By doing so he would set off actions and reactions in Karachi, a kind of nuclear fission that would burn for decades, exploding ever outward like the city itself.

THE MOMENT THAT Jinnah's plane touched down—5:38 p.m. on August 7, 1947—can fairly count as the birth of Karachi as we know it today. We could consider earlier moments, like 1729, when a group of merchants relocated to Karachi's harbor after a nearby harbor silted up, or 1843, when Britain's conquering General Napier seized the province of Sindh, using Karachi as his headquarters and laying the foundations of the modern city. The city grew steadily in the century after Napier. But Jinnah's arrival signaled the start of something new. Karachi's population would more than double in the few years that followed.

Even in those early days of August, the flow of migrants toward Pakistan was increasing. Although there was no television, and most Indians lived beyond the reach of All India Radio, the idea of moving had spread through newspapers, letters, and political meetings. For many Muslims, the new national capital was a natural destination, where they could hope for jobs in business or the new government. Some Muslims were educated and ambitious, "civil servants, lawyers, scholars, doctors, and entrepreneurs" who, in the words of one historian, "migrated to the new Islamic state, there to carve out careers unimpeded by competition from Hindus."

Some migrants must have been surprised, then, to discover that Karachi had nearly as many Hindus as the places they had just left.

A Hindu temple stood near the Muslim shrine of the Prophet Mohammed's great-grandson; another temple was across the street from city hall. Hindus lived in mansions, and ran fine stores on Elphinstone Street. Although Sindh was an overwhelmingly Muslim province, which explained why it was about to become part of a Muslim country, 51 percent of the *city* was Hindu, and other religions were practiced as well. Neither Muslim leaders nor the members of other religious groups knew how to handle this awkward reality. And the non-Muslims were getting anxious, as anyone could see by handing over pocket change—one and a half *annas,* a couple of coins—for a local newspaper. The headline about being "Swamped Over By Outsiders" appeared in the *Sind Observer,* and its editor was a deeply concerned Hindu.

Well before Jinnah arrived in Karachi, the *Observer* was sending signals of distress, which Jinnah would have seen if aides forwarded news from the future capital. The *Observer*'s headline on July 1 was "Profession and Practice." The unsigned commentary probably reflected the views of the Hindu editor, Shri K. Punniah:

> Apologists of the partition of India have been profuse with protestations that the minorities both in Pakistan and the rest of India would get a fair deal. Mr. Jinnah had been saying all along, "Let us part as brothers." . . . During the recent league council meeting at Delhi he seems to have told the Sind Ministers that minorities should be treated not only justly but generously. So far, however, we have very little proof. . . . We understand that behind the scenes, political plots are being hatched to reduce the Hindus to impotence.

The Hindu Punniah could not easily be persuaded that his rights would be protected in a majority Muslim state.

In a reflective moment, Jinnah might have noticed the irony in these words, since Jinnah had lately been arguing that *his* people should not be placed under majority Hindu rule.

THE PARTITION OF INDIA could look so clean on a map—Muslims over here, Hindus over there, borderlines in between. It was never that simple, as the life of the Karachi editor Punniah made clear. An old photo portrays him as a respectable man, with a wispy mustache and heavy black eyebrows floating above his round black-rimmed glasses. He is not a young man—there does not seem to be much hair on the back of his head—but his skin is smooth, his cheekbones are high, and his sharp eyes look skeptically at something to his left. By 1947 Punniah had edited the *Sind Observer* for a quarter of a century (except for one brief and glorious interval when he was fired and then rehired after defying his boss's order not to cover a news event). He lived in a palatial house with his wife, a physician of whom "it was said that she knew half of the population of Karachi (all women) personally and the other half were delivered with her assistance."

Punniah was born around 1882 in southern India, more than a thousand miles from Karachi. He was a schoolmaster's son who failed an examination to enter school, and ran away to Bombay. He worked as a water carrier. He worked as a clerk. He took a modest newspaper job. By his mid-thirties he was living in the city of Madras and editing an English-language paper, campaigning, according to one account, against "Caste, Idolatry . . . Communalism, Drink, and a number of social evils." Then he migrated to Karachi, where an ambitious Hindu could rise. Hindus in the province of Sindh were far more likely to be literate than people of other faiths. They formed so much of the merchant class that one of their languages, Gujarati, became the local language of business. Their cosmopolitan spirit was reflected in the pages of the *Sind Observer,* an English-language paper where international news appeared between ads for fine jewelry and British "Super Ten Saloon Cars." Hindus played such a large role in the capital of this Muslim province that Punniah later wrote of the city's "mutual toleration, on account of which the Hindus lived for centuries on good terms with their Muslim neighbours."

Muhammad Ali Jinnah knew the minorities in his new nation could bring Pakistan strength, since so many were people of education and means, people like Jinnah himself. He came from a minority sect of Islam—his family was Shia. His doctors, his steward, and even his late wife were non-Muslim. He was comfortable with people of many faiths, and sought their aid as he organized Pakistan. In 1947, he met with a Zoroastrian shipping magnate from Karachi, and asked for help in forming a national shipping line.

He must have believed that he could get the minorities' aid. In 1947 Karachi's religious communities "were not divided," remembered Bibi Inder Kaur, one of the city's many non-Muslim residents, who told her story decades later to oral historians. She was a member of the Sikhs, who had ruled their own expansive kingdom in northwest India until the British relieved them of it in the mid-nineteenth century. Kaur's family prospered in Karachi, where she bore three children by her husband, a doctor, and plotted behind his back to get an education.

Then again, diversity had limits. Her Hindu neighbors refused to touch the doorway of her home, because they knew that her Muslim servant touched it. In Punniah's *Sind Observer*, people were straightforward about their religious preferences in the classified ads:

> *Wanted:* a Muslim Typist and Stenographer.... *Wanted:* Influential and reliable Chief Agents for Karachi, one Hindu and one Muslim.... *Wanted:* an M.A. in English Literature or B.A. in English Honors for Literary Work. Christian preferable.

The truth was that British India was riddled with divisions of religion, caste, region, and race. The British embraced and emphasized these divisions, which complicated India's long fight for independence. In their farsighted moments Indian political leaders tried to work together; Jinnah himself brokered an alliance between Hindus and Muslims in 1916, and worked to maintain that unity for years afterward. But communal differences gradually widened. Eventually Muslims demanded their own state, a demand that intensified after 1940. As British rule neared its end, communal attacks increased across India.

Karachi remained more peaceful than other cities, but hummed with tension. The *Sind Observer* was said to back Hindu nationalists, and the local chapter of a Hindu nationalist group called the RSS had been meeting in Karachi for years. Members of the society pledged themselves to "the protection of Hindu religion, Hindu culture, and Hindu society." They recruited young men like L. K. Advani, a nineteen-year-old with a dapper mustache and dark-framed glasses—a fashion similar to that of the old Hindu journalist Punniah. Advani, from an affluent family, was a product of St. Patrick's Catholic school and an admirer of Charles Dickens's *A Tale of Two Cities.* He would remember a city where it was "common for Hindus to pay homage at the shrines of Sufi saints and for Muslims to celebrate Hindu festivals." Nevertheless a friend persuaded Advani to join the RSS, which was active in communal riots in much of India.

Jinnah's Muslim League had an armed wing known as the Muslim National Guards, and not all Muslims shared Jinnah's openness toward other religious communities. As soon as the division of India was announced, some Muslims in Karachi began talking of seizing Hindu property, or of rigging the electoral system to limit the power of religious minorities. These were the proposals that generated alarming articles in the *Sind Observer* and other papers, and early in the summer of 1947 some Hindus began to leave Karachi.

Jinnah found this galling. The Hindus were fleeing from *him,* doubting his words of assurance. Weeks before arriving in Karachi, he began a long-distance effort to calm the situation. He summoned a friend in the Karachi press corps, a Hindu editor whose paper took a more sympathetic view of the situation than Punniah's *Observer*: M. S. M. Sharma of the *Daily Gazette.* In mid-July, Sharma agreed to meet with the Great Leader in New Delhi, and later wrote that Jinnah made a personal appeal:

> "Do stay on in Karachi," he thundered as if delivering a public lecture. . . . "You cannot go out of Karachi." . . . Now that he had got Pakistan, he had no longer any grudge against the Hindus. In fact, he was anxious to revert to his old and familiar role of "Ambassador of Hindu-Muslim Unity." He proposed that he should continue as the champion of minorities in Pakistan as he had been, for several years now, the champion of the minorities in India. . . . "I am going to rely on your help. I am going to take no refusal."

The Great Leader enlisted the editor's help in a news conference that was about to begin, dictating questions that Sharma was supposed to ask about minority rights. Jinnah stepped before the press corps and delivered his answer: "The minorities, to whichever community they may belong, will be safeguarded. Their religion or their faith or belief will be protected in every way possible. Their life and property will be secure. There will be no interference of any kind with their freedom of worship." His statement of reassurance received a gigantic headline in Sharma's Karachi newspaper, and front-page treatment in others.

Careful readers of the news conference transcript in the *Daily Gazette* would nevertheless have noticed a moment of awkwardness when the performance wandered off script. Jinnah was asked a deceptively simple question. "Will Pakistan be a secular or theocratic State?"

Jinnah, the old lawyer, ducked.

"You are asking me a question that is absurd," he said. "I do not know what a theocratic State means." Twice the reporters clarified the question, and twice more Jinnah dismissed it. He had never explained the role that he intended for Islam to play in the Islamic state. He kept his goals vague, necessarily so since his supporters didn't agree on much. Any real answer had to wait until after he arrived in Karachi on August 7, and even then, as he moved into the old colonial Governor's House, Jinnah stayed quiet for days.

On August 9, Punniah's *Sind Observer* tried to stay calm: "Hindus of 'Pak' Should Not Feel Panicky" read one headline. Other headlines offered reason for panic. Seven people were killed in the Indian city of Amritsar. The *Observer* gave space to a Hindu politician who charged that "Muslims in Pakistan were intimidating the minorities with a view to making them leave their homeland." The Hindu leader was quoted as saying, "Violence must be met with violence. . . . Be brave and throw away all luxuries of life." In Karachi, the Pakistani Muslim leader Liaquat Ali accused an Indian leader of "inciting Hindus," and threatened "repercussions." From the northern reaches of Pakistan came this report: "One Thousand Shots Exchanged in Peshawar." News arrived from Larkana, a town in Sindh, that three Hindu women had been abducted from their homes "by a gang of about 37 Muslims armed with lathis, lorhs, and hatchets."

THRONGS MIGHT HAVE surrounded him at the airport, but once he reached the Governor's House Jinnah was in some ways alone. His wife was dead. He was attended by his sister Fatima, the woman in white satin who had arrived with him on the plane. They had kept quiet about the old man's illnesses. ("There is nothing wrong with me," Jinnah would write one of his advisors shortly before his death. "A little rest in Quetta has done me a lot of good.") Now he faced the challenge of creating a national administration from scratch. India would inherit New Delhi with its old infrastructure of colonial power; Pakistan would inherit nothing comparable. "There is no Government of Pakistan but it is being created overnight," wrote Shahid Hamid, an army officer who knew Jinnah and helped to create that government, and who later published a chronicle of his experiences. "There are no Government offices, no Ministries, and no office furniture or stationery. Typewriters are a luxury."

Until recent weeks the new country didn't even have a flag, and Jinnah had to put up with Britain's last viceroy presuming to design one. Lord Louis Mountbatten suggested a flag with a small British Union Jack in one corner. Jinnah thought not. He approved a flag nodding to Islam rather than empire: white crescent and star against a green background. A vertical white stripe was added along the pole, meant to represent religious minorities. Karachi authorities encouraged everyone to fly the banner on Independence Day, but the Illumination and Fireworks Committee ran out of flags and had to advise people to improvise with "any flags and buntings for decoration which they may have in stock."

In this unsettled situation, the Great Leader tried to maintain his cautious pace. Some days earlier he had met a Muslim military officer who expressed hope for quick promotion upon joining Pakistan's army, and the old man made a face. "You Mussulmans, either you are up in the sky or down in the dumps. You cannot adopt a steady course. All promotions will come in good time, but there will be no mad rush." Unfortunately for Jinnah, the world was in a mad rush. The mid-August independence date had only been set in June. Everything that was India—the civil service, the army, the bank reserves, and above all the land—was supposed to be divided in weeks. "As the time for Partition gets closer everybody seems to be in a spin," wrote Shahid Hamid. "Some are preparing for the coming celebrations while others are more concerned with avoiding the impending bloodbath."

From the far side of India came news that Gandhi was walking the streets of Calcutta, urging the Hindu majority not to attack Muslims. His fellow Hindus booed him, blaming him for failing to prevent the division of their nation. A Hindu politician declared Gandhi's peaceful methods "obsolete."

Shahid Hamid wrote a chronicle of those days that noted for Sunday, August 10, "Rioting by the Sikhs has started." This was happening to the northeast of Karachi, in the province of Punjab, the Sikhs' ancestral homeland, which would be sliced in two between India and Pakistan. On Monday, August 11, Hamid recorded killings at a rate of more than two hundred per day.

This was the day that Muhammad Ali Jinnah would finally be called upon to speak in Karachi.

That day he put on the soft brimless cap that was becoming known as a "Jinnah cap" and walked into what was known as the Sindh Secretariat. Its wood-paneled assembly chamber was an architectural sign of change; the Sindhis had won the right to organize a provincial assembly just a few years before. Today a different group was gathering at the hundred-plus desks, men charged with writing a constitution for the new nation of Pakistan. Muhammad Ali Jinnah expected to be chosen that day as their leader.

That morning the *Sind Observer* reported, "Lahore and Amritsar are scorched-earth cities and parts of Calcutta too. . . . Hundreds of thousands have left their homes on account of fear and want of food and are wandering about like helpless and unwanted refugees." In a Sindhi town outside Karachi, a man was taken into custody for the alleged manufacturing of bombs.

Pakistan had little to hold it together except the frail man in the chamber, hunched over as he signed his name in the register.

There was some preliminary discussion. A lawmaker proposed rethinking the Islam-accented national flag, which troubled religious minorities, but Jinnah's top lieutenant said it was too late. Jinnah was chosen as expected to be president of the constituent assembly. And in a hint of Karachi's electricity-challenged future, the power went out before he could speak. The microphone at the lectern went dead, and the old man's words were just a buzz to people in the galleries. Jinnah spoke anyway, as the sixty-odd members of the assembly leaned in to hear him and reporters raced down from the press gallery to get within range. The speech had an improvised feel to it. "I cannot make any well-considered pronouncement at this moment, but I shall say a few things as they occur to me," he told the assembly.

"A division had to take place," Jinnah continued, trying to reassure them that they had been wise to break away from the rest of India. "There are sections of people who may not agree with it, who may not like it, but in my judgment there was no other solution."

Scratchy recordings of other speeches from that time demonstrate that Jinnah spoke English in the cadence of the nineteenth century in which he had been born, drawing out his words, pausing often for effect. He spoke in a steady tenor as commanding as his stern gaze. It was the language in which he had studied law in London, the language of Winston Churchill, a contemporary he admired. Without referring directly to the spreading catastrophe, Jinnah set a lofty goal for the men at the desks before him:

> Now what shall we do? Now, if we want to make this great State of Pakistan happy and prosperous we should wholly and solely concentrate on the well being of the people, and especially of the masses and the poor. If you will work in co-operation, forgetting the past, burying the hatchet, you are bound to succeed. If you change your past and work together in a spirit that every one of you, no matter to what community he belongs, no matter what relations he had with you in the past, no matter what is his color, caste or creed, is first, second and last a citizen of this State with equal rights, privileges and obligations, there will be no end to the progress you will make.

History does not record whether Jinnah was conscious of any irony in his speech. "Change your past," he advised the assembly. Not try to understand or overcome the past, which would be difficult enough—change it. Maybe it was fitting that Pakistan's founder asked the impossible. He might as well, because when it came to getting people's cooperation to help "the masses and the poor" gain "equal rights" regardless of "color, caste or creed," the past was going to be hard to handle no matter what he did. Jinnah himself had just finished arguing for years that a minority group was not a minority at all but a separate nation. Even as he appealed for unity on August 11, he declared that "a united India could never have worked," which was why "a division had to take place." It was not going to be easy to end the divisions there.

Nevertheless he tried, and the realities of Karachi in 1947 make it plain why he had to. Jinnah needed everyone who could help him. And so the founder of the Muslim state told the assembly to banish religious differences from public life: "You will find that in course of time Hindus would cease to be Hindus and Muslims would cease to be Muslims, not in the religious sense, because that is the personal faith of each individual, but in the political sense as citizens of the State."

The banner headline on the next day's *Sind Observer* suggested that the speech was exactly what Shri K. Punniah, the Hindu editor, needed to hear:

JINNAH REASSURES MINORITIES
Will Be Treated Alike Irrespective of Caste or Creed

Two days later the *Observer*'s editorial column declared that Jinnah's speech "dispelled the fears of those who were told to expect a theocratic State." At the *Daily Gazette,* Jinnah's friend Sharma was practically out of his mind, declaring that Jinnah's speech "deserves to be written in letters of gold and handed down to posterity to receive the countless blessings of the unborn generation."

That, at least, was the hopeful line of the moment.

On August 12, the day after Jinnah urged his countrymen to "bury the hatchet," news came of forty people killed and thirty injured in Pakistan's future cultural center, the historic city of Lahore.

On August 13, although Karachi itself remained quiet, rioting spread.

A British general took a plane to key cities along the border, later recording, "Several houses were burning in Amritsar City as I flew over it and four or five villages within ten or fifteen miles of the city were apparently completely destroyed by fire and still burning. . . . Muslim League National Guards also appear to be acting in furtherance of disorder."

That same day the viceroy arrived in Karachi for the independence celebration. Lord Mountbatten—brilliant, impatient, handsome and vain, traveling with an elaborate uniform he had designed for the occasion—paid his respects to Jinnah that evening. "The atmosphere was tense," the army officer Shahid Hamid wrote, for Jinnah and Mountbatten had grown to bitterly mistrust one another.

The viceroy was splitting the subcontinent among men who had all supported some version of a united India in the past. But at key moments, every effort fell apart. Jinnah insisted that his people could not even discuss a united India until after Muslims were granted parity, with power equal to the far more numerous Hindus. Faced with this demand, the Indian National Congress, led by Jawaharlal Nehru and aided by Mountbatten, finally preferred to shove Jinnah to the margins, giving Muslims a separate state and keeping it as small as possible. Jinnah didn't even know how small it would be on that evening in Karachi; the viceroy had delayed revealing the final boundary lines. Later that night, at an event with over a thousand guests, the Great Leader looked "frail, tired, and pre-occupied," according to Shahid Hamid, but had to remain at the event as long as the viceroy did. Hamid carried a message across the room from Jinnah to Mountbatten, asking the last representative of British rule in India to hurry up and leave.

The next morning, August 14, was Independence Day in Pakistan, whose leaders had chosen to mark the occasion a day ahead of India. Green-and-white flags flew from the homes of those who could find them. Thousands of people saw Jinnah ride in an open car through the city. A newsreel crew took footage around the city, aiming the camera down streets lined with stone-fronted buildings. Many people were outside. Horse carts and bicycle riders competed for space with cars and the odd camel. As the newsreel announcer would later put it, Karachi presented "a peaceful aspect" in those final hours before everything changed.

AT HIS PRESS CONFERENCE in July, Jinnah's Hindu friend M. S. M. Sharma posed a question that carried great import for the days ahead:

Question: Would you like the minorities to stay in Pakistan or would you like an exchange of population?

Mr. Jinnah: As far as I can speak for Pakistan, I say that there is no reason for any apprehension on the part of the minorities in Pakistan. It is for them to decide what they should do.... I cannot order them.

"Exchange of population" was the phrase for millions of Hindus moving to India while millions of Muslims moved to Pakistan. Jinnah was saying that he saw no need for it. Few leaders imagined that masses of people would abandon their homes.

They were mistaken. Millions crossed the dividing lines.

Some crossed willingly, like the family of Arif Hasan. The future planner, whom we last encountered as he offered his theory of the Ashura fires, was four years old when he arrived at Karachi's train station from Delhi. "I remember quite vividly," he told me. "Landing at the railway station, being greeted by Pakistani flags and 'Long Live Pakistan' slogans. I remember going to a refugee camp near the railway station." They didn't stay long in the camp; the boy's father earned better quarters. He was the secretary of a Delhi think tank called the Indian Institute of International Affairs, and brought the organization's library with him on the train. Suddenly Hasan's father was the secretary of the new Pakistan Institute of International Affairs, and his family was put up at a former military intelligence school. Hasan's father joined a cadre of educated people who came to Pakistan. While their motives varied, they knew, as one migrant put it, that most Muslims were "illiterate and there would be a good chance of domination in the new country as 'we' had made Pakistan."

If the migration to Pakistan had been limited to these elites, it would have been less painful, but vast numbers of Muslims came as refugees, fleeing murderous bands of men. Hundreds of thousands, at a minimum, didn't make it across the border. A mob was waiting for one Pakistan-bound train in Amritsar, India, having thrown a switch to divert it to a spur track. Attackers climbed on board with machetes. After they finished, an Indian journalist was allowed to look: "The 2,000-odd bodies of the dead were still in the train," he wrote later. "They were poor, unarmed, defenceless peasants." The journalist said that similar trains full of bodies were rolling eastward out of Pakistan. It was becoming one of the worst episodes of mass violence in history.

Shahid Hamid, the military aide, wrote, "People have gone mad."

Many people who survived the madness sought shelter in Karachi.

Westbound Muslims made it across the dividing line in the province of Punjab, which could not absorb them all. Many were shuttled southwestward to Sindh, the next province along the rail line, until the smaller cities and towns of Sindh resisted taking any more. The national capital became the last resort. There was nowhere beyond Karachi but the sea.

In the age now beginning—which we can think of as the age of the instant city—Karachi was one of many urban areas that received people fleeing some political nightmare. India's partition was not the only event to transform a city in the 1940s. In China, for example, the civil war that ended with a Communist takeover sent masses to British-controlled Hong Kong. That city, which was partly emptied during the war, refilled beyond capacity, climbing in a decade from 600,000 people to 2.5 million; the overflow filled refugee camps. In more recent decades, global estimates of refugees and displaced people sometimes grew and sometimes fell, but commonly numbered in the millions. A United Nations report listed "instability, civil war and repression" among the factors prompting people to migrate to cities. Consider a few data points from 2008: Amman, Jordan, was the semipermanent home of an estimated half million people who fled the war in nearby Iraq. Refugees from other conflicts clustered in Cairo, Egypt, and Baku, Azerbaijan. Kabul, more secure and prosperous than other parts of war-torn Afghanistan, had a population that was believed to have climbed by more than a million in a decade. And Karachi was still hosting a camp for Afghans who had lived there since their country's war in the 1980s. Governments hoped for refugees to go home, but history showed that not all of them would.

Cataclysmic events seemed to tilt the surface of the earth, raising the angle until human beings tumbled downhill into the city at the bottom of the slope. The partition of India was the greatest convulsion of all, tilting the ground on which millions of Indians stood. And Muslims began tumbling downward into Karachi's reluctant embrace.

THE PEOPLE REACHING the bottom of the slope included Abdul Sattar Edhi. In the middle 1940s, the future founder of the Edhi ambulance service was a teenager in a town that would become part of western India. Years later he would remember his restless childhood. He struggled to concentrate in school, and even struggled to concentrate when his friends took him to his first movie. He fidgeted in the dark. Many years later he would say he was consumed with a single question: "What will I be?"

In September 1947 Edhi's family joined a group traveling by train to the coast, and then by sea to Karachi, wisely avoiding the carnage on the border. The young man's first sensations were the sight of decrepit buildings and "the heavy smell of fish." The group went ashore, where the elders of the group had secured a building at the edge of town.

The young man looked about the crowded streets with dark, deep-set, serious eyes. Heavy eyebrows lurked above them. He had a hooked nose, and thick lips added to his somber expression. As soon as he was able, Edhi grew a scraggly black mustache and beard. He was twenty-one years old.

His father gave him enough money to begin working as a street peddler. He made himself into a human display case, holding pencils and matches on a tray while draping towels over his forearms. Soon Edhi switched to selling *paan*, a mixture of leaves and nuts that people chewed like tobacco. He learned to make several plugs of *paan* per minute, but the repetitive task grew boring, and he considered again what he wanted to be.

The young man saw signs of ethnic and religious tension. One day he noticed the "intensity in the eyes" of a turbaned man on the street. The man abruptly leaped "like a ferocious tiger" and stabbed another man to death. They came from differing groups—the attacker was ethnic Pashtun, the victim Sikh. In the evenings, when he returned to the room where his family was staying, he saw the building next door. It was a Hindu temple, recently built and also recently abandoned as some Karachi Hindus fled.

Near the airport where celebrating crowds had mobbed Jinnah just a few weeks before, a constable fired twenty-three shots, killing five people. Again the attacker was Pashtun, a member of a group that came from the far northwest of the new country, with their own language and a conservative brand of Islam. Authorities raced to tamp down rumors that it was an ethnic or sectarian attack, but they believed the emotion spread by the killing incited an incident the following morning, September 4. A Sikh man was walking outside the Jubilee Cinema, the same theater that celebrated "the Independence of Hindustan & Pakistan" with a special film premiere. Authorities said the Sikh was "stabbed to death by a person or persons with a long knife." The chief magistrate immediately ordered a curfew in much of the city.

It began to seem that some Karachi newspapers were downplaying events. It was not a news blackout, rather a dampening of the horror—murders tucked into inside pages, calamities quickly referred to but not really explained. A façade of normal life continued. A writer mused in the *Daily Gazette* about the novels of James Joyce and H. G. Wells. A cosmetics company advertised a facial cream called Afghan Snow. Advertisements promoted *Sinbad the Sailor*, with Douglas Fairbanks and Maureen O'Hara, playing in a Karachi cinema.

Jinnah, now governor-general of Pakistan, had made an outraged broadcast on the new radio station, declaring that his people had created Pakistan "by moral and intellectual force and by the pen which is mightier than the sword.... Are we now going to besmear and tarnish this greatest achievement ... by resorting to frenzy, savagery, and butchery?" Days later, several hundred Pakistan government employees descended on his office. They demanded to know what Jinnah intended to do about the slaughter of Muslims in India. Whatever the Quaid-e-Azam told the government workers apparently did not console them. They left the meeting and poured into the streets shortly after curfew, four to five hundred strong as they passed the India Coffee

House on Victoria Street. At a tram station they "attacked a passenger bus with fist blows" and then ransacked the shops of *paan* sellers.

More than twenty "goondas," or hoodlums, descended on the railway station. They killed Sikhs and Hindus with knife thrusts.

HINDUS AND SIKHS were not the only ones worried about their future. Leading Muslim politicians in the province of Sindh were anxious about the potential power of the new arrivals flooding the city. The whole province was "Swamped Over By Outsiders," as the newspaper headline complained: the accompanying story referred to politicians arriving in Karachi from across the new nation, where the "outsiders" would vastly outnumber the locals in the assembly charged with writing a national constitution. A few dozen out-of-town legislators would make trouble enough; the widespread migration to the capital triggered further anxiety. They were upsetting the political balance. And the naming of Karachi as the national capital further dismayed Sindhis, who feared that their province's largest city would be taken away from them. Their fears proved justified, because for a time the city was formally detached from the province.

Even before independence, a leading Muslim politician issued a warning. Sindhis, with their own language and long history, sympathized with the Muslim migrants "who have suffered in Hindu dominated areas," but, continued Agha Ghulam Nabi Pathan, "Sind Muslims . . . are simply unable to do anything for these immigrants who, naturally on arrival at Karachi are subjected to any amount of inconvenience, not to speak of the disappointment that is natural in such circumstances . . . it is likely that the public health of Karachi itself may be endangered."

Endangering the public health? Like the Irish immigrants to nineteenth-century New York, or North Africans in twenty-first-century Paris, the newcomers to Karachi appeared to be a threat. On behalf of Sindhis, Pathan said they were unwelcome. "The notion that Sind can provide room for immigrants in Government services is altogether erroneous," he said. "No applications for Government jobs in Sind or at Karachi can therefore be entertained." Pathan offered a vague but ominous forecast of what would happen if the newcomers were not stopped. "The situation," he said, "may lead ever more to worse results."

The results were already bad enough. So many thousands of people were arriving that they overwhelmed all available housing. On September 19, 1947, Muhammad Ali Jinnah visited a refugee camp, where the elegantly dressed leader met a few stunned survivors. He had been urging his countrymen to help however they could. Yet Karachi had passed the limits of its tolerance. Jinnah's own minister for refugees had just announced a new policy, summarized in a banner headline across the front page of the previous day's *Daily Gazette*:

NO MORE REFUGEES FOR KARACHI

Every train bearing newcomers was to be stopped well short of the capital. This, at least, was the plan, but nothing would stop the refugees, who numbered about half a million in Karachi by May 1948.

As Pakistan approached the anniversary of its independence, Jinnah went away from his capital, hoping to improve his health in the mountain air to the north; it was in this period that he cheerfully wrote his United Nations ambassador that "a little rest in Quetta has done me a lot of good." The only question was whether tuberculosis would kill him before cancer could. Finally he came back to Karachi to die; on September 11, 1948, the government said Jinnah had perished of "heart failure."

The *Sind Observer* ran an archival photo of the Great Leader in a quiet moment. He was wearing his *sherwani* unbuttoned. He was seated, resting his left elbow on the arm of a chair. His face was so thin, the skin so taut, that he almost looked young again. He was looking downward, in prayer or in thought. It was the expression of a man who had been asked for advice on a difficult question, and was considering how to say what must be said. Pakistanis would never know the answer.

At Jinnah's funeral the next day, the coffin was carried on a gun carriage past massive crowds. He was laid to rest in the city where he was born. It was said that six hundred thousand people turned out to offer prayers.

If that estimate was even remotely accurate it confirmed the change that Partition was bringing to the city. The number of mourners was considerably greater than the entire population of Karachi had been just over a year before.

IT WOULD TAKE YEARS to build the Great Leader's tomb, which finally rose as one of the great national symbols of Pakistan. Once I went to see the dead man at dusk, on a low hill overlooking the central city. The tomb is a square building, its white walls leaning slightly inward. A white dome soars overhead. On each wall an archway allows in visitors and light. Inside I saw Jinnah's coffin encased in stone, looking as thin as the man himself. Soldiers stood at the four corners of the coffin. Now and again they shouldered their rifles and made a ritual march around the grave, the slap of their boots echoing off the dome.

On the way out I paused at the doorway, looking out at the low buildings of Karachi, which stretched away forever in the blue evening haze. The lights were just starting to come on, as a prelude to another evening of power outages. The tomb was surrounded on all sides by gorgeously landscaped parkland, with walking paths and benches and shrubs. Families sat in the evening breeze, and boys played cricket until dark.

Scholars still puzzle over Jinnah's 1947 speech in which he urged his countrymen to "change your past" and work together regardless of "color, caste or creed." Some historians have suggested that Jinnah must have been a hypocrite,

Jinnah's tomb, 2010.

or that he was rambling, even losing his mind. How could he propose unity as he led Muslims into a division so profound?

Akbar S. Ahmed—who in 1948 was a Muslim youth just arrived in Karachi after a train ride from India, and who would become a prominent scholar of the Muslim world—has offered a more sympathetic interpretation. Jinnah supported a Muslim state, Ahmed says, but not just any Muslim state. He wanted to follow a Muslim ideal of according full respect to non-Muslims, an ideal that is as old as Islam itself. To Ahmed there is scant contradiction between Jinnah's words and deeds. This speech in August and the short speech on the day of independence combine to form what he calls Jinnah's "Gettysburg Address."

The results on the ground suggested that Jinnah was drawing distinctions too fine for his people to bear. And if we make comparisons to American texts, an earlier one may be instructive. We may take Jinnah's August 11 speech in the same spirit as America's Declaration of Independence. The Declaration expressed great dreams—which, for some signers, were self-delusions. America's founding fathers proclaimed that "all men are created equal" knowing that a number of the founders would go home to their slaves. Still the words took on their own life, and the Declaration found its most profound meaning when later generations of Americans challenged each other to live up to it. That is a way to understand Jinnah's speech of August 11, 1947. He laid out the highest aspirations, which were no less genuine because his actions were leading to a different result. His words had power, and would outlast him. Much of Pakistan's history—and Karachi's history—would be driven by the tension between the aspiration and the act.

I see that tension at play when I leaf through old copies of the *Sind Observer,* handling the yellowed pages carefully to keep them from falling apart. The *Observer* devoted adoring coverage to the death of Pakistan's leader: "A Great Loss to Pakistan . . . Quaid-i-Azam Will Go Down in History as One of the Greatest Men." He was "beloved," and Pakistanis were now "orphans." Those were the words of the *Observer* in 1948, although it was a different newspaper than the year before. Gone were the ads for luxury automobiles and jewelry. Gone, too, was the skeptical tone about Pakistan's treatment of minorities. The editorial column in which the paper aired its anxieties and its grievances was no longer in print. And something else was notable by its absence at the top of the front page:

Shri K. Punniah's name was gone.

5 | SHRINE AND TEMPLE

One Karachi landmark gives a different impression of the instant city than we have seen. It conveys a more generous spirit than the convulsions of 1947 or the explosion at the Lighthouse Bazaar. At this shrine by the sea, Karachi seems spiritual, openhearted, quirky, tolerant, and diverse.

It's the shrine of Abdullah Shah Ghazi, the descendant of the Prophet Mohammed, who is revered in Karachi and beyond. He's laid to rest at the top of a long run of stairs. One time I visited was after dark, and the building was draped with strands of red, green, and yellow lights. Street musicians added to a festive atmosphere, as did a nearby amusement park where people boarded carnival rides.

It was Thursday night, just before the Muslim day of prayer and usually the busiest time to visit. Even though Friday is officially a workday, Thursday counts for many as the start of the weekend, so closely connected to the day of prayer that in Urdu it is called *Jummay raat*—literally, "Friday night." On this night before Friday, pilgrims passed through the great metal gates of the shrine and removed their shoes out of respect.

A pilgrim named Razzak arrived without any shoes at all. He mounted the stairs on weary feet and squeezed into the crowded rooms. Here, some people snapped padlocks onto steel window bars, believing it would help the saint remember their prayers. Others pressed against the marble sarcophagus, dropping rose petals or covering the tomb with little green cloths. Razzak edged up to the tomb and made off with one of these cloths, tying it around his head like a bandana. When I met him downstairs a few minutes later, he explained that the cloth had the power to heal him. An illness had cost him his job as a laborer

The shrine of Abdullah Shah Ghazi.
[Rizwan Tabassum/AFP/Getty Images]

in the city of Multan, and when he took a train to Karachi in hope of finding a cure, the first thing that happened was that somebody stole his shoes.

But now he had what he needed. He felt better already.

On the plaza where we spoke, a young man and woman sat on a blanket, not touching but obviously together. Forbidden to date, boys and girls sometimes visit the shrine and miraculously encounter each other. Nearby, up shadowy steps, a tiny orange glow and an acrid smell confirmed that men were smoking hashish. A recent crackdown on drug use at the shrine apparently was not a complete success. Nor was it certain that anybody *wanted* complete success. Pakistan has a strong tradition of Sufism, a mystical brand of Islam whose followers seek a closer bond with God, sometimes with the aid of drugs. More broadly, many Sufis focus on their relationship with God rather than worrying whether everybody else follows the same religious dogma. This is what the editor Shri K. Punniah meant when he wrote in the 1940s of Karachi's "mutual toleration," which he linked to its "Sufi culture."

A more explicit sign of tolerance stands a short walk up the street: an old

Hindu temple. As at the Muslim shrine, people enter through long stairways, although they lead down instead of up. They're descending a bluff overlooking the beach. Near the bottom, the white stone steps double back into the rock face, and the faithful enter a cave. Within the earth itself they pray amid display cases filled with the many-armed statues of their gods. This temple is dedicated to Shiva, the god sometimes called "the destroyer of the world." Many Hindus believe Shiva is responsible for change, overseeing death and destruction and the ending of bad habits. Shiva works in concert with two other gods: Brahma creates the world, and Vishnu preserves it until the time that Shiva destroys it so that Brahma can start over again. It's a process that a naturalist might call the cycle of life, or that an economist might call creative destruction.

Monday evening is the most popular time to visit Shiva's temple, and one Monday near sunset I met Makwana Narindas, a construction contractor who said he'd just spent two hours praying inside.

"What do you pray for?" I asked.

"For me and all the public," he said. A friend who'd prayed with him added, "For our country and our family. For us. For all the problems."

"And there are so many problems that it takes two hours for you to finish?"

Mr. Narindas laughed out loud, but a third worshipper who'd overheard us broke in. "No, no, no problem," he said. "We are happy. We are happy. We are happy." All the men insisted that life was good in Pakistan and that their rights were well protected. "We come in peace," one said, as if their intentions might be questioned.

The Hindu temple offers one of the most spectacular views in Karachi. I saw the sunset through a row of nearby Roman arches—the entrance to Kothari Parade, a pedestrian walkway donated in the 1920s by a Zoroastrian business-man. The promenade pointed toward the hazy expanse of the Arabian Sea. The park had recently been restored during the administration of the city's Muslim mayor, Syed Mustafa Kamal; topiary shrubs were cut in the shapes of animals, like at Disney World.

The scene offers testimony to the tolerance that forms one strand of Kara-chi's persona. But Karachi has a very small percentage of Hindus to worship there. Shiva, the god of destruction, portrayed inside his temple sitting cross-legged in meditation, must have been deep in thought during the destruction of Karachi's Hindu majority beginning in 1947.

Temple of Shiva.

Soon after independence about two hundred thousand Hindus disappeared, roughly half the city's original population, as hundreds of thousands of Muslims replaced them. Hindus went from 51 percent of Karachi's population to about 2 percent. Karachi became overwhelmingly Muslim. The result should be a lesson for all cities, because after the Hindus were swept away, the people who remained found other divisions among themselves. They divided by ethnicity, language, class, and Muslim sect, which they would still be doing more than sixty years later when the Shia procession was bombed at the Lighthouse Bazaar.

Karachi grew less stable as it became less diverse.

SOME OF THE HINDUS left Karachi within weeks of independence. Nineteen-year-old L. K. Advani fled in September, saying he and other members of the Hindu RSS wanted to avoid police questioning about a bomb that exploded in a Muslim neighborhood. Advani caught a plane to New Delhi, vaulting over the writhing border areas. Once on the far side he would begin a political career, becoming an architect of a Hindu nationalist party and eventually deputy prime minister of India.

When some older and more established Hindus departed, it became clear that much of the skill and education of the city's elite was disappearing with them. Stores were closing. Factories were shutting down, just as thousands of Muslim refugees expected jobs. Muslim leaders understood the problem: although the Muslims included men and women of great education and eloquence, their numbers were dangerously small. Across the province before independence, not even 5 percent of Muslim men could read, and fewer than 1 percent of women. This lack of education reflected extreme poverty, for most Muslims lived in the countryside, where a few landlords dominated the lives of millions of poor farm workers. The educated men and women among the newcomers were hardly enough to compensate.

Hindus who were resented for their presence in Karachi soon discovered that they were also resented if they tried to leave. Officials declared that departing Hindus could take along almost none of their possessions. They were searched for valuables as they lined up to board ships at the wharf. The Muslim chief minister of the province, M. A. Khuhro, would be remembered as sympathetic to the Hindus; he showed up at the wharf to make sure the searches were not too harsh or stringent. But the yellowed newspapers of the era leave the impression of a political leader struggling under conflicting pressures. Khuhro, a meaty-faced man with a mustache that followed the line of his frown, said at the wharf that he "could not reconcile himself to the idea of Hindus evacuating with all their belongings, while Muslim refugees arriving in Karachi generally came as paupers."

Whether through hope for the future or fear that they would lose all their property, many Hindus remained in Karachi for months after independence. Jinnah himself repeatedly offered them reassurances, and just after the New Year in 1948 an official in East Pakistan said the national government "will give the fairest deal to all minority communities . . . to live in peace and honour." Three days later the newspaper *Dawn*, the voice of the Muslim League, carried a headline that suggested neither peace nor honor:

KARACHI'S SUDDEN OUTBREAK OF
VIOLENCE NOW WELL IN HAND

Something had happened on the streets. *Dawn* never managed to give a full account, merely passing on official responses to the incident, while describing the tragedy in the most general way ("There was a sudden flare up of communal disturbances in Karachi yesterday, resulting in some deaths. There was also a certain amount of looting.") The details were too awkward or inflammatory to print: a mob attacked a convoy of refugees from the north.

The refugees were Sikhs, of the same faith as those blamed for slaughtering Muslims on the trains in Punjab. A mob killed dozens of people in the street ("some deaths"). The violence spread beyond Sikhs. Thousands of Hindu shops and homes were looted. Hindus had to be "taken to safe places." Over a period of days, some 180 people were killed. The finance minister of Pakistan had just departed a luncheon for visiting British officials when he and his colleagues "saw a number of people engaged in looting houses. They at once stopped the car and rushed to the assistance of the victims with sticks they had snatched from the hands of the looters." The man overseeing Pakistan's economy spent part of his day rounding up looters and holding them until police could arrive.

INCIDENTS LIKE THESE were enough for Bibi Inder Kaur, the Sikh doctor's wife who had found Karachi a tolerant city on the surface. "We had never really thought of leaving," she told oral historians decades later, but "we saw that our neighbors were looking at us differently, looking askance at us. Where my husband's clinic was, that was the place where they started killing Sikhs." Soon she was at the docks with her family, trying to crowd onto a ship. "There were no tickets for berths," she remembered. "All we could hope for was deck space." Two long lines snaked along the pier, one for women and one for men; as the lines dissolved into a frantic crush of humanity, she was separated from her husband. She clutched a baby in her arms; two more daughters were in line with her. "And the crowds! The rush! Because everyone wanted to get onto the boat somehow. The coolies threw in our luggage. . . . With all the pushing and jostling my two young daughters got left behind. When I reached the deck I realized they were not with me. I thrust my youngest daughter into the arms of a Sindhi woman standing next to me and, wailing loudly, went to look for the other two. My god! What if someone had seized them and whisked them away? Pulled them to one side? I was so worried but I found them at the end of the queue."

Struggling to redeem the disaster, the provincial chief minister Khuhro traveled with Pakistan's finance minister to a camp full of Muslim refugees. The finance minister made a furious speech, accusing refugees of bringing shame on both Pakistan and Islam. Weeping refugees surrendered the loot they'd ransacked from Hindu homes, making a giant pile of "cotton sheets, shirts, beddings, coats, blankets, children's clothes, vessels, utensils, electric fans, beddings, chairs, books, gramophones, silverware, brassware, Singer sewing machines, telephones, radio sets and bicycles." But by then, many of the rightful owners of these stolen goods were leaving town. The final great exodus of the minorities was under way, their homes wrecked, their leaders disappearing, their newspapers silenced. M. S. M. Sharma, the Hindu editor of the *Daily Gazette* whom Jinnah had personally asked to stay, moved to India after the riots. Only six months earlier, he had been helping to form a Sind Minorities Association, and publishing editorials urging Hindus to fight for their rights within Pakistan. If his view had prevailed, Pakistan might be a different country today. Now he was leaving, even though Jinnah personally arranged for guards outside his house. His fellow editor Shri K. Punniah of the *Sind Observer* was already gone. The last paper to bear Punniah's name on the masthead had been published back on November 27, 1947.

Churning with anger, Punniah and his physician wife relocated to Bangalore, in southern India. In the summer of 1948 Punniah, now sixty-six years old, agreed to write an article for an Indian magazine to mark the upcoming anniversary of independence. He wrote bitterly that Pakistan was "evolving into a Fascist State," adding inaccurately that the Muslim nation would be ruled by "medieval Shariat laws"—*shariat* being the word for Islamic jurisprudence. He said the selection of Karachi as Pakistan's capital was destroying the city and province he had known. "The Hindus have left and are leaving, and the Sindhi Muslims will, in the course of time, neither have a name, nor a habitation on account of being swamped." Punniah delivered the article to the magazine editor and then traveled to attend the All-India Newspaper Editors' Conference in Bombay. He went out for a walk through the city where he'd begun his newspaper career many decades before, and apparently suffered a heart attack. The former editor of the *Sind Observer* was found lying dead in the street.

A SMALL NUMBER of minorities chose to stay in Karachi, like the family of the Hindu I met after his two-hour prayer at the temple of Shiva. There were also a few Zoroastrians, followers of an ancient Persian faith even older than Islam. Known as Parsis, they had been part of the city's elite for generations, and their attitude was epitomized by Ardeshir Cowasjee, the youthful son of a Karachi shipping magnate. Cowasjee wasn't going anywhere. Cowasjee's father was the Zoroastrian businessman who agreed to help Jinnah assemble a Pakistani shipping firm.

More than sixty years later, when he was a droll and influential newspaper columnist, Cowasjee welcomed me into his stone house in Karachi. He lived surrounded by the images of his parents, ancestors, and his wife's relations; formal portrait paintings hung in the dining room, and three white busts stood watch at the door. They represented generations of life in the city. Cowasjee liked to point at them one by one, giving updates on their condition: "Dead . . . dead . . . dead . . ." He wore a finely cropped beard that gave him the look of an aristocrat, although the first time I came to his house he wore a bathrobe. His wardrobe announced that he was home, he was comfortable, and he would be damned if he would make himself uncomfortable for anyone. The second time I visited he greeted me in short-sleeved pajamas, and we ate lunch by the picture window overlooking his garden. His cook laid strips of mangoes atop thick slabs of fish, which was delicious even though Cowasjee said Karachi's fish came from some of the world's most polluted water. As we spoke, he recalled a prophecy that he heard in the late 1940s.

"Jinnah told my father," he said, "that each government of Pakistan would be worse than the one that preceded it."

THE NATIONAL LEADERS who followed Jinnah—and there would be many, as the government changed every few years or sometimes every few months— had their chances to improve the capital city. The 1951 census found that a city of around four hundred thousand had been transformed into a crowded metropolis of 1.13 million. Muslims had arrived even faster than Hindus could leave, and the more fortunate and educated brought tremendous energy with them. The city suddenly had a vast labor force, just as industrialization was intensifying in the developing world.

Electricity and technology were boosting the economies of cities, attracting more workers at the same time as rural areas became less appealing. In Nigeria, the wealthiest farmers began moving to cities, shifting their spending, taxes, and investment away from the countryside. People followed the money: metropolitan Lagos exploded from 267,000 people in 1952 to more than a million in 1963. Cities all across Nigeria grew as migrants left behind a depopulating countryside of "derelict . . . mills, empty houses, broken bridges and deteriorating roads," joining what a Ford Foundation report from the era called an "urban revolution" unequaled in Africa's history. The challenge, there as everywhere, was how to manage the sudden growth. In Hong Kong, a devastating fire called attention to the refugee camps filled with hundreds of thousands of people from Communist China. The government began a massive housing program, supplemented by health care and public education, providing for the workers who powered the industries that were beginning to make Hong Kong a great manufacturing center.

In Karachi, Indus River Valley cotton had been shipped through the port for generations, mostly to English mills; now Pakistanis made more textiles themselves. In 1947 the western section of the country had two hundred thousand spindles used to weave cotton fibers into thread; within a few years the number shot to 1.3 million. The better-educated and better-connected refugees became industrialists or managers. The lower-paying factory jobs drew hardworking migrants from the impoverished countryside, including ethnic Pashtuns down from the mountains near Afghanistan. This migration would increase in size and importance over time.

The trouble was housing. Architects in Karachi reported a "minor building boom" in the early 1950s: "Foreign, particularly American, speculators had shown considerable interest in new buildings here." But the foreigners were interested in the upper end of the market, such as concrete houses on the beach in an area called Hawkes Bay. This did little for refugees still homeless. For hundreds of thousands of people, Karachi was a tent city, a squatter city, where people lived beneath rags or in the open air. The "large open spaces" that Jinnah once praised for their "feeling of space and ease" were now full of tents, and many of those spaces would never be open again.

At 25 Victoria Road, one of the city's more fashionable addresses, stood a cavernous house with a tennis court. After partition, there were people sleeping on the tennis court. The masters of the house were the family of Akbar S. Ahmed, the scholar whom we last encountered as he interpreted Jinnah's view of minorities. In 1947 he was a child newly arrived with his family from India. As a railway superintendent, his father had a job and a claim to the house, but less fortunate people were constantly arriving on their doorstep from Delhi. "There were many people living with us," Ahmed recalled. "They were in the corridors, they were all over the house. I remember, because it really disturbed me then, there was a boy who was a little bit older than me, about four or five years older. And he would be sleeping on a tin box, a large tin box, which contained blankets and things. And this tin box was just outside the kitchen. And he would be sleeping on that tin box with a sheet round him, wrapped round him, and the sheet going over his head like a shroud." People said the boy had lost his family on the journey from India. He lived for two years with Ahmed's family before slipping away into the streets.

Even in the crowded house, Ahmed knew he was privileged. Once he was taken to see a refugee camp, "this sea of little more than shacks."

In the summer of 1950, the monsoon brought several inches of rain in thirty-six hours. Wind and water lashed the tents and huts that some refugees had been living in for years. "What was left at night—rags tied to bamboo sticks, the last remnant of their thatched roofs—was completely washed away the next day," the newspaper *Dawn* reported. Two children who lived with their families under a row of trees outside a railway station died of exposure. A girl playing in a puddle was electrocuted by an exposed wire in the water; her brother leaped in to save her and also died. Angry refugees began organizing protest marches, sloshing through the rain to the prime minister's house. The protesters became so rambunctious that soldiers arrived, loading some into army trucks and hauling them off, so it was said, to shelter somewhere in the "suburbs." It was a hint of the technique that authorities would eventually attempt on a much larger scale.

This intervention wasn't enough to keep the city quiet. Late in the morning of August 16, 1950, a senior official named O. M. D'Sa was working at city hall, the Karachi Municipal Corporation Building with its onion domes, when he heard a noise outside. Through a window he saw about two hundred protesters approaching the building "chanting slogans." The protesters were refugees, angry that officials had torn down a place of worship they had built without authorization in a public park. D'Sa picked up the phone to call police. The line was dead. The crowd grew until thousands surrounded the building. The boldest slipped through a side gate, walked into the first office they found, and "pulled out chairs, tables, and cycles from the room and threw them into the court yard. There they set them on fire." O. M. D'Sa could do nothing to stop them. Some city employees were suspected of joining the melee. Four armed constables looked on and made a strategic decision to do nothing. Protesters raced through the building, throwing the city's account books out of the windows, where others set them on fire. People ransacked offices, knocked over cabinets, and broke almost every window in the sprawling building. Police finally arrived to a welcome of stones thrown by the growing mob. The police responded with tear gas.

IT WAS TELLING that the location of a place of worship would ignite the disturbance at city hall. The most immediate problems at that moment were housing, planning, and land use. And yet what drove people beyond reason, leading them to smash windows and light fires, was when these disputes were overlaid with religion.

Pakistan in the 1950s was unusually vulnerable to religious disturbances. The country was still struggling to answer the question that the national founder Muhammad Ali Jinnah avoided in his press conference in July 1947: "Will Pakistan be a secular or theocratic State?" Reporters pursued him on this question for several minutes, as we have seen. They provoked the old man to bark, "For goodness sake, get out of your head the nonsense that is being talked about. What this theocratic State means I do not understand." Jinnah responded as if he sensed a trap, or an insult—a presumption that Muslims could not govern themselves according to modern ideas. Jinnah began to answer this question more clearly as independence neared, when he said that citizens would have an essentially secular relationship with the state. But this was not written into law. The constituent assembly that Jinnah led failed to finish its work on a constitution before he died.

Despite its name, Jinnah's Muslim League was not really a religious party, but rather an organization of elite leaders committed to safeguarding the political interests of people who were Muslim. And the League was under pressure from men who saw the world differently. Even as Jinnah spoke of a state where the people overlooked color, caste, and creed, another political leader in British India believed it was time for government by the one true faith. His name was Abul A'la Mawdudi. He founded his own political party, Jamaat-e-Islami—

which can translate as the Islamic Group, or Islamic Party—and he chose Pakistan in 1947. He was in his mid-forties then, a journalist and scholar who lagged far behind Jinnah in stature, but would have decades to spread his influence after Jinnah was gone. With his black-framed glasses and whitening beard, he became a constant presence. And his intellectual descendants are with us today, for while Mawdudi was not precisely an extremist, he was one of the intellectual fathers of modern extremist ideas—ideas visible everywhere from the wreckage of the World Trade Center to the Shia procession bombed in Karachi on December 28, 2009.

In these pages, we have presumed that cities draw strength from their diversity. Mawdudi presumed no such thing. He considered the incredible diversity of South Asia's religious beliefs to be a serious problem. Nor was he alone. Conservative Muslims had railed for a century or more against the many varieties of Islam that could be found across the subcontinent. Converts to Islam who retained some of their Hindu traditions were an abomination; even Shia Muslims were unacceptable. And the influence of India's Christian colonial masters, the British, was insidious. Mawdudi's innovation was to do more than complain: he argued that Muslims must seek political power to ensure the proper application of Islamic law. Islam should apply to all of the earth—"not just a portion, but the whole planet"—because all humanity should enjoy its benefits.

It is revealing to contrast Jinnah's speech in Karachi on August 11, 1947, with one of Mawdudi's from the era. When Jinnah said that "Hindus would cease to be Hindus and Muslims would cease to be Muslims," he was speaking in the modern language of the secular state. Mawdudi spoke in the modern language of ideological revolution, using present-day terms to express what he professed to be an ancient creed. He offered a sweeping, Leninist view of his cause in Lahore in 1939:

> Islam is not the name of a "Religion," nor is "Muslim" the title of a "Nation." In reality Islam is a revolutionary ideology and programme which seeks to alter the social order of the whole world and rebuild it in conformity with its own tenets and ideals. "Muslim" is the title of that International Revolutionary Party organized by Islam to carry into effect its revolutionary programme. And "Jihad" refers to that revolutionary struggle and utmost exertion which the Islamic Party brings into play to achieve this objective.

Mawdudi said he believed in democracy, and his party contested elections, but his vision allowed for no source of law except Islam. Muslims who created any other law were apostates. Political leaders with whom he disagreed were not simply mistaken; they were modern versions of the ancient rulers from the time of *jahiliyya,* the age of pagan beliefs before the coming of Islam. The twentieth century was a new age of *jahiliyya,* and it was time for a new awakening. His was a narrow and rigid Islam, deeply concerned with specific religious commands like the prohibition on alcohol, and his party suggested that any Muslim who did not follow his view of Islam was not really Muslim at all.

Mawdudi's rhetoric infuriated Pakistani officials, who found reasons to put him in jail for a time in 1948 and even had him put on trial and sentenced to death in 1953. The sentence was commuted, however, and the wily political leader would live to influence another generation. His party built an infrastructure in key parts of the country, including Karachi. His activists became known not only for their strict beliefs but also for their relative freedom from corruption. Jamaat-e-Islami gained support among Karachi's dislocated refugees, many of whom were seeking to define their identities in this unfamiliar place, and some of whom turned more deeply to religion. In November 1955 Jamaat-e-Islami held a conference in Karachi attended by two thousand people. The streets of the capital city reflected a battle of ideas. People painted graffiti for and against the *mullahs.* Secularists painted slogans in English, the language of the elites, while religious parties painted graffiti in Urdu, the leading language of the refugees. Questions about religion's role in the government affected the interminable debates over Pakistan's constitution in Karachi, and when the basic law was finally ratified in 1956 the country would be formally named the Islamic Republic of Pakistan. In 1958, Jamaat candidates won the Karachi municipal elections.

Mawdudi was never directly linked to religious violence, but the years of his rise in Pakistan were years of religious intolerance. Sunni Muslim refugees began agitating against civil servants and other officials who happened to be Shias. And meetings of a Muslim minority known as Ahmadis were disrupted by hundreds of angry conservative rioters. Jamaat-e-Islami provoked the agitation; one of Mawdudi's arrests came after his publication of an attack on Ahmadis. Religious leaders argued that Pakistan would not be a properly Islamic state unless the Ahmadis were formally declared to be a religious minority, not Muslim at all.

As people rioted against these alleged apostates, Pakistan came full circle. From 1947, the country had unwittingly conducted a vast human experiment: what would happen if a diverse place suddenly cleansed itself of many of its minorities, so that almost everyone was, on the surface, the same?

Now the results of the experiment were coming in.

Muslims, the single "nation" championed by their leaders just a few years before, proved to be strikingly diverse. They always had been. Now some looked within their numbers and began singling out new minorities to replace the ones they had lost.

6 | GROUNDBREAKING

D uring Pakistan's chaotic first decade a movie about Partition opened in Karachi. Abdul Sattar Edhi went to see it, and fidgeted. He couldn't pay attention.

Maybe part of the reason was that the young migrant from India was thinking of his future. Tired of selling *paan* on the streets, he joined his father in what amounted to a check-cashing business. Later he volunteered at a dispensary—what Americans would call a pharmacy—and in 1951 he opened his own dispensary, measuring eight by eight feet. It was in Mithidar, a neighborhood of "narrow, unpaved allies" and "shakily balanced buildings, the beginning of one not distinguishable from the other." Here Edhi made his living among the poor, selling medicine to those who could pay, and giving it away to those who could not. The young man was trying one identity and then another, moving closer to the ambulance service that would make him famous.

Karachi, too, was weaving toward its future. It was the seat of one short-lived national leader after another. A scholar has listed the ways in which the leaders met their ends: "Assassination . . . Dismissed despite a parliamentary majority . . . Paralysis . . . Intrigue . . . Infighting." And then, a decade after Jinnah, Pakistan came under the hand of a leader who vowed to address the problems that past leaders had not. He had the power to do it, for he ruled by the gun.

General Mohammad Ayub Khan deployed soldiers in Karachi in 1958, and set the pattern for more than half a century of his country's history. He began the army's involvement in politics. He built much of the modern state, but left it weak and unstable. He was the first of several Pakistani coup leaders, each of whom took power with energy and conviction, only to depart frustrated and reviled. Pakistanis remember him vividly even today, sometimes with nostalgia and sometimes with bitterness. Much of the country's trouble—which became the region's trouble, and finally the world's trouble—can be traced back to Ayub.

It's less well known that Ayub's coup was an emblematic moment in the age of the instant city.

During his years in office, the general put his name on a book explaining his fateful steps. He weaved Karachi into the explanation. Pakistan's first dictator said the swiftly growing capital city was unhealthy and rebellious. In evaluating the record of the government that he displaced, he emphasized its failure to address Karachi's problems, and when defending his own record, Ayub listed his achievements in urban development.

Ayub altered the map, spreading the city over hundreds of square miles. He shaped the city that was visible in the security cameras on the day of the Ashura procession on December 28, 2009. He built neighborhoods such as Sau Quarter, where the Shia marcher Mohammad Raza Zaidi woke on his final morning alive. And he built Jinnah's long-delayed tomb, putting the old lawyer to rest in more ways than one.

A picture from another December shows Ayub beginning his work. The

Ayub at groundbreaking, December 1958.
[Times of Karachi]

photo is from December 1958, preserved in a frail old copy of a newspaper called the *Times of Karachi*. The image shows the general himself, in a khaki uniform, his army cap firmly on his head, his sleeves crisply rolled up above his elbows. Ayub Khan holds a shovel in hand. He's bending over, feet spread wide, to dig up a scoop of earth. Smiling dignitaries stand behind him as he works. He is laying the foundation stone for new Karachi construction, posing for the quintessential mid-twentieth-century photo announcing Progress.

AYUB KHAN WAS ONE of the senior army officers at the time of Pakistan's birth, fresh from a distinguished career serving Britain in the Army of India. An old photo showed a dashing young soldier, almost handsome enough to play himself in a movie, with wavy hair combed back from his forehead and dark eyebrows looming over big handsome eyes. Or, if not Ayub, Sean Connery could have played such a role; those were the eyes, winning and clever and mischievous.

He was a veteran of the Allied war against Japan, and a man who was ready for anything—anything except Karachi. The city was "humid and unhealthy," he complained later, with "an enervating climate which saps one's energy and efficiency." The water and sewer systems were built for a fraction of the current population, and the "unhygienic conditions prevailing throughout the city had a serious effect on the health of the government servants. The whole administration looked worn out after the first few years." Worse, "the town also became a centre of agitational politics: politicians found that they could collect mobs with the help of industrialists and businessmen and bring all kinds of pressures to bear on the government."

Ayub believed that all this needed to change.

Strictly speaking, none of this was Ayub's business. But the army became active in politics as Ayub rose in the army. By 1951 he was commander in chief. And in 1953 he made a powerful new friend. He met with a visitor from America, Secretary of State John Foster Dulles. As a leading figure in the cold war against the Soviet Union, Dulles was seeking anticommunist allies. Ayub didn't miss the opportunity. The American stepped off the plane in Karachi to find an honor guard of oversized Pakistani cavalrymen awaiting him; he would later gush about the tall lancers, who "sat there on these great big horses, and were out of this world." Later Dulles sat with General Ayub. The man in uniform presented a strategic assessment of the Soviet threat that almost perfectly matched the concerns of the bespectacled American in the suit. When he got home to Washington, Dulles declared, "I believe those fellows are going to fight any communist invasion with their bare fists if they have to."

American tanks and other weapons were soon flowing to Ayub Khan's army.

A few years later the U.S. ambassador to Karachi, James Langley, would say that Pakistan's claim to American support was "a hoax." The Pakistanis were using the Soviet threat to stockpile American resources for the next of their periodic wars against India. The cost of meeting American commitments sometimes exceeded $500 million in a single year, an immense payout in that era. During a meeting with advisors in 1957, President Dwight Eisenhower complained that the United States was "doing practically nothing for Pakistan except in the form of military aid. This was the worst kind of a plan and decision we could have made." Eisenhower's lament foreshadowed almost identical complaints that would be made by future generations of American policymakers and analysts; his statement in 1957 could just as accurately have applied to 1987, or 2007, when the United States was building up the military's power at the expense of the rest of the state. Yet Eisenhower felt helpless. "Now we seem hopelessly involved in it," the president said. The Pakistanis were at least providing bases for American spy planes, and Ayub's power grew.

On October 4, 1958, the general caught a train to Karachi from the army headquarters in northern Pakistan. "The hour had struck. The moment so long delayed had finally arrived," he later said of that decisive night. "As I settled down in my railway saloon I knew that an era was coming to an end. I was going to Karachi where an agonizingly prolonged political farce was drawing to a close." Ayub intended to lower the curtain himself. Shortly before independence in 1947, as Ayub must have known, senior Muslim military officers gathered to meet Muhammad Ali Jinnah, their future leader. "Pakistan's elected government will be that of civilians," said the old lawyer, "and anyone who thinks contrary to democratic principles should not opt for Pakistan." Although Ayub opted for Pakistan, he now doubted that his country was ready for democracy.

HE ARRIVED IN KARACHI on October 5. By now the general looked heavier and more burdened than the dashing young officer he had been. His hairline had crept up his forehead and his mustache had grown thicker. His jowls had thickened too. Most changed were his eyes. He still had the look of mischief, but he increasingly gazed at the world through a near-permanent squint, the kind of hard and penetrating expression that would cause other men to look down.

Those piercing eyes would have seen a city filled with energy as he rode a car around town. A photograph from the era shows tram cars rolling down Jinnah Road in front of the old city hall. The faces of movie stars look out from billboards over the entrance of the Lighthouse Cinema. More advertisements hang from the balconies of the apartment building next door. Farther up Jinnah Road, thousands of people were living in improvised shelters, as they had since 1947. There was a chance that Ayub could have passed one of the first of the Edhi ambulances in traffic, for Abdul Sattar Edhi had purchased his first vehicle in 1957, driving it around town himself.

Ayub went to see Pakistan's president, Iskander Mirza, who had summoned him to Karachi. In President Mirza's view, democratic politics had reached a dead end. The jowly, clean-shaven president was under pressure to hold national elections, and feared that he would lose. Jamaat-e-Islami was on the rise, having just won the municipal elections in the capital city. Jinnah's old Muslim League was restive too, threatening civil disobedience in Karachi if a national election didn't come soon—and the new leader of the Muslim League, too, urged greater emphasis on Islam. But Ayub Khan had army brigades on hand in case anyone caused trouble. On October 7 the president abrogated the constitution, declared martial law, and issued a proclamation denouncing "the ruthless struggle for power, corruption . . . and the prostitution of Islam for political ends." Ayub Khan was named the martial law administrator. He immediately issued new regulations, stating that anyone who disobeyed him would face "rigorous imprisonment" or death.

Behind the scenes, President Mirza moved to head off a potential threat, writing President Eisenhower to assure him that Pakistan would maintain its commitments to "the free world." He need not have worried. The American government had seen the coup coming, and while finding it unwise, had decided in advance to accept it. U.S. ambassador Langley had already received a telegram from Washington noting that while the United States could consider cutting off military aid to Pakistan, there was "danger" in this course. Langley was instructed to diplomatically express faith in democracy, but to acquiesce in the coup "if only by implication." Soon Secretary Dulles, the cold warrior so enamored of all those Pakistani cavalrymen, sent a personal note to "my dear President Mirza," helpfully suggesting that the destruction of Pakistan's constitution in a military coup was not really that much different from the American system of constitutional amendments.

Nor did the people in the streets of Karachi voice any stronger protest. City life went on quietly. Business continued. The Palace Theater was promoting an American movie that could be seen in "Air-Conditioned Luxury," Jimmy Stewart and Doris Day in *The Man Who Knew Too Much,* a cold war drama that began on the crowded streets of Muslim Morocco.

Pakistanis were initially hopeful that the military would sweep away the failures of the old government, although within days the U.S. embassy was reporting "uneasiness and nascent fear" among many people who were beginning to understand "the absence of any checks on the police." Two days after the declaration of martial law, the police picked up M. A. Khuhro. The Sindhi leader and onetime provincial chief minister, whom we last saw as he struggled with the departure of the Hindus, had gone on to a dramatic and controversial career as a national politician. He arrived at his house one day to find a deputy superintendent of police waiting to arrest him for alleged black market activity, the sale of an unregistered 1958 Chevrolet.

A generation of politicos was being elbowed offstage. Even President Mirza had to go: Ayub tired of him after three weeks, deposed him, and put him on a plane to England. The general promised an early return to elected government, a promise that yielded the same result as most such promises around the world. He effectively froze the political process for years. Pakistan's reckoning with its many ethnic and religious differences—the diversity that strained the nation from its birth—would have to wait for some later time.

Ayub concentrated instead on construction. "I am a man in a hurry," he would say in days to come. "There are so many things to do and there is so little time to do them." And he made some hurried decisions about urban development.

"The capital must be moved out of Karachi," he declared at an early cabinet meeting. He wanted the government beyond the range of the mob. He appointed a commission to study the advantages and disadvantages of Karachi as a capital, putting it in the charge of his close aide Yahya Khan. After a thorough investigation the commissioners agreed with the opinion of the general who had said he would imprison or kill anyone who opposed him. The new capital would be built many miles to the north, near the military headquarters of Rawalpindi, where the climate was less humid and the generals could forever keep the politicians nearby.

"I mentioned in the Cabinet," he recalled of another meeting, "that we should take up the construction of the Quaid-e-Azam's mausoleum." It would be under a military ruler's orders that Pakistan would finally complete Karachi's monument to Jinnah. Ayub also raised with his advisors the subject of the people still living in tents in Karachi. "The resettlement of displaced persons, refugees from the time of Partition, had been delayed too long," he said later. "It was essential to solve this problem quickly in the interests of the displaced persons as well as the economy."

Soon he traveled to a patch of vacant land several miles east of the city, where he posed with his shovel in front of the photographer from the *Times of Karachi*. At the time of the ceremony, Ayub had been in sole control of the country for barely six weeks. He was still consolidating his power. It was a time for only the most urgent tasks. But in Ayub's view, this *was* an urgent task: he was addressing what his administration called a national emergency. This project would become, in Pakistani parlance, a new housing colony, built for the benefit of refugees who had lived so many years in tents. "The ultimate shape of this colony," Ayub declared in a speech, "will be that of a satellite town in which all modern necessities and amenities like schools, hospitals and parks, sanitation and roads will be provided."

The general was planning to solve one of the city's enduring problems by building what Americans called a suburb.

AYUB WAS ABOUT TO apply the world's cutting-edge thinking about cities, so it is instructive to note how cities were changing in the years around 1958. Metropolitan areas were growing not only in population but in geographic area. American cities especially were transforming, expanding beyond their formal borders. Millions moved into newly built suburbs, taking advantage of the mobility of a growing fleet of cars.

A spectacular expression of this growth came in the northeastern United States, where in 1961 the geographer Jean Gottmann published a book declaring that all the cities from Boston to New York to Washington had grown together. He called this behemoth "Megalopolis," and said it prospered even though it had few natural advantages over other parts of America—gold mines and oil wells were elsewhere. It just had migration. Immigrants offered up their labor and ideas in cities that had to "rely on their wits to thrive." The region was a center of transportation, technology, finance, government, education, entertainment, and media—the knowledge economy as it existed in 1961. Once cities like this began to grow, they often continued growing. A separate study from the era argued that "migration and employment growth perpetuate one another." A growing urban population created the demand for more goods and services, "thereby drawing more migrants to fill new jobs."

This explained the change in Los Angeles and its suburbs, which were growing at a stunning rate, from four million people in 1950 to 6.5 million in 1960. Los Angeles made almost anything that was wanted for a comfortable life in suburban cold war America: "furnaces, sliding doors, mechanical saws, shoes, bathing suits, underwear, china, furniture, cameras, hand tools, hospital equipment, scientific instruments, engineering services and hundreds of other things." The city expanded as entrepreneurs produced all the things that were needed for a growing Los Angeles. Growth fed upon itself; a city grew because it grew.

This was also an era of grand urban plans around the world. Whole sections of New York and Chicago were flattened to make room for towering redbrick housing projects. In Brazil, engineers and construction crews were in the midst of building a new national capital where no such city had existed before. Brasília would be inaugurated on April 21, 1960.

Some plans worked, and some didn't. Many of the new public housing projects in America destroyed intricate communities to make room for buildings designed on an inhuman scale. Still other plans were swiftly defeated by the relentless pressure of human nature. In Tokyo, which was flattened during World War II, planners saw a chance to erase the ancient and convoluted street grid and build what one scholar called "an entirely new urban form," with a series of dense downtowns "nestled against a background of green space, green corridors and broad tree-lined boulevards." It didn't happen. American bombs destroyed buildings, but didn't destroy the claims of property owners, who resisted giving up their land. It was quicker and easier to build along the old streets. A glance at history might have shown this would happen; the world's most famous example of urban planning, Sir Christopher Wren's redesign of central London after a great fire in 1666, was never put in place. Landowners rebuilt on the same properties as before. So it was with Tokyo: partly planned but also partly organic, it was swiftly growing into the largest city on earth.

This was the historic moment in which Pakistan's new ruler Mohammad Ayub Khan plunged his ceremonial shovel into the earth in December 1958. Ayub embraced global trends in city planning. And although he could not have realized it, he was also embracing a global trend of frustrated dreams and unintended consequences.

SUCH WAS the general's eagerness to get started that he laid the foundation stone of his new suburb first, and brought in his chief planner afterward.

Ten days after the general stopped at Korangi for his photo opportunity, a man went to the airport in Athens, Greece, that city of cities. Constantinos Doxiadis caught the midnight flight on SAS Airlines to Beirut, and from there on to Karachi.

An American met him upon arrival at the airport and gave Doxiadis a ride into town as well as a memo on the situation. The American represented the Ford Foundation, which had close links to the American business and government establishment. Ford had been assisting with planning and development in Pakistan since 1951, bringing in advisors from Harvard University; now Doxiadis was part of Ford's team.

After a preliminary meeting, Doxiadis was driven to the Mauripur airport to begin a helicopter tour of the city. Sitting in the front seat beside the pilot, he soared over central Karachi with camera in hand. East of the city, they flew over a fishing village and a military air base; Doxiadis made note of a Zoroastrian landmark called the Tower of Silence. As the chopper continued on over the mostly silent waste that was Korangi, Doxiadis snapped photos of arid land.

The Greek planner in the front seat was an exuberant man with deep-set eyes, a big-toothed smile, and a mustache peppered with gray. He worked in the seemingly ordinary realm of street grids and concrete walls, but his plans required a touch of the visionary. He wanted to understand, forecast, accommodate, and even shape the behavior of millions. He once wrote a book in which he imagined himself at his office window, falling into a dream state as the sun set over Athens. The philosopher Plato spoke to him, followed by Sir Thomas More, the author of *Utopia*. Frank Lloyd Wright joined the discussion of how to build the ideal city, as did H. G. Wells and George Orwell.

His acts were as grand as his dreams. At the close of World War II the Athenian oversaw substantial rebuilding in his battered nation, using American money provided by the Marshall Plan. He coined the term "ekistics" to describe the scientific study of human settlement, and he founded a firm that grew over many years to employ a staff of four hundred. They worked everywhere from Baghdad to Rio de Janeiro to cities in the United States—an urban renewal project in Philadelphia, the waterfront in Louisville, the redevelopment of Washington, D.C. *Time* magazine once described Doxiadis as a man who had "helped resettle 10 million humans in 15 countries."

As he considered the plan for a suburb at Korangi in 1958, Doxiadis recorded misgivings in his diary. "Several aspects of the problem begin to worry me," he wrote. The site had been chosen before his arrival. And it was several miles outside of town. Anybody who lived there would have to pay to commute to their jobs in the city, and, he told his diary, "I wonder if they can." The suburb was expected to house the poorest people in Karachi, so poor that when Doxiadis asked for their typical income and began calculating the cost of electricity and food, he wasn't even sure how they could afford to live in Korangi at all. For these people, unlike American suburbanites, a car was an impossible dream; even bus fare was too much. He pondered what he saw when the helicopter passed over the central city:

> During this flight I am impressed . . . that in many places the people manage to have a house, a small one, a hut built on a very tiny plot between industries . . . or between big blocks of houses. This is a clear proof that people tend to live as close as possible to their working places, transportation is their big problem, they cannot afford to cross big distances.

But there had already been a big photo opportunity miles outside town. Ayub's government was promising to build thousands of houses there within six months. "It is the pet scheme of the Government," the new planner wrote, "the only one on which they concentrated their attention up to now."

Doxiadis accepted this. It was the price he paid for becoming, in effect, the chief planner to the king.

He worked for the government of Pakistan for much of the next decade. Doxiadis's firm planned the new capital city, Islamabad, laid out in a green valley in the northern reaches of the country. Broad lawns surrounded public buildings. Future generations of American visitors would get the feeling that

Doxiadis at his Athens office in 1959, showing Pakistan's rehabilitation minister a plan for Karachi.

[Constantinos A. Doxiadis Archives, © Constantinos and Emma Doxiadis Foundation]

they had arrived in an American urban renewal project from the 1960s: Pakistan's presidential palace brings to mind the Kennedy Center in Washington, no coincidence since the two buildings had the same American architect, Edward Durell Stone. In Islamabad, General Ayub Khan and his chief planner seized the rare opportunity of a blank slate. The city grew so rapidly that in time heavy traffic overwhelmed its broad thoroughfares, but it stood apart for decades as probably the most orderly and comfortable metropolis in Pakistan. Islamabad worked.

Karachi was not a blank slate.

Facing a mass of refugees and a military ruler's problematic concept, Doxiadis responded with a faith that matched the era, not lowering his expectations but raising them. By January 1959, he had persuaded the government to let him expand the plan for Korangi. He wanted to accommodate half a million people "in a self-contained community rationally planned." This, in turn, became part of an even larger scheme to develop suburbs around the metropolitan area; a second major settlement, North Karachi, was laid out even farther away from the central city. "It was a grand plan, a really grand plan," the Karachi architect

Arif Hasan told me when I mentioned the suburbs. Construction began on "schools, community centers, markets."

It is hard not to like the planner who envisioned all this. Doxiadis wanted to create communities where poor people could thrive. In our age of energy shortages and climate change, his ideas seem prescient: he planned buildings that would function efficiently in Karachi's intense heat. Schools would take advantage of traditional South Asian methods of climate control. They would have perforated concrete walls to increase air flow, as well as "wind-catchers" on the roofs—scoops positioned to capture the prevailing ocean breeze and channel it through classrooms. He left spaces for gardens in front of and behind houses, knowing that shade from plants would keep away heat. The planner also sought to learn from old South Asian homes, many of which were surrounded by verandas, or covered porches, that kept the brutal sun and monsoon rains away from the walls. He opposed importing Western construction practices.

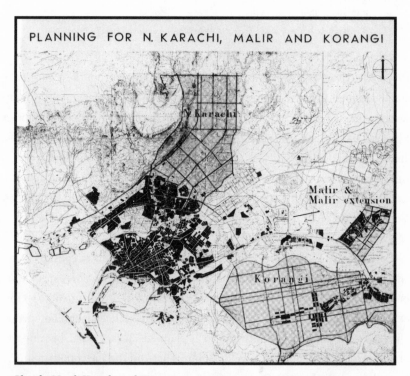

Plan for North Karachi and Korangi.

[Constantinos A. Doxiadis Archives, © Constantinos and Emma Doxiadis Foundation]

They were too expensive. Better to build houses with sun-dried bricks, which local women in rural villages could earn a living by making.

Reading Doxiadis's diary entries from his visits to Karachi makes me feel that I am in the hands of an enlightened man, open to other cultures, thoughtful and wise. Not all of his beliefs withstood time—the wide roads that he favored have been proven the world over simply to encourage more traffic—but his diaries seem to reflect the best global ideas of his era for designing the instant city.

This leaves only one question to answer.

Why did he fail?

CONSTRUCTION CREWS WORKING for the Karachi Development Authority began the project with impressive speed. Within a year and a half of General Ayub Khan's photo opportunity, the government said it had resettled 13,079 families in new homes. The swift construction became a showpiece for the military government. In December 1959, Ayub Khan displayed it for Dwight Eisenhower, the American president who had accepted the coup and who now made the powerful symbolic gesture of visiting Pakistan. In between a formal lunch and a formal dinner in Karachi, Ayub and Eisenhower boarded a helicopter and flew over the new suburb at Korangi. Looking down, the two presidents saw Pakistani schoolchildren arranging themselves to form the words of an Eisenhower campaign slogan, "I Like Ike." Another group of children formed a crescent and star.

Other visitors in the same era looked at Korangi's denizens more closely. A small survey of residents being encouraged to move showed them to be a cross section of the lower end of the service economy in the developing world: they included government workers, shopkeepers, street hawkers, tailors, unskilled laborers, household servants, rickshaw drivers, water carriers, makers of cheap "country made cigarettes" that were rolled in leaves instead of paper, and at least one *qawal,* or musician. Most earned the equivalent of a few dollars per month. Most had been living in tents or huts in some of the more squalid sections of the city. Many had been living on land that was now being cleared for the long-delayed construction of the tomb of Mohammad Ali Jinnah.

The families obtained their government-subsidized suburban houses on a rent-to-own basis. Their rental payments were supposed to help finance additional houses for additional refugees. And that was the first problem. People didn't pay.

Doxiadis had been right to doubt whether Karachi's refugees would be able to afford suburban living, even with government subsidies. He was right to wonder. By November 1960, the development authority reported that "the residents not paying their nominal rent are delaying to some extent the rehabilitation of the thousands of other families still living in huts." By early 1961 the failure to pay was so widespread that the entire program had received a "serious setback." Hundreds of families were evicted for nonpayment, and there

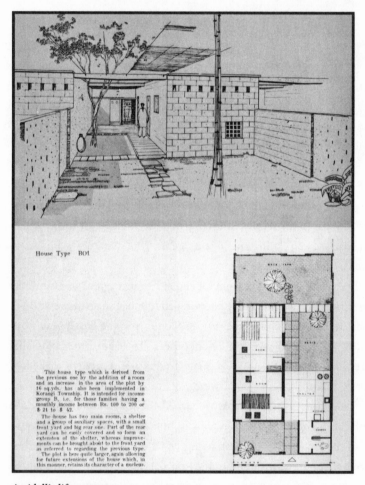

House Type B01

This house type which is derived from the previous one by the addition of a room and an increase in the area of the plot by 16 sq.yds. has also been implemented in Korangi Township. It is intended for income group B, i.e. for those families having a monthly income between Rs. 100 to 200 or $ 21 to $ 42.

The house has two main rooms, a shelter and a group of auxiliary spaces, with a small front yard and big rear one. Part of the rear yard can be easily covered and so form an extension of the shelter, whereas improvements can be brought about to the front yard as referred to regarding the previous type.

The plot is here quite larger, again allowing for future extensions of the house which, in this manner, retains its character of a nucleus.

An idyllic life, on paper.

[Constantinos A. Doxiadis Archives, © Constantinos and Emma Doxiadis Foundation]

must have been many more in arrears, because there was "great reluctance" to evict anyone at all. There had to be reluctance. The government couldn't easily throw people back on the streets. This was Ayub's signature project in Karachi, and one of the great justifications for his coup. When people were evicted, they returned to the center city and built new huts in the same neighborhoods that the government was working so hard to clear.

Nor were the residents the only ones failing to keep their promises to pay. The government, too, failed to provide funding as quickly as expected. Construction began slowing down.

A greater problem loomed, and a comparison with Doxiadis's work in Islamabad is instructive. The plan for Islamabad gave considerable attention to the location of homes for poor people. The great planner said the poor should not be fully segregated from the homes of the middle class **or the** wealthy. Instead there should be "gradual integration" of people in different income groups, "both to help the lower-income people to mature, and to assure the comfort of the higher income-classes." In other words, maids and gardeners should not be forced to live too far from their employers. This design was meant to avoid the sort of low-income ghettos that were developing in Western cities.

In Korangi, this "gradual integration" did not happen, though Doxiadis expressed a desire for it. It was exactly the opposite, according to a confidential report by Doxiadis's firm. Only the poorest people were being moved miles out of town, and their commuting costs were painful. People who had once walked to their low-paying jobs now had to pay bus fare at the end of a long working day. "The people living there became poorer than what they were before," the planner Arif Hasan told me. Some couldn't afford a bus, including Mumtaz Ahmed, who in 1959 was a teenager whose family was moved to Korangi from the area near Jinnah's tomb. Ahmed found himself crowded on the back of a truck with many other people each day, riding all the way back to the central city to work in his father's modest shop. When I met him half a century later, he still recalled the indignity: "On trucks you take cattle, not people," he said. Some people found the commute so frustrating and expensive that they abandoned their new homes and moved back to the center city.

In theory this problem could be solved, and Constantinos Doxiadis had been planning a solution all along. If people no longer lived close to their jobs, then jobs would have to move closer to the people. Wide sections of Korangi and other nearby areas were designated for new markets and factories. Within a few years many businesses set up operations there. The evidence suggests that they succeeded only too well: all the industrial plots were filled, creating new jobs more quickly than the Karachi Development Authority was able to build affordable homes.

Employees of new markets and factories had to live somewhere. It might have been apparent what would happen next.

On November 29, 1963, Americans, along with much of the world, were still reeling from the assassination of President John F. Kennedy seven days before, but Karachi's chief planner remained focused on his work. Doxiadis took one of his periodic driving tours of Korangi under construction. He made, as always, precise observations of everything he saw. He noticed a long line for the bus at 7:30 in the morning. He passed high schools under construction, and made notes about the progress of plantings. He also noted something new and disturbing on a number of properties, which would have to be stopped before more properties were "spoilt." Doxiadis noticed that, for the first time, people had been building unauthorized shacks in Korangi. These sad homes resembled the houses that the government had been trying to demolish in the central city. The problem that Ayub had vowed to solve—and that Doxiadis had been hired to eliminate—was simply moving to a new location.

"**WE DID NOT** have the institutions and expertise for implementing such a large-scale development," remembered Arif Hasan, who in those days was about to begin his career as an architect and planner. There were, for example, not enough experienced engineers, leading to continuous mistakes. A postmortem by one of Doxiadis's aides reached the same conclusion. "There is no control or guidance whatsoever," the aide said. "Nobody was interested in keeping up with the project." One housing agency "is practically non-existent," while another "has no interest," and the city government "does not have the capability to do anything." Communal spaces and sports areas were "abandoned," while schools were "not maintained at all" and were deteriorating.

As the years went on, Karachi would have less talk of the scientific study of human settlement. There would be no more discussion of the "gradual integration" of the well-off and the poor. The government turned to cruder tactics to push people out of the center city and into new settlements. "They started dividing up the land in different locations," Hasan told me, "picking up the refugees, putting them in trucks, dumping them on these plots of land."

"Whether they wanted to go—" I interjected.

"—or not," Hasan said, finishing my sentence. "You cleared a place, you put them in trucks, you gave them all a piece of paper, you gave them that land, you made an access road to that land, and then you forced someone to provide transport over there, and you supplied water through tankers, and you left that place to its fate."

Hasan admitted that his country's first military ruler accomplished one thing in Karachi that politicians had not. The general finally cleared the refugees out of some of the central city. But the way that Ayub did it fostered "the beginning of poor-rich segregation," pushing society's weakest members toward the periphery. Karachi's well-off kept control of the central areas, like the seaside neighborhood of Clifton, with its shrine of Abdullah Shah Ghazi and cool ocean breeze. They maintained the Stock Exchange as well as the old British section of town, now a zone for consulates and nightclubs and upscale hotels. Some long-established poorer neighborhoods did remain near the center—zones like Mithidar, where Abdul Sattar Edhi kept his pharmacy, and where many of the streets were too narrow for his white ambulance. But large numbers of people in temporary shelters were strongly advised to try their luck a few miles away in the desert.

The Karachi resettlement was so large, and its beneficiaries so poor, that it would have strained the capacity of any government. And now Pakistan's government was distracted. In the mid-1960s, Ayub Khan was seeking to bolster his legitimacy by holding a referendum on his rule, then a presidential election (and arranging to win them both). Next he was maneuvering his country into a disastrous war with India. Then he was struggling to keep his job amid a rising tide of street protests, including some in Karachi. As pressure slowly increased, little signs appeared that Ayub's administration had not managed to get its hands around some of the basic functions of government. In 1964, a Lieutenant Colonel N. Ahmed surveyed a random selection of properties around Karachi. "It is very interesting," he wrote, "that 159 structures out of 205 surveyed were not assessed and as such were not paying any taxes." The lieutenant colonel found this breakdown even though he limited himself to *legal* buildings that had received permits, and ignored "the large bulk of un-authorised constructions undertaken in this rapidly expanded city."

The final judgment of Ayub's urban policies would have to wait until after he was forced to step down in 1969, so disdained that he could hardly speak in public for fear of assassination. (He turned over power to General Yahya Khan, the aide who had led the effort to choose the location for the new capital, and who would preside there as the country slid toward civil war.) In 1971 consultants from the Investment Advisory Centre of Pakistan completed an examination of Karachi. Working for a private client, the organization interviewed the residents of more than ten thousand households, helping each to fill out questionnaires. The resulting "Socio-economic Survey of Karachi" was a savage evaluation: "One-fourth of the people of Karachi are still shelterless, whose living 'staggers the imagination.'" Only about half the city lived in solid homes; many of the rest lived in *juggis,* or improvised shacks, "which may be graded poorer than even probably the huts of the primitive communities."

That same year one of Doxiadis's aides took a driving tour of the Karachi suburbs and wrote up a postmortem for his boss. Doxiadis's vision was being erased. People were building squatter homes all over Korangi's new street grid. They even built homes in the yards of existing houses.

North Karachi, the other big new suburb, was mutating. People turned markets into homes. They turned homes into shops. Residents had transformed the heart of the suburb into a "big cattle-breeding area," while a "very rich mosque" had been built in a location nobody had planned. Nobody was building factories in North Karachi, although two cinemas were under construction on land designated for industry. None of this would have mattered if the community functioned, but the streets were "full of mud, garbage, and dirt," and the inhabitants were extremely poor. North Karachi had become the first stop for the newest migrants from the countryside. And there were many such migrants, for rural areas remained in the hands of a few wealthy landowners, known as "feudals," and offered little opportunity for the growing population of poor people. When people arrived in North Karachi, however, their new homes were almost impossibly remote from the jobs and opportunities of the central city. The entire project was "ruined," although the aide made one grudging admission about the residents. Some neighborhoods "are self sufficient in a rather primitive way, considering that everyone does as they please."

By then, the two men who had imagined a different Karachi had both published books. In his ghostwritten memoir, Ayub told a version of the story of his Karachi development, in which everything had gone according to plan. He recalled the triumphant laying of the foundation stone for Korangi in 1958, and went on to mention the swift construction of the first few months. Then he changed the subject.

Constantinos Doxiadis's books included a brief and intriguing work published in 1966. In the introduction, Doxiadis alluded to the doubts that had begun to overshadow the self-confidence of his age. People were turning cities into "dystopias," he said. "Here is reality and here are our dreams—why don't they lead anywhere?" The world population was exploding, urban areas were growing even faster, and cities seemed unable to adapt:

> It is true that man is lost within his growing settlements; it is true that he is confused by the new forces; and thus he is often led to the wrong action. . . . This city cannot survive in this way. There are too many vested interests in every sense of the word—economic, political, cultural, public, and personal—to allow us to remodel it as we should. Is it doomed to become a victim of its past which has created so many commitments for it?

By 1971, Karachi's population was estimated at 3.5 million—more than three million higher than it was on the day when Mohammad Ali Jinnah's plane touched down a quarter century earlier.

7 | SELF-SERVICE LEVITTOWN

Karachi had planners after Constantinos Doxiadis, some of whom influenced the city's growth, but Karachi residents did not follow the planners' instructions. Instead power passed to thousands of people like Nawaz Khan, who had no reputation, no books to his credit, no theory of ekistics, and no architectural firm that bore his name. He just had a few bolts of cloth.

Many years later, as an older man, Nawaz told Karachi researchers his story, which says much about the forces that were shaping the city. He was a migrant from Pakistan's North-West Frontier Province, one of the ethnic Pashtuns who lived along the border with Afghanistan. He obtained fabric, smuggled duty-free from outside Pakistan, brought it to sell in Karachi, and decided to stay. In the 1960s he found an undeveloped plot of land in the northern reaches of the city. The land belonged to the government, but nobody paid attention when Nawaz built a house. He invited Afghan nomads to settle alongside him—they were fellow travelers in the smuggling trade—and two hundred families built homes on "his" land. Suddenly Nawaz was a community leader.

One day a stranger arrived in the neighborhood. The visitor identified himself as a representative of a new political party—the Pakistan People's Party, whose charismatic founder, Zulfikar Ali Bhutto, was climbing toward supreme power. The People's Party man invited Nawaz to become the party's local representative. More than that: Nawaz was encouraged to attract new residents to his settlement, who might then become voters for the party. Nawaz might someday win public office himself.

Nawaz took the opportunity to rise with Bhutto, a Sindhi aristocrat who was young and eloquent and energetic. Bhutto's patriotic stands and speeches as a diplomat made him the most popular politician in Pakistan. He kept a house in Karachi at 70 Clifton, which was fast becoming the most famous home address in the city. And Bhutto had a shrewd organization behind him, as demonstrated by the invitation to Nawaz.

Now the smuggler turned community leader became a real estate developer, marking out individual plots of public land as if he owned them. He sold the plots to other migrants, and by the time the Karachi Development Authority tried to recover the land it was too late. His political connections ensured that Nawaz and his new neighborhood could stay. Many years later, the settlement was "regularized"—meaning that the government gave the residents legal title to land that Nawaz had taken and sold. The fabric smuggler was confirmed as a prosperous and influential man, while the migrants who stuck by him gained a chance for electricity and other services. Nawaz named the neighborhood after the official who sponsored him within the People's Party.

This was how Karachi was growing—person by person, neighborhood by neighborhood. Private interests—both personal and political—overcame the efforts of public servants. In the 1970s the government undertook a variety of new development schemes, and even developed a master plan for the city. But it could hardly keep up with the city's accelerating growth. The civil war that came in 1971 convulsed the country, and when it was over, Pakistan was split in two: East Pakistan became Bangladesh. Karachi became the destination of another mass migration: years after the war, Bengalis fled their impoverished new country and migrated to Karachi seeking work.

The breakaway of Bangladesh was a symptom of ethnic discord all across the country. Secessionist movements arose, including one in Karachi's province of Sindh. These movements, and government crackdowns, added to the poverty and instability of the countryside, encouraging still more migrations to Karachi. All this and more happened in the 1970s, during the decade-long saga of Zulfikar Ali Bhutto's great climb and Shakespearean fall, which captivated the whole country, and which we will shortly revisit.

Karachi was on its way to a population of 5.4 million by 1981. In the absence of consistent government, many of those millions were as thoroughly on their own as if they had moved onto some wild frontier.

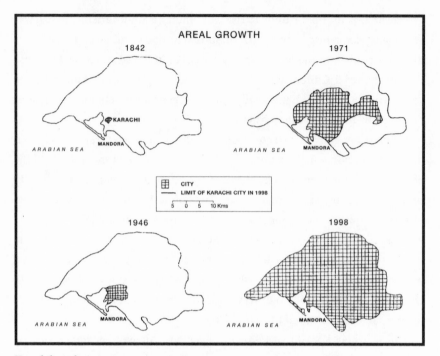

AREAL GROWTH

Karachi's explosion. *[Government of Pakistan]*

AN IRREGULAR NEIGHBORHOOD like Nawaz Khan's was commonly called a *katchi abadi*, which translated simply as "temporary settlement." That proved to be a euphemism. There was nothing temporary about it. Rather than try to move people to new locations, the government settled for a more modest solution. Residents campaigned to have their existing settlements brought within the law. From time to time the Pakistani government approved sweeping legalizations of *katchi abadis,* like the one that proclaimed an amnesty for unauthorized neighborhoods whose residents could prove their homes existed as of March 23, 1985. Yet it took many years to register the neighborhoods, and new settlements constantly appeared. They became such a permanent problem that the provincial government of Sindh included a Minister of Katchi Abadis.

When I sat with the man who was serving as minister in 2010, a gregarious People's Party politico named Rafique Engineer, he handed me results of the most recent survey available. His paper showed 539 irregular neighborhoods in Karachi that were home to about 2.5 million people. And as Rafique knew, his numbers were almost two decades out of date. Some of those settlements had since been brought within the law, but more were appearing constantly. It was commonly estimated that something around half of Karachi's people lived in unauthorized homes.

In other words, half of the inhabitants of the largest city of a nation founded by a lawyer—a lawyer whose face and name where everywhere—were now living in the realm of the extralegal. And this was typical of cities across much of the developing world. Karachi's *katchi abadis* were rough equivalents of the vast settlement called Kibera that was growing at the edge of Nairobi, or the crowded slum of Dharavi in the heart of Bombay, or the *favelas* that climbed the steep hillsides of Rio de Janeiro (and which the Athenian planner Doxiadis, in his plan for Rio, had proposed to demolish). Governments were struggling, and often failing, to deal with social and economic change. Western advice frequently went astray, as in the exploding Nigerian city of Lagos, where one study reported that United Nations–led efforts to create a city plan "had no tangible results." A study of Lagos in the early 1970s produced a description that could have applied, with only minor revisions, to Karachi and many other cities around the world—and that in many cases would still apply today:

> Chaotic traffic conditions have become endemic; demands on the water supply system have begun to outstrip its maximum capacity; power cuts have become chronic as industrial and domestic requirements have escalated; factories have been compelled to bore their own wells and to set up stand-by electricity plants; public transport has been inundated; port facilities have been stretched to their limits; the conditions have degenerated over extensive areas within and beyond the city's limits, in spite of slum clearance schemes; and city government has threatened to break down amidst charges of corruption, mismanagement and financial incompetence.

Every one of these problems was only going to get worse, because Lagos kept attracting people. For all its problems, the city remained a better place to make money than the impoverished countryside, with its hollowed-out economy. A more recent study found the poverty rate in Lagos to be less than half that of the countryside.

For many people around the world, life in urban slums meant survival.

But in the scramble for even the most basic resources, observance of the law became a luxury.

The instant city was going off the books.

WHENEVER I WONDERED what was happening in the far reaches of Karachi—and the spring of 2010 was such a time—I met with a woman who understood as well as anyone how the city was changing. She was the person to whom other experts deferred; if I started asking detailed questions about illegal housing they would say, "You should talk with Perween Rahman." She was thin and raven-haired, with a musical way of talking and eyes that lit up when she spoke. She had that priceless quality that marked so many people in Karachi: the worse the situation became, the more amused she seemed.

I found Rahman at work inside the largest informal settlement of all, a section of northwest Karachi that is sometimes referred to as "Asia's largest slum," but is known locally as Orangi, pronounced *oh-ran-gee*, with a hard "g." Here she worked for one of the few organizations that seemed to have adapted to the realities of Karachi's unauthorized neighborhoods, and even transcended

Perween Rahman.

them. She directed the Orangi Pilot Project–Research and Training Institute. The Orangi Pilot Project, or OPP, was by far the most famous slum development organization in Karachi, and well known overseas; the Research and Training Institute, or RTI, evolved from it. Rahman knew the *katchi abadis* so well because the OPP-RTI helped people obtain services for their irregular homes.

Rahman's job required her to keep track of land developers and other characters who were, to a greater or lesser degree, criminals. She had developed a unique perspective on these men, whom government officials angrily denounced as "land grabbers" or "land mafias."

"Everybody says land mafia, land mafia," Rahman told me with a characteristic smile. "We call them land suppliers." Why be judgmental? The government officials who attacked "land grabbing" were often grabbing land themselves.

Rahman did not necessarily condemn unauthorized housing. The situation was too far gone for that. "We are looking at it from the point of view of the poor—where can they settle? We've seen that, for the poor, this land is the only option they have in this city." At the same time, she appeared startled by the many square miles of public land being chopped up into little plots for sale, beginning around 2006. "Now everybody is a land supplier," Rahman said. "The government, the political parties, the police, the members of the national assembly, the members of the provincial assembly, the councilors, the *nazims*"—that was the word used for the leaders of the eighteen municipalities, or subdivisions, of the city. "Everybody is a land supplier."

Rahman led the way into a corner office, where we talked by the light from the windows; the power had gone out, and most people had gone home, as it was late on a Friday afternoon. She showed me a printout of a Google satellite image of the far north fringes of the city. I saw villages, fields, and here and there a crowded neighborhood. Then she began placing layers of colored tracing paper over the image. Each color illustrated the widening sections of land that had been subdivided or built upon, year by year. An estimated one hundred thousand plots of land were being subdivided annually. About a third became houses right away, while speculators bought the rest.

She said the activity had gone beyond the scale of mere corruption. It had spun beyond the authority of the state.

"This," she said, "is a new form of alternative government."

PERWEEN RAHMAN KNEW all about alternative government. It could be argued that the OPP institutions had become an alternative government for Orangi. True, they gave no orders, and had no police. Still, they were doing what Ayub Khan, his Athenian planner, and many well-intentioned officials and consultants since then had failed to do—improve people's living conditions on a vast scale.

Rahman was educated as an architect, and found a job at an architectural firm after graduation. The job didn't work out. "I was designing a hotel," she said, "and I didn't understand what I was doing." She had an epiphany: there was too great a distance between the upscale hotel and the poor districts of her city. She didn't know whom she was helping. She was wasting her time. "I ran from the office without taking my pay," she told me.

She fled to Orangi, about as far as possible from upscale hotels. Her base was the OPP-RTI office in the heart of Orangi, around the corner from a dusty and ramshackle market street, at least an hour's drive from the center city, and sometimes two. Orangi was a sunny and welcoming and pleasant place to work, except for the days when it was not. Days after the Ashura bombing of December 2009, a deadly gun battle took place a few minutes' drive from Rahman's office. On another day a group of armed men burst into the office, demanding that the OPP give over some of its space to allow them to open, of all things, a karate studio. "It was the start of a land grab," Perween explained. The gunmen were linked with the major political party of ethnic Pashtuns. Rahman's colleagues called for help, and eventually another group of gunmen arrived from the People's Party, offering their support. "If you start, we start," the People's Party men said to the rival gunmen in front of the OPP's front door. In time everyone calmed down and went home.

The OPP had good relations with many people, because it operated on the principle of self-help. It didn't wait for the government to provide the poor with basic services like sewers. Instead its employees met with residents and explained how their lives might be improved if they *chose to lay sewers themselves*. The OPP, and the community activists who worked with it, moved lane by lane through Orangi, a district whose population was swiftly surpassing one million people. If the residents of a particular lane decided that they wanted to build a sewer, the OPP and the activists lobbied the government to build the major sewage artery to which the local sewer line would connect. Then the OPP provided technical information, like the angle of incline necessary for the sewage to flow downhill. The street-by-street digging was left to the people. Thousands got sewers this way.

This method was the brainchild of Akhtar Hameed Khan, a former civil servant and social scientist who made the OPP the final project of his long and creative life. Perween Rahman remembered him as the elderly man who'd hired her: "He was a man who would say, 'I'm your grandmother, not your grandfather. Why? Because the grandmother gives love. The grandfather scolds, and he's aggressive. But the grandmother loves, and through love, she's able to encourage and make people grow.'"

Hameed mixed that gentle approach with pragmatic thinking. He started the Orangi project in the early 1980s with grants from the Bank of Credit and Commerce International, or BCCI. The bank and its founder would soon become notorious in the West for allegations of massive fraud, but Akhtar Hameed Khan made sure that some of the profits went to a good cause.

By the time of his death in 1999, the OPP had evolved into three separate institutions, and expanded its services well beyond sewers. It was part of a network of experts and activists who gave advice on building homes with solid walls and strong roofs. One day I visited the home of an OPP-affiliated activist named Shamsuddin, who recounted the decades-long saga of how he and his neighbors maneuvered to get their homes hooked up to electricity. He organized people to put up their own poles ("I became a state within a state," he said), and finally persuaded the electric utility to string the wires. We spoke of this while sitting on the carpet in Shamsuddin's living room, beneath his electric ceiling fan. The only chair was covered with papers and books, but it was a solid house, a "*pucca* house" in the local parlance, far better than the huts where so many people lived and died in decades past. I didn't know what Constantinos Doxiadis would have thought if he had toured the local streets, but the lane outside Shamsuddin's door was straight and orderly. On the commercial streets in his neighborhood, little shops alternated with storefront English schools, every school a sign of people's desire to get ahead.

Such results seemed almost inspiring under the circumstances—but they took decades to achieve. And the city was spiraling further out of control, as Perween Rahman was forever learning. In her work, she met local residents and government officials. She asked simple questions, and often heard jaw-dropping answers. What happened to all the water that the city piped in from the Indus River? Rahman wrote a paper documenting that much of it was stolen with tanker trucks and sold to citizens at premium prices. Why did monsoon rains cause such floods in the city? Rahman showed me a massive wall map that the OPP-RTI had prepared, illustrating how many storm drains and sewers emptied into a marshland that was now being clogged with development.

Illegal developers, Rahman reported, were sweeping across the far reaches of the city like prospectors in a gold rush. The poor people who moved into these neighborhoods were entirely at the mercy of their local land supplier. If he was humane and delivered what he promised, they might grow to love him like a father. If he took their money and failed to deliver, they had no recourse. This was what Perween Rahman meant when she spoke of "a new form of alternative government." She said of the construction projects at the city's edge, "They are self-governing systems. Because nowadays the land suppliers have started providing water, started providing electricity, road, sewage systems. So then what is the role of the municipality?

"And the question comes, where are the planners of this city?" she asked, before answering her own question:

"They are redundant."

AS WE SPOKE I thought of the day in 2008 when I'd gone to find an illegal settlement under construction. It wasn't hard. It simply required traveling in any direction, although I chose a zone at the edge of the city where construction was said to be especially active.

This zone spread out along the periphery of Karachi, where a brand-new highway called the Northern Bypass had dramatically improved access to many square miles of real estate. The highway swerved around the central city much as interstate beltways skirt the edges of American cities. And just as American interstates opened vast rural lands to development, the Northern Bypass was inspiring a desperate lunge of land acquisition and construction around the edges of the metropolis.

My driver steered the car to a section known as Tasier Town, which stood within a couple of miles of the new highway. It was in the farther northeastern reaches of the city, a bit farther than the street grid of Doxiadis's "ruined" old suburb in North Karachi. We stopped in a settled area to ask directions, and were pointed down a two-lane road. A market area appeared to the right. A wide expanse of sand stretched off to the left. Someone had posted a sign on a little roadside building there, a 2007 order from the High Court of Sindh directing that nothing should be built on that property. Behind it, on the vacant land, we saw homes under construction.

We turned left onto a dirt track, rolling past a few forlorn and half-finished houses between vacant lots. On the far side of a swale, we spied some activity around a pair of attached homes. A pickup truck was parked to the left. A barrel-chested man stood by the truck, staring at a side wall of concrete blocks. A nasty jagged crack cut through the blocks from top to bottom, where the foundation must have settled unevenly. This was a universal scene, recognizable anywhere in the world: the man was a contractor, contemplating a screwup. He was trying to think of the easiest way to fix it or cover it up. After a moment he signaled two men on the back of the truck, who began unloading new cinderblocks from the truck bed.

The sun was heating up now as the two laborers heaved the concrete blocks onto the ground. The contractor, Wahab Khan, showed me around the partially built neighborhood, including a completed model home. A banner on the front wall proclaimed that this could be yours for 350,000 rupees—about five thousand dollars at the exchange rate of that time. Wahab unlocked the gate of the house and led the way into a tiny walled courtyard. Beyond the courtyard were two tile-floored and windowless rooms, and a bathroom at the back. A drainpipe ran from the bathroom to the dry creek behind the house.

Two rooms, a bathroom, a courtyard. In those respects it met Doxiadis's old standard for a proper house for the poor, although the location was bad and the street was dirt. I noticed an electrical outlet and asked where the power came from. Wahab led the way out and pointed to the horizon, where a row of electrical poles spread out along the main road. "What we do," he said, is "we put our own hooks on those main lines." A web of smaller electric wires led away from the main lines, held up by bamboo poles, taking the stolen electricity toward houses in various stages of completion. "And when the government comes here, they just, you know, remove these lines. And when they go away, we put the hooks back."

Wahab Khan, it turned out, was more than a contractor. He was the man in charge of what amounted to the local version of Home Depot, where he agreed to take me next. He had set up operations on a sandy lot, where he kept a spinning cement mixer that made the concrete blocks he had just dropped off at the cracked house. His laborers were dumping wet concrete into the steel brick mold that worked like a giant ice-cube tray, cutting eight blocks at a time.

The local Home Depot was called a *thalla,* and Wahab, as the boss of it, was the *thallawalla.* Like his workers—and like so many newcomers to Karachi— he was a Pashtun from Pakistan's war-torn far northwest. On this lot he sold most of the basic materials to make a simple house. Concrete blocks and roofing material were cheap. Human beings were even cheaper. Wahab's laborers lived under a little thatched roof near the concrete mixer.

Wahab said there were certain expenses. Police sometimes came by and declared themselves to be shocked—shocked—that illegal construction was under way. The cops could not possibly overlook such an obvious violation unless they were paid. Sometimes they jailed a whole construction crew, and it would take a couple hundred dollars to get them out. (I later described Wahab's account to the commander of the provincial police, Muhammad Shoaib Suddle. Could it be true? He seemed surprised that I needed to ask: "Of course we all understand that without—you know—protection, these things cannot prosper." Two years after that, residents told me their bribes had become standardized, which was good for business; people paid five thousand rupees per home plot to the top official at the nearest police station.)

I said goodbye to Wahab and went back into the illegal development, along a narrow and straight dirt lane. Little ridges of dirt marked out the future home lots on either side. I chatted with several men who were laying PVC pipes in a trench, building a sewer line that would dump into the seasonal stream. One was a migrant from Baluchistan, the vast and arid province to the west. The laborer, Fawaz Mohammad, said there wasn't much work at home, so he had migrated to Karachi in search of 250 rupees a day, about $3.57 at that time. He walked to work each day from another settlement where his boss arranged housing, five or six men to a room.

Fawaz Mohammad couldn't afford to bring his wife and one-year-old daughter here from Baluchistan. He said he caught a bus back home to visit every six months or so.

Who was paying the men to dig the sewers? "A rich man," was all one said.

Down the lane, I found two women on their haunches in the dirt. They were crouching over the tangled branches of a bush, which they were chopping with little hatchets to make firewood. Behind them stood two concrete-block row houses in which the two women lived with their families, side by side.

Razia and Shinaz were relatives. They had sixteen children between them, many of whom swirled about as we stood talking in the dusty lot.

"Nobody goes to school?" I asked Shinaz.

"No," she answered.

I realized afterward that there was probably not a single member of that family who could have read the sign by the road that forbade construction.

The women showed us around their homes, which were laid out like the model home we had seen, with a tiny walled courtyard in front and two main rooms behind. One had a portion of the courtyard walled off to make a third room, a kitchen. However, the families did not have the money to finish their homes with plaster or tile. The walls were bare concrete blocks, the floors dirt. They had not been able to buy roofing material either, so their homes were open to the weather. They were sleeping under the stars.

One woman's husband was a fisherman, who was away on a boat for days at a time. The other husband ran a fruit drink stand in another part of the city. A third male relative lived with them; the women freely described him

Suburban life: two Bengali families. *[NPR]*

as a "drug addict," although he was standing right there. Both women worked cleaning homes. Each said she earned about twenty-five hundred rupees per month. The monthly payment on each house was two thousand.

Do you have enough to live on? I asked.

"Look at our children's faces," one said. "Don't you think they're underfed?"

Even so, the women seemed grateful. Both families were Bengalis, meaning they or their ancestors came from what had once been East Pakistan—the far-away province that broke away to form Bangladesh in 1971. Ever since the war, Pakistani authorities had treated Bengalis as a national security threat. This made their lives hard, and also made them perfect customers for the developers. In the early stages of an unauthorized settlement, developers commonly reached out to the weakest and most vulnerable people. They were the only ones who would pay for a home where life was so hard, and where property ownership was so doubtful.

Shinaz and Razia spoke like first-time homebuyers. They were optimistic. Whatever the downsides, they preferred this place to the rooms they had rented in years past. They represented the most powerful force in the instant city: the desire of millions of people—simple, quiet, humble, and relentless, no matter what the odds—to make their lives just a tiny bit better than they were.

8 | CASINO

M illions of people pursued their modest ambitions in the instant city. Some pursued gigantic ambitions.

In my research I began to hear stories about a man who dreamed of transforming Karachi, starting with some prime real estate by the beach. His property stood within a few blocks of the shrine of Abdullah Shah Ghazi and the Hindu temple of Shiva. The stories I heard said the man wanted to build a different sort of temple, not religious at all, although its builder invested it with his own kind of faith. This man dreamed of a building that combined the romance of Paris, the glitter of Macao, and the allure of old Beirut.

He began construction in the 1970s, when Karachi was asking the same question posed by cities all over the world: What do we have to offer, and how can we compete in the global marketplace? What can make our city distinct? Karachi was still so new; it could become anything. But there was competition for the city's identity. The man who dreamed of Paris had to contend with other men whose dreams ran more toward Mecca.

I went looking for the dreamer who envisioned Paris on the Arabian Sea, and found him at a local club for the city's elite. It was called the Karachi Gymkhana, and it occupied one of the finest addresses in the city. High walls surrounded the compound, and when I arrived at the security gate a guard said that only members were allowed. Luckily I had an appointment with a man whose name opened doors.

I stepped along a curving driveway toward a building that vaguely resembled a ski lodge. It had a Tudor design of wood and plaster, as well as a steeply sloped roof, as if a snowstorm might start any minute. Beneath the roof, however, the old building was adapted to the South Asian climate. A wide veranda offered a shaded space where club members could have drink in the breeze. The veranda also kept sunlight away from the rooms within.

The man at the front desk directed me down a hallway that was open to the breeze, and into a cool central room. Here I sat on a plush couch and waited for my appointment with Tufail Shaikh—onetime nightclub owner, impresario of dancing girls, and Karachi business legend. People sometimes called him by his nickname, Tony.

I had heard a story about Tony Tufail, one that in outline was familiar to longtime residents, though few people knew the details. I wanted to learn more, because the story captured a moment when Karachi's fortunes changed, along with those of Pakistan, with wider implications for the world.

Tony Tufail was the man who dreamed that Karachi, that overwhelmingly Muslim metropolis, would be the perfect place to build a casino. People said that he actually built a giant casino on Karachi's beach. They said it was filled with gambling tables and plush furniture, though it was never allowed to open. Anjum Niaz, a freelance writer, professed to have walked inside during the 1980s, when the cavernous building was completed but unused. The interior, she wrote, "was covered with cobwebs. Yet the damask on the furniture and the curtains hadn't lost its majesty, nor the emblemed cutlery and crockery made of finest bone china lost its lure."

Artist's conception, Clifton Beach Casino. *[Collection of Tufail Shaikh]*

ALL THIS HAPPENED decades ago, so when I began asking after Tony Tufail in 2010 I did not know if I would find a withered old man or an active one. Nobody answered at his home number. Then I heard that he played cards almost every afternoon at the Karachi Gymkhana. I left a message there, and within a few days he returned my call, speaking in a strong and clear voice. "Karachi was a *completely* different place in the seventies," he said as we talked.

I asked to meet him at the Gymkhana. And here he was now, extending his hand as he walked across the room. He had a strong handshake. He wore the long-tailed shirt and baggy pants that were traditional in his part of the world, though with a hint of his individual style. Tufail's pants were white, and the long shirt a deep royal blue. He had a full head of fine black hair, and a high-boned face that seemed almost Hawaiian in character. His smooth-shaven skin hardly seemed to have a wrinkle. His sole concession to age was a pair of metal-framed glasses.

"You should come to my house," he said, "where we can talk, and have a cold drink. But first you should look around the Gymkhana."

We walked out through the veranda and across a perfectly clipped lawn to inspect the facilities. "Gymkhana" was a familiar word across South Asia and Iran, not perfectly translatable into English; a gymkhana could resemble a gymnasium, a country club, an Elks Club, or all three. This complex had every-thing from an outdoor swimming pool to an indoor poolroom. We studied the table tennis area and a building full of squash courts—the building was open to the weather on the north side, designed so that a breeze might work its way inside but direct sunlight never would. Several people along the way stopped Tony Tufail to say hello; he had until very recently been the club president.

According to a plaque inside the veranda, the building dated back to 1886. The first president of the Gymkhana had been a Leftenant Colonel B. Simpson—and his name served as a reminder that the uppermost layer of Karachi's elite used to be entirely British. The Gymkhana was near the Sind Club, which had its own list of past British colonial officials, as well as rifles and the head of a tiger mounted on the inside walls. The architect Yasmeen Lari, who once invited me for lunch in the Sind Club's dining room, informed me that in colonial times this neighborhood was the "white" area, where the British could live at a slight remove from the "blacks" in the rest of Karachi. It was not the most harshly segregated city in British India, she said, but all the same the members of the Sind Club posted a sign that read, "No Dogs or Natives Allowed." Now, she said with a laugh, "*we* are the ones who live in the white area."

At the Sind Club the elite lunch crowd was nearly all "natives," uniformed servants as well as the clientele—here was Yasmeen with her husband the distinguished historian of Sindh; here was an elderly woman who'd run a magazine for many years, dropping by to chat; and over there was Ardeshir Cowasjee, the Zoroastrian shipping magnate turned acerbic columnist, with his short gray beard and his vest, dining alone. (I said hello, as we'd met before, and told him I was still writing about the city's development. "What a terrible subject, have you nothing else to write?" muttered Cowasjee, who chose to write about it constantly himself.)

This was the complex of privilege that Pakistan's new elites claimed when the British era ended in 1947. Pakistanis had expanded and updated it, as I could see when Tony Tufail led me out onto the great circular cricket field that was part of the Karachi Gymkhana. Across the field we had a spectacular view of two vast modern hotels, the Sheraton and the Pearl Continental.

It was one of the most impressive views of Karachi I ever saw, except for a single thing. Near the great slabs of the two hotels stood a third huge building, or rather the skeleton of one. It was all concrete floors and pillars, about fifteen stories high. It looked like a construction project, some sign of great things to come, except I happened to know that it wasn't. It was a construction project in suspended animation; the building was completely unchanged from when I had first seen it eight years earlier. "That's the Hyatt," Tufail said. It belonged to a friend of his. Or it did, until the government took control. "Zia stopped construction."

Zia-ul-Haq? I asked. The military ruler who took power in 1977?

Yes, he said.

How could the project have been left for dead for more than thirty years at one of the most visible corners of the city? Almost every foreign visitor for decades who stayed at the Sheraton or the Pearl would have looked at that monstrosity and wondered, as I did, what had gone wrong.

"Zia stopped construction," Tufail went on, "because my friend was a supporter of Zulfikar Ali Bhutto. Just like me." Bhutto—the founder of the People's Party—was the man whose great rise and fall defined the 1970s and had great significance for Karachi. His face appeared on political posters even today, frequently alongside his famous daughter Benazir Bhutto, as if they were still running for office, as if neither one had been killed on the job.

Tony Tufail led me back to the main building and showed me the card rooms before we left. On our way to his car, which was waiting at the front entrance, I noticed a vast painting on the veranda. It showed thousands of figures streaming across the landscape. They were painfully lugging their belongings while a train passed in the distance. It was a painting of masses of people moving at the time of Partition in 1947, and it was hung in a place where every club member would see it. Tony Tufail had been among those moving masses, born in Delhi and brought to Karachi at the age of nine.

We drove through Karachi's old white area, past the coils of barbed wire that protected the road in front of the American consulate. Nearby, I knew, stood the stone-walled compound of the chief minister—the leader of the provincial government—as well as the homes of other high officials. These VIPs lived within layers of security, all of them backed up protectively against each other like soldiers on a hilltop preparing for a last stand. Reality had a way of leaking into the white area, of course, the way that water will find its way into the best-built ship. In 2002, a bomb blew up a bus outside the Sheraton. In 2002, 2003, 2004, and 2006, attackers struck the American consulate. Now armed guards stood everywhere.

"Were there always so many guards in the city?"

"No way," he answered.

On our way toward the beach we passed the metal gate and the outer walls of 70 Clifton, the old compound of Zulfikar Ali Bhutto. We passed the temple of Shiva and the shrine of Abdullah Shah Ghazi. We passed the property where Tufail's casino had once been, then turned around and studied the property a second time on the way to his house.

"Somebody told me you had actually finished the building," I said.

"Yes, yes, in July 1977," he said. "Invitations were printed, tables were set, everything was ready."

Tufail had survived the setback. He said he still owned some real estate, which he had bought for speculation up in Hawkes Bay—the same far-off beach area where there had been talk of a "minor building boom" in the 1950s, thanks to some American speculators. Tony had talked with Americans recently, looking to move his property, but found no international interest. "People are shy of investment in this country," he said, because of the problem with terrorism.

So what else was he doing?

"Basically I am entertainment, I had a hotel. I sold it."

"Which hotel?"

"The Excelsior."

"You're entertainment in a city without enough entertainment."

"Look, one time this city was full of life," he said, becoming agitated. "You could walk along the street at four in the morning. Nothing, no guards were required. The gates were open, no guards."

A guard pulled open the gate to Tony Tufail's driveway. As soon as we walked in the door, I knew we were in a special place. The living room was one floor up from the door, but rather than mounting stairs we followed a long ramp that doubled back on itself—the sort you'd see in a football stadium or Grand Central Terminal, perfect for moving masses of people. Tufail told me that the man who designed his house was the same man who designed his casino. That same architect had designed a casino in Beirut, which was the very reason Tony Tufail was inspired to bring him to Karachi. Tony was a regular visitor to Beirut many years ago, when Zulfikar Ali Bhutto was alive and Tony was a younger man.

"I'M A MECHANICAL ENGINEER," Tony told me, smoking a cigarette. He got his engineering education in London, then came back home. "My brother owned a hotel here, called Excelsior. He died in 1965. Then I took over the hotel. Since then I've been in the entertainment business. I had two nightclubs here in Karachi. In those days Karachi was swinging. We had nightclubs, we had hotels, we were free, we were . . ." He trailed off. "Things have changed. Life has changed."

We sat in an expansive living room with a garden just outside the window; a gardener came by watering the shrubs as we talked. "You want a beer?" he said, and I declined, explaining that I had been up most of the night and felt too tired to start drinking in midafternoon. Only later did it occur to me that he might have been disappointed, that we might have come to his house in the first place because we could have a drink in private, but Tufail, the perfect host, betrayed no hint of this. He signaled a maid to bring tea.

Tufail's Excelsior Hotel stood in the central part of the city, an area known as Saddar. It was a center of public life—through which the annual Ashura processions moved, for example. It was a zone of historic stone buildings and restaurants. Many Karachi residents had vivid memories of the neighborhood in the decades after 1947. Akbar S. Ahmed, the young migrant and future scholar, spoke of going there with his mother to a bookstore that was, for him, like magic. Arif Hasan would remember poolrooms and restaurants for every class

"Tony" Tufail Shaikh.

of people: "You had bars where the taxi drivers went. You had bars which were more expensive." Kamran Asdar Ali, a Karachi native who grew up to become an American anthropologist, recalled "constant talk within my household and those of my middle class friends of how in the 1950s our mothers and aunts would go to watch movies without chaperones. They would wear saris showing their bare midriffs . . . and walk without hesitation through the elegant streets."

Saddar included the Jubilee Cinema, where the "all India premiere" of a movie from Bombay had come at the time of independence. In fact there were many theaters, like the Nishat Cinema, where a young man named Masih ul Hassan went to work as a ticket-taker in 1964. Hassan told me that Indian movies were banned after the disastrous war of 1965, but the theaters stayed in business. Pakistan was developing an Urdu-language movie industry, and Western imports were hits. People watched *Lawrence of Arabia* when it premiered in central Karachi at a cinema called the Bambino.

And of course Saddar included the Excelsior.

"What were the nightclubs like?" I asked Tufail.

"We had all the artists from Paris, Lebanon, all over the world. We even had the striptease. We had floor shows, belly dancers. Karachi was full of life." And of course there was alcohol, which flowed freely.

"I used to go and book the acts. I used to go personally abroad. Mainly Beirut. Plus we had these agents all over the world, they would send their acts. It's been a long time, but I also had contact in Paris with a strip joint called . . ." He tried to think of the name. "Very famous—still there."

"The Moulin Rouge?" I suggested.

"No, not Moulin Rouge, it was a competitor. I used to get some of my artists from there. And Egyptian belly dancers." It bothered him, not recalling the place in Paris; I told him not to worry, it would come to him. Tufail went on to say that the Excelsior drew some customers from abroad, as well as dancers. "Karachi was full of foreigners," he said.

I later ran across a reference to Tufail's main enterprise in an essay called "Karachi Before Prohibition," written by a gentleman old enough to remember the years leading up to the 1970s:

> As the booze flowed and as the locals developed a preference for fading continental blondes, a number of seedy establishments cropped up in different parts of the city. The Excelsior . . . was a pioneer of the sleazy joints where cabaret meant strip tease. Posters and advertisements regularly billed the performers as stars of the Folies Bergere [a music hall in Paris] but the girls . . . whimsically shaking their partially unclad bodies . . . invariably turned out to be bawdy campaigners from the nightclubs of Istanbul or Beirut. The client who had already tucked away a quart . . . never knew the difference. Nor did he particularly care, as long as the girls were white, voluptuous and available.

Some people looked down on Tony Tufail; he didn't care. Tufail had ambitions far grander than the Excelsior Hotel. And he had a chance to achieve his ambitions, because in the 1960s, one of his customers was Zulfikar Ali Bhutto.

BHUTTO WAS A MAN whose hairline began receding early, and who exhausted himself through overwork. But his large and expressive eyes, the commanding way he carried himself, and above all his eloquent speeches set him apart from other politicians.

He was the son of a wealthy landowner, a feudal leader in Larkana, in rural Sindh. As a son of privilege, Bhutto studied in America, at the University of

Southern California, and later at Berkeley. Before coming home he also worked as a volunteer in a 1950 United States Senate campaign, but his candidate lost. Her name was Helen Gahagan Douglas, and she was demolished in a famously nasty election. A rising young Republican named Richard Nixon smeared her by suggesting she was a Communist sympathizer, and went on to become the most important American political figure of the next quarter century. Although Bhutto played no significant role in the campaign, he was getting an education in politics. He had certainly seen nothing to overturn his belief that politics required both ferocity and deception.

He was still a very young man, just thirty years old, when he joined the first cabinet of the military ruler Ayub Khan. Ayub later made him Pakistan's foreign minister. And somehow Bhutto turned a progression of disasters to his own advantage. Bhutto's dubious advice played a role in Ayub's decision to go to war with India in 1965, a miscalculation that ended in a bitter stalemate; yet Bhutto remained a hero for his verbal defense of his country. Bhutto fell out with the general who sponsored him, but when he left the government he became Pakistan's most ferocious spokesman for democracy.

"How did you know Bhutto?" I asked Tony Tufail.

"When I came back from England after my studies, my brother knew him, and introduced me." In the mid-1960s, when Tony took over the Excelsior, Bhutto was a frequent customer. ("He used to bring his wife also," Tufail stressed.) This was around the time that Bhutto, still not yet forty, had left Ayub's government to chart his own course. Tufail would follow him. "He formed his own political party, and I was with him. I was not active in politics, but I was a founding member. When the party was being formed, I was there."

The guiding spirit of the Excelsior became part of Bhutto's entourage. "Whenever he was in Karachi he used to call me," Tufail said, and Tufail would drop what he was doing and head to 70 Clifton, Bhutto's Karachi home. Tufail said he would simply do whatever his friend needed, talking with visitors, dealing with small problems, waiting. He might stay there from noon until one o'clock in the morning, whatever Bhutto needed.

The office at 70 Clifton still exists, spacious but not ornate. When I visited, it was easy to sense what it might have been like to have Bhutto sitting behind the desk. He had passed on his charisma to his strikingly beautiful granddaughter Fatima, who welcomed me into the house. Tiny in stature but forceful with language, she had become both a journalist and a celebrity. She let me admire a painting that hung on the wall, showing her grandfather shaking his fist as he addressed a great crowd. It is an impressionistic painting, Bhutto clear and dramatic in the foreground, the people represented by countless dots behind him.

The man in that painting told people that power belonged to *them*, that they would be in charge if he were in charge, and many believed. ("Who am I to make your decisions?" he told a mass rally during a speech on foreign affairs, saying that if they wanted, he would tell other countries to "go to hell.") His party stood for "bread, clothes, and shelter," for socialism, and for the poor. Behind the scenes he was always maneuvering, always shifting course, always grasping for the top. He *did* want to be the man who made the decisions. In 1970, the east and west wings of Pakistan finally held elections for parliament, and the People's Party did very well—in West Pakistan. A party from East Pakistan actually won more seats and the right to form a government. Rather than submit, Bhutto seemed to encourage the breakup of the country through his words and deeds. What followed was Pakistan's catastrophic civil war, in which the army massacred countless Bengalis and still lost control of the east when India's much larger army intervened in 1971. Bangladesh was gone, Pakistan's

Fatima Bhutto in her grandfather's office.
[Tracy Wahl]

military was crushed, and the Pakistani government lay in ruins. There was nobody left to run the country but Zulfikar Ali Bhutto, who promised to pick up the pieces—"very small pieces," as he said in a speech to the nation.

In many ways he did. His speeches restored his country's morale. First as president and then as prime minister, he established a more democratic government, or at least a more popular government. He rammed a new constitution through the parliament in 1973. Less successfully, he began a massive intervention in Pakistan's economy. He nationalized key industries and companies, to the dismay of the business community. He grew increasingly deceptive and autocratic. In a famous episode, he spoke at a New Year's Eve celebration attended by many of Karachi's business leaders, and he offered them reassurance: there was no truth to "wild rumors" that he was about to nationalize all banks. The next day, January 1, 1974, he nationalized all banks.

That same day, Bhutto also took over the ships run by the family of his neighbor Ardeshir Cowasjee, the Zoroastrian heir to a shipping fortune in Karachi. Cowasjee never forgot: when I met him decades later, he still had paintings of his ships on the walls of his home. Nevertheless Cowasjee accepted a position in Bhutto's administration, serving as the head of the Pakistan Tourism Development Corporation. And so it could have been Cowasjee who was called upon to bring the casino to Karachi, except that the prime minister's capriciousness intervened. Bhutto moved Cowasjee to a different job and then, for reasons never explained, had Cowasjee thrown in prison for two and a half months. (When I asked him why he thought Bhutto imprisoned him, Cowasjee said he truly didn't know, although "I might have called him a damn fool." He told me that while in his cell he received a message that he would be released if he would write an apology. "I said, 'I will be happy to write an apology. I will write it. Just tell me what I have done.'") His detention proved be a useful spur to a career change. After his release, Cowasjee wrote several letters to the editor of the newspaper *Dawn,* which captured enough attention that he was given an opportunity to become a columnist. He would turn himself into one of the most significant voices on the city's development, a crafty and erudite critic of corruption and land theft.

During these increasingly wild years the nightclub owner Tony Tufail was frequently at Bhutto's side, and more than once they spoke of the future of Karachi. In Tufail's memory, Bhutto's dream for the city began with its modern gateway, the Shahrah-e-Faisal—the road from the international airport. They spoke of a road that would match one of the grandest avenues in Paris.

"You know he planned to make it the Champs-Elysées, from the airport to the Metropole," Tufail said, mentioning one of the popular hotels of the time in central Karachi.

Tufail knew exactly which visitors he wanted to see rolling down the road from the airport. The new oil wealth of the nearby Persian Gulf had made millionaires of countless Arabs, who suddenly had money to spend on pleasures that their own countries did not allow. Many traveled to Europe or the United States. Some chose Beirut, that friendly and scenic city on the Mediterranean, which allowed casino gambling among other diversions. But in the 1970s, Lebanon was descending toward civil war, and that created an opportunity for Karachi.

"We knew there was trouble in Beirut," Tony Tufail told me, in explaining the rationale for the casino. "We knew we would get all the Arabs here."

"You were trying to make it the new Beirut?"

"The economy would boom," he replied. "We had so many plans, all those hotels were being built, like the Hyatt you saw. It was a part of that scheme, to get five-star hotels, casino, nightclubs, so people would come here. Otherwise, why would they come here? We had to offer them enjoyment."

With the prime minister of Pakistan behind him, Tufail worked for years toward his goal. He wanted the best of everything. He obtained the property by the beach—he considered it the best real estate in the city. He commissioned the architect of the Casino du Liban, outside Beirut, to work his wonders in Karachi. And having no experience in running a casino, Tufail brought in a man who did—Stanley Ho, one of the world's richest men, the man who for many years controlled the concession for gambling in the Portuguese-controlled city of Macao, on the Chinese coast. Tufail showed me a photo of himself standing with the gambling king; Ho's company would bring in the gaming tables, the poker chips, the roulette wheels. Tufail, of course, would handle the entertainment—the dancing girls. "People who don't want to gamble, they can come and watch the floor show, have dinner, enjoy the evening. People who want to gamble, they can gamble."

Wasn't it always going to be a problem to open a giant casino in an overwhelmingly Muslim country? I asked him. Certainly people did anything and everything in private, but a casino could hardly be more public. If it had been easy to build a casino in a Muslim country, the Arab sheikhs would probably have already built them at home. (Beirut, the model that Tufail wanted to follow, was in an unusually diverse and open country, where the largest single religious group was historically Christian.)

Tufail said this had been worked out. The casino would be regulated so that the Arabs with their suitcases of money would come and go without polluting the Muslim masses of Pakistan. "This was foreigners only," he said. "Plus we made a provision," he added, that Pakistanis who paid high income taxes could come—"people who are rich people. Otherwise it was restricted only for foreigners."

In the mid-1970s, the Clifton Beach Casino began to take shape. When I met Tufail, he still had an artist's rendering in a picture frame. It showed a single building, with a car dropping off customers at the front door. Each of the two planes of the enormous roof were curved upward, as if tracing the ascent of a jetliner. The building would cover approximately one hundred thousand square feet, approaching the size of a modern-day Wal-Mart in the United States.

"It was my dream," Tufail told me. "When I visited Lebanon and other places, I saw these casinos. And I thought that in my country I could attract people there."

He started another sentence, failed to finish it, and apologized. It was his fate to see his ambition crushed.

"It's been thirty years," I said. "You're not over this even now, are you?"

"No," he said. "No, I'm not."

TUFAIL'S PATRON Zulfikar Ali Bhutto appears at first glance to be a global—and globalized—figure, with his foreign education, his diplomatic background, and his support for the democratic socialism that was so widespread in his time. He was as eloquent in English as he was in Urdu, and looked equally comfortable in fine Western suits or South Asian dress. He was indeed one of the brilliant lights of the developing world, who thought of his country in global terms. He was also an old-fashioned Sindhi landlord. And he was a politician. His power depended on maintaining his hold on his people, all those dots in the painting on his office wall. And so, like any politician anywhere in the world, he was forever sensitive to local conditions. He was forever adjusting course. He did not lack courage, and wanted to accomplish great things. But that very ambition caused him constantly to calculate his own best advantage. If he believed that the greater political good required him to sacrifice someone—seize the banks, throw an old supporter in jail, or ruin a few lives—he would do it.

Bhutto began to make concessions to conservative Muslim leaders.

There was, for example, the case of the Ahmadis. In the 1970s agitation rose again against this same Muslim sect that had been the focus of riots in the 1950s. Some conservative Muslims considered the Ahmadis apostates because of their differing interpretations of religious history and scripture. Bhutto himself was a member of a minority sect, the Shias, but he did not stand up for the Ahmadis. His national assembly passed a measure declaring them to be a religious minority, not Muslim at all, which cost them many rights in the Islamic republic. The move was seen as fine political judo, as it bolstered the PPP's religious credentials and undercut political rivals. And if there was a price to pay, Bhutto did not think he was the one who would pay it. Ahmadis would suffer second-class status and persecution across Pakistan for decades to follow. Scores were killed in twin bombings in Lahore in 2010.

Bhutto's act was not completely out of character; his party had always mingled religion with patriotism. He was in this way not much different from any number of American politicians. But it was hard for him to buy off fundamentalists for very long. He was a whiskey-drinking, hard-living man not known for his piety, and conservative politicians did not trust him. (It would be hard to understate the importance of alcohol in the equation. The founder of the religious party Jamaat-e-Islami, Abul A'la Mawdudi, could have had Bhutto's Karachi in mind when he declared public morals had "deteriorated over decades due to the onslaught of cinema, obscene pictures, songs, mixed society, drinking and other evils." He also blamed the recent breakup of Pakistan on the failure to follow Islamic rules, especially the drinking habits of national leaders; the party's student wing blamed the country's troubles on "wine.") Bhutto's list of enemies was rapidly growing, and although he did not seem to realize it, that list included a deeply conservative leader of the army. General Zia-ul-Haq had a pointed mustache, hooded eyes, and a disarming way of feigning obedience. Bhutto considered Zia unthreatening enough that he appointed the general chief of the army staff.

In the March 1977 election for parliament, major religious parties joined a broad coalition that opposed the prime minister, and this was the moment when Bhutto's PPP committed its fatal mistake. Just like the American president Richard Nixon in the United States a few years before, Bhutto's side played dirty in an election that he probably would have won without cheating at all.

After election night, when absurdly high vote totals began pouring in for the PPP, the opposition charged fraud. Protests and calls for Bhutto's resignation mounted, and the prime minister began losing his grip on power.

In Karachi during those chaotic months, Tufail was setting up the gambling tables and lining up the acts for the Clifton Beach Casino. He was, as he remembered, simply waiting for final approval to open. The approval wasn't coming. His patron was still trying to buy off the conservatives. In May 1977, under Bhutto's direction, Pakistan's national assembly proclaimed Friday, the Muslim day of prayer, as a holiday; it would remain so for the next two decades,

The assembly also banned all forms of gambling.

At the beginning of July, the situation swung wildly. Each day's banner newspaper headlines contradicted those from the day before. One day Bhutto had reached a settlement with opposition leaders; the next day he hadn't. On July 4 he told advisors that he really, truly, was close to an agreement that would end the crisis. But early in the morning of July 5, word spread that he had run out of time. Tufail Shaikh's telephone rang about two o'clock; a leading newspaperman was calling to say that the military had arrested Bhutto. Taking advantage of the post-election tension, General Zia-ul-Haq had seized control.

Tony Tufail described that late-night phone call to me as we spoke in his living room. Talking with me, he seemed as distressed for his friend as if the call had just come. I wondered, "Did you immediately ask yourself what does this mean for your casino?"

"You know, I take it as it comes. I had a shock. I was dazed. And I got up and, in those days, I had a drink. And then I was thinking, 'What now?' And then I thought I will have to start all over again."

The first stage of grief is denial. And after he had his drink and calmed down, Tufail persuaded himself that his casino was not really gone. "I thought he would allow it, Zia would, because, it was made for foreigners." In the first hours of his coup, General Zia encouraged everyone to live in denial; he did not claim that he was out to change the country, promising he would hold elections within ninety days—"Election in October next" as a headline put it—and even saying that he expected the people to return Bhutto to power. Zia never got around to holding those elections. As his own October deadline receded into the past without a vote, the newspapers were filled with statements that were such masterpieces of obfuscation they suggested the general had a sly sense of humor:

QUETTA, Dec. 4 . . . General Mohammad Zia-ul Haq, who was talking to newsmen soon after his arrival at the Quetta Airport this morning, told a questioner that although political activity was undoubtedly essential for the evolution of the country's politics, yet there were things higher than politics. Politicians, he hoped, would "appreciate" larger national interest.

As long as Zia was holding power, he intended to use it. Two days after the coup, the mustached general spoke a sentence about religion at the end of a public statement. It must have seemed to some readers like typical boilerplate—"Pakistan, which was created in the name of Islam will survive only on the basis of Islam, for which Islamic system is most essential"—but Zia turned out to mean it. Tony Tufail could not have been encouraged to read a few months later that the new military government was making plans to remodel the economy "in accordance with the injunctions of the Holy Quran." And in truth his hope should have faded when one of the early martial law regulations was announced:

AMPUTATION OF HAND FOR THEFT

The military began building a case against Bhutto, publishing "white papers" on the crimes of his government. Islamist political parties led the way in demanding "accountability," by which they meant Bhutto's execution. The aged Maulana Mawdudi declared the prime minister a "moral criminal and a murderer." The deposed prime minister was blamed for crimes ranging from murder to election fraud. He was even accused of getting the government to pay much of the bill for a Carrier air-conditioning system, shipped from America and installed in his Karachi home at 70 Clifton.

A group of military investigators descended on Tufail's casino, questioning the plans, questioning the finances. Finally, as Tufail remembered it, General Zia himself came to the casino to receive the results of the inquiry. Tufail said he spoke up for the casino as a "national project." The general replied that if the casino were already open he would not interfere, but as it had never opened, he would not allow it.

General Zia had Prime Minister Bhutto put on trial for his alleged involvement in murder. He was accused of ordering gunmen to open fire on a political rival, a burst of shots that missed its target but killed the rival's father instead. Even if the charges of Bhutto's involvement had been true, they were minor compared to the murder of democratic government. Bhutto remained defiant even after his conviction: "We will meet one day," he wrote Zia from his jail cell. "You pursue me now. Wait till I pursue you." Bhutto was hanged after midnight on the morning of April 4, 1979.

NOT FAR FROM the Excelsior Hotel and nightclub, in the Saddar district of the city, Masih ul Hassan reported for work as normal on April 4 at the Nishat Cinema. He arrived in time for the morning show, as it was called, the playing of a movie before the matinee—in those days it started at 11:30. Having heard of Bhutto's overnight execution on the radio, Hassan expected the cinema to close. But as he told me years later, customers were waiting at the ticket window. "The people said, 'Forget Bhutto and give us our tickets.'"

The morning customers went in to see Eli Wallach in an old spaghetti western called *Ace High*.

It was good that people took in a picture while they could. The coming decades would be a time of decline for the movie business. Many of the old theaters closed; few new ones opened. The Jubilee Cinema was torn down and replaced by an apartment building. The Urdu-language movie industry was fading; Bollywood movies were still banned. Cinemas would never be outlawed in Pakistan, but some conservative Muslims frowned on them, and after Bhutto's hanging, the new government began imposing restrictions that damaged the film industry.

Pakistan was now living through the most overtly Islamist government in its history. The government intruded into cultural habits large and small. Women remembered going to the movies with bare midriffs and without chaperones in the 1950s and 1960s; now every part of that equation—the clothing, the movies, the freedom—became problematic. Visitors from abroad noticed the difference as soon as they landed. An unsympathetic survey of Pakistani tourism written near the end of Zia's rule described a different world from the one Tony Tufail had known:

> Even after dusk and before dawn, facilities for tourists continue
> to be spartan. All night clubs have been closed, strict prohibition

is enforced (unless the non-Pakistani tourists want liquor in their room or in rooms designed for hotel guests who declare themselves to be "habitual users")! . . . Folk dances as well as belly-dancing have been axed. Muzak is gone. In its place are Muslim calls to prayer over the hotel's intercom and convenient instructions in each room as to which direction faces Mecca.

Of greater import was Zia's support for Islamist political groups across Pakistan. Jamaat-e-Islami, one of the religious parties that had opposed Bhutto, had a student wing—these were the students who blamed the country's trouble on wine. Militant and sometimes thuggish student leaders were given offices and official sanction on university campuses, even as other student political activities were banned. A generation of students was pressured to conform to stricter interpretations of Islam. Sometimes a young man was beaten if he sat too close to a young woman. Upon graduation, Islamist student activists received preference for teaching jobs, extending their influence to another generation.

Far more radical groups were founded during Zia's time, and their influence, too, lasted for decades. These were the years when the United States was supporting a covert war against the Soviet Union, which had invaded nearby Afghanistan. Pakistan under Zia became the willing supply base and safe haven for American-supported *mujahideen* fighters whose activities long outlasted the Soviets. Men attracted to the war from across the Muslim world would continue fighting into a second generation. Long after Zia's death in 1988, the military and intelligence agencies he once commanded would cultivate and guide the recruits of the Taliban—the extreme fundamentalists who eventually took over Afghanistan, gave shelter to Osama bin Laden, and altered history.

The Pakistani leaders who came to power in the years after Zia's death took various approaches to mixing Islam and the state. Zia's first real successor was Benazir Bhutto, leader of the winning coalition in the 1988 election and daughter of the man Zia had deposed. "Wait till I pursue you," the father had written from his jail cell, and though he never lived to do it, Benazir pursued the dictator through the 1980s, becoming the most famous person in Pakistan and eventually the world's most famous Pakistani. During a turbulent decade after Zia's demise, she led the People's Party through four free elections, twice winning power as prime minister and twice losing it again; through it all she cast herself as relatively liberal and pro-Western. Her two defeats came at the hands of a rival party led by Prime Minister Nawaz Sharif, who talked like an Islamist but sometimes behaved like a pragmatist—his administration restored Friday as a day of work rather than prayer, finding that a Monday-through-Friday work-week was more efficient in the global economy. Under both prime ministers, Pakistan continued its dealings with the Taliban and other extremists. Finally both leaders were exiled after yet another military coup in 1999.

The extremist groups remained. They included Sipah-e-Sahaba, founded in the 1980s as a political party of the fundamentalist Sunni Deobandi sect. Its platform called for an act of parliament declaring that Shias were not Muslims, just as Ahmadis had been labeled non-Muslim years before. The organization was suspected of murdering countless Shias in Pakistan. A later military ruler, Pervez Musharraf, banned Sipah-e-Sahaba in 2002, but years after the ban I was still able to visit Dr. Mohammad Fiaz, the general secretary of the party in Karachi, at a mosque where the group operated under a different name. Dr. Fiaz denied that his group was involved in killing Shias, and pointed out that members of *his* group were frequently killed. It was true. All kinds of people were killed in Karachi. Names of the group's many martyrs were painted on a black wall at the entrance to the mosque, and we went to visit the grave of one of the men who was buried on the grounds. Nevertheless, Dr. Fiaz and an aide told me that the organization was still patiently working toward its original goals: the restoration of the caliphs, the ancient line of rulers of the Muslim world who guided both Islam and the government; and the passage of a law declaring Shias to be *kafirs,* or apostates.

Many groups that were less well known became part of a not-so-underground network that spread across both rural and urban Pakistan—what one security specialist called an "infrastructure" of extremist groups, ready to be activated when called upon. Some would be linked in one way or another to al Qaeda. Some would eventually threaten the Pakistani state. Many of their members were constantly forming splinter groups. This ever-evolving web of organizations would still be active on December 28, 2009, the day the bomb exploded at the Ashura procession in Karachi.

BEFORE I LEFT the home of Tony Tufail, he directed me to an inner room. Here he kept framed photographs of himself standing with Zulfikar Ali Bhutto. Tufail told me that after the coup his passport was taken away. He was forbidden to travel abroad for a decade. No Paris, no Beirut. For a few years the casino remained fully equipped on the Karachi waterfront; these were the days when the writer Anjum Niaz toured the "majesty" of the mothballed interior. Eventually Stanley Ho, the gambling king of Macao, had the gambling tables taken away for use elsewhere.

Tufail held on to the slowly decaying building for years, then he finally sold "the best location in Pakistan" to a Karachi development firm. Tufail made a profit. The buyers used the giant building as the setting for a children's amusement center until the time came to attempt something larger. The buyers imagined a project that was more easily compatible with conservative Islam, but as we will see, their high-flying dream, like Tufail's, would be shaken by the turbulent religious forces that were increasingly let loose upon the instant city.

A few days later I telephoned Tufail with one more question. He answered me and then added, "I remembered the name."

"Excuse me?"

"The name of the cabaret in Paris," he explained.

Oh, yes. The competitor to the Moulin Rouge, the place where he said he found some of the dancing girls who took the stage of his nightclub so long ago. What was it?

"It was the Crazy Horse Saloon."

NIGHTCLUBS NEVER RETURNED to Karachi after Zia's coup, but fragments of the old cultural district survived. Good bookstores were still doing business in 2010, English books in front, Urdu in the back, and just about everything terribly cheap. Some of the books were imports, but some of the best were by Pakistani novelists who savaged their country's recent history—Mohammed Hanif's *A Case of Exploding Mangoes* so eviscerates General Zia-ul-Haq that if the dictator were not already dead, the book surely would kill him. For a few small bills you could walk into an open-fronted market and buy almost any video, or have them copy any video you brought along. Numerous newspapers were for sale on the streets, and while the journalists made a pittance—the publisher of one notable paper, the *Daily Times*, went at least half a year without paying many reporters at all—they maintained a loud public debate. A few miles away, one of Karachi's great philanthropists had even opened a horse-racing track, with regular Sunday events and all betting creatively reconfigured so that it did not run afoul of Islam's ban on gambling. Karachi was nothing like Tehran, another Muslim megacity, where many of the richest parts of the culture were samizdat—banned books smuggled in suitcases from outside, banned movies screened secretly in people's apartments, banned messages shouted from rooftops under the protection of the dark. Much more of Karachi's culture was still in the open.

A few dozen cinemas remained in business. They were easily identified by giant billboards over the doors, typically showing a thirty-foot image of some Bollywood hero and the indescribably beautiful woman he loved. The Nishat Cinema occupied a prominent place on Muhammad Ali Jinnah Road, and that is where I found Masih ul Hassan behind the steel grate of his ticket booth, the place where he'd worked since 1964. Hassan had rich brown skin and a close-cropped gray beard; his long shirt, or *kameez,* was a shade of gray that suggested it might have been a different color many washings ago.

Leaving another man to watch the till, Hassan came out from his ticket booth and led the way around to a tiny office. Here he opened a cabinet and took out some ledger books showing past movies and gate receipts. These items, along with Hassan's long memory, testified to the shifting zeitgeist of the city.

He said the cinema recovered for a time after General Zia's death; Hassan especially remembered Arnold Schwarzenegger's *Terminator 2,* which played for sixteen weeks in the early 1990s and was his favorite film. Later the business suffered more blows; Urdu films continued fading, and at least in Hassan's memory, American films lost some popularity for several years after the September 11, 2001, attacks and the subsequent war in Afghanistan. But the theaters gained a boost when the government began allowing Indian films to be shown for the first time in decades.

On December 28, 2009, the cinema was closed for the Ashura procession. It remained closed for three days after the bombing and fires nearby. Then it reopened for the New Year with *Avatar,* which was a gigantic hit. Hassan's handwritten ledger showed huge weekly receipts. American movies were back. The science-fiction film about earthlings colonizing a distant planet—a story that some saw as a fable criticizing America's overseas adventures—was in its fifth week when the cinema closed again for the Shia procession on February 5, 2010. Hassan was lucky it was closed. "People threw stones at the theater," he said, in their fury after the February 5 bombing.

As Hassan and I spoke, a movie was playing in the theater, a Bollywood production called *Kites.* He said I was welcome to step in to see it. Of course it featured an Indian hero and an indescribably beautiful woman. The actors spoke in three languages. ("How do you say, 'I love you' in Hindi?" the heroine asks in English, and the hero cheerfully teaches her to say, *"Mai ullu ki puthee hoon,"* or "I am the daughter of an owl," an owl being a creature spoken of in South Asian slang as a derogatory term.) The audience roared. A few days ago the city had been shut down by a spate of political killings, but now there was no sign of tension.

It was nearing eight o'clock when I said goodbye to Hassan and left the theater. Outside, the area was mostly quiet. Vice existed, it just kept a low profile. Prostitutes were known to pick up customers some distance up Jinnah Road, in the spacious park around Jinnah's tomb. Gambling dens also operated quietly (although one such establishment would appear in news headlines the following year when it was bombed).

I was working that evening with Amar Guriro, who assisted my research for this book, and as we stepped out into the cool and humid night, I recalled something he had mentioned about Karachi. Alcohol had never been completely outlawed in Pakistan, at least not for non-Muslims, and Amar said that Karachi still had several dozen licensed liquor stores. They tended to be run by Hindus, and in theory their customers would be non-Muslim. But of course in South Asia, Muslims and Hindus tend to look the same.

Deciding to visit a store, we climbed into a car and rolled through the quiet streets of the old central city. We came to a darkened street of old stone buildings and stepped through an arched gateway into an alley. The alley was strewn with trash. Off to the right I saw a lighted window. Several customers stood in front of the window, waiting their turn to take wrapped packages from the men inside.

I simply meant to observe, maybe chat with the store owner, but a man standing in the alley approached me. "You want a drink?" he asked in English. "Where you from?"

"America."

"America?" he said. *"Parley-vous Frances? Parley-vous Frances?"*

"No," I said. *"Non."*

"You want a drink? Come have a drink with me, I have a room where we can go, you are my guest."

"No, thank you," I said.

"Would you like some wine? How about some wine? *Parley-vous Frances?"*

He then said a considerable amount in French, although I didn't follow it.

Amar and I looked at each other; Amar spoke four languages but not this one. Later the man switched back to English. "I love Paris," he said, leaning into my face. "To me, Paris and Karachi are the same. You can drink."

He was not a young man. He had just a bit of very short gray hair, and a gray beard. I can't remember his eyes. I may have been avoiding them. He wore a white *shalwar kameez*. His name was Lodhi; he gave his full name, a grand one several words long, which I am choosing to withhold, as he said he was Muslim.

He led the way to the window and signaled the men inside, who passed him a selection of alcohol to choose from, all of it Pakistani-made. I declined all the bottles, saying I preferred beer anyway. Of course Mr. Lodhi turned back to the window and came back with two tallboy cans, blue with gold lettering, or so they seemed in the awful light. Each can said "Murree's Millennium Brew." It came from an old brewery up near Islamabad. I tried to pay, but this could not possibly be allowed. I was in Pakistan. I was a guest.

Mr. Lodhi was still insisting that I come to his room. "You are my guest," he said.

Amar and I shrugged. We were here to learn. Mr. Lodhi had of course taken a beer for himself, and he led the way into one of the darkened stone buildings, down a short dim hallway. Then he climbed a steel spiral staircase. At the top of the stairs we emerged in a room with its window covered by a sheet.

The light was bad, but in my memory the walls were some kind of dirty pink. A dirty sink hung on one wall; an old television sat dead on a corner shelf. A thin flowered mattress lay on the floor, and on this mattress four men sat playing cards.

The card players, I came to learn, were employees of the liquor store. They were all Hindus, and little posters of two gods hung on the wall above them. One of the pictures was of blue-faced Shiva, the god of destruction. The workers spent their downtime here. Mr. Lodhi was apparently such a regular customer that he knew about their break room, which he must have used so often that they barely noticed him.

We sipped Millennium Brew and talked a little while. Mr. Lodhi offered a theory: "You can tell the psychology of Karachi by the way it drinks," he said.

I asked if he meant that liquor sales go up when people are distressed. Yes! he answered. That was exactly it.

"Let's ask the employees," I said, and we inquired of the card players if this were true. Do sales go up when there is violence or trouble in the city?

No, they said. It's a steady business.

PART THREE

NEW KARACHI

9 | ICON

Several times after the Ashura bombing I visited the shrine of Abdullah Shah Ghazi. It served me as a weather station, where I checked Karachi's climate.

The shrine of the Prophet's descendant includes a market area. Vendors in souvenir booths sell seashells, and boxes covered in seashells, and mirrors framed by seashells. In other booths, men stir pots of rice, which they dole out whenever a pilgrim to the shrine donates rupees to feed the poor.

When a pilgrim gives, the poor materialize out of the night. One second they're invisible among the tourists on the poorly lit plaza. The next second a hundred people appear, scrambling for a place in line in front of one of the rice sellers. The seller's ladle clangs against his pot. He fills the tiny plastic bag in each man's hand, feeding as many as the donation allows. People near the front of the line walk away with a hot meal, while hungry people near the end fade into the crowd until next time.

One evening, watching the poor men vanish and appear like ghosts, I recalled something I'd heard from the shrine guards. They said the number of pilgrims was running below normal, maybe because of fear. Religious shrines were being bombed that year in other Pakistani cities. So I asked a rice seller if his donations were down: "How's business?"

The seller replied with an old saying. "It's like the wind. Sometimes it blows hard, and sometimes not at all."

Across the street from the market, through a burnished metal gate, I saw the lights of an amusement park. The lights blurred as the rides spun. This was one of the most upscale sections of Karachi, the district known as Clifton. When I walked uphill from the amusement park, I encountered two things: a bus stop shelter adorned with an ad for skin-whitening cream, which was popular among women who could afford it; and a new real estate development. An earthen ramp led down into an enormous pit, close to a hundred feet deep and the size of a small city block. It was going to become an office tower, positioned on prime real estate between the Muslim shrine and the Hindu temple of Shiva.

During my visits I saw workers toiling through boiling afternoons and well into the night. Welding sparks flew at the bottom of the pit as crews erected steelwork for seven basement floors. The Icon Tower, as it was to be called, had a permit to soar up to sixty stories high. Once I walked into an air-conditioned trailer next to the pit and sat with a company official who refused to confirm the precise height but said flatly, "We're building Pakistan's tallest building." It was designed by Karachi's most distinguished architectural firm and financed by a Pakistani developer who professed to be wealthy enough to pay for the building in cash—the developer didn't want to borrow, because lending for interest was forbidden under Islam. The company official, Zain Malik, brushed

Artist's conception of the plan for the Icon Tower.

aside concerns about terrorism or the economy. "According to us, it's the right time to build," he said. Karachi had a lot of pent-up demand for upscale space. How was business? In Zain Malek's view, the wind was blowing.

I later learned that at least two men involved in building the tower were closely allied with the president of Pakistan, Asif Ali Zardari. Not surprisingly, the project overcame all questions raised before the government about its environmental impact. The Icon Tower had a very long way to go, but was moving visibly upward. It was going to dominate Karachi's skyline, if the builders could finish before Zardari lost his job.

And if they could finish before Karachi slipped further toward chaos.

Construction would continue even after October 2010, when bombers struck the nearby shrine of Abdullah Shah Ghazi. The bombing killed a number of people on a Thursday, *Jummay raat,* the busiest night of the week.

THIS WAS KARACHI in the months after the Ashura bombing, destination of pilgrims and home of the poor, a field of operations for the makers of buildings and bombs. The instant city mixed the good with the bad, battering people with the impartiality of a typhoon.

Even in the terrible year that was now under way, Karachi had much to recommend it. Businessmen saw opportunity in the city's outrageous expansion. Workers saw opportunities too, which explained why many migrated to Karachi, or commuted from their home villages. The UN human development index, measuring education levels, health, and income, showed Karachi doing worse than the West, but far better than rural areas of Pakistan. Medical care was more easily available, and so was education. Although Pakistan's school system was appalling—more than 40 percent of the country could not read—Karachi's literacy far surpassed that of the surrounding countryside. Young women, especially, had much more freedom to go to school. Even in poor neighborhoods, little storefront schools lined the streets, like the "English Primery School" I noticed one afternoon in Orangi. What these basic schools lacked in sophistication, they made up in motivation and low prices; experts saw them as a useful alternative to inadequate government schools.

But Karachi was struggling to exploit its advantages, as I could see when I traveled a few miles along the waterfront from the Icon Tower site. Near the harbor, a highway ran parallel to railroad tracks. Beside the tracks stretched a bare concrete platform, a stop on Karachi's circular railway, which moved in a loop around the entire central city. This stop was named Wazir Mansion, after the nearby birthplace of Muhammad Ali Jinnah.

The railway could have been the heart of Karachi's mass transit system, swiftly moving people to and from their jobs. It could encourage prosperity. It could use energy efficiently, and increase the value of real estate near the train stops. It *could* do this, except that the railway stopped running years ago. The silent train stop was a symptom of a government that frequently drifted toward chaos. City and provincial officials told me that they wanted to revive the railway, and they even attracted the interest of a Japanese firm, but for the moment there was no commuter rail in one of the world's largest cities.

Instead, upscale residents relied on a swiftly expanding fleet of cars, which consumed expanding quantities of fossil fuel. The poor depended on overcrowded private buses, which were commonly set on fire during Karachi's ethnic riots.

As for real estate near the train stops, the long sweep of the railroad tracks gave me a clear view of the land along the far side. It was one of the most spectacular vistas in Karachi. Across the tracks, for as far as I could see, ran a line of concrete buildings, low and tangled and backed up by a sea of more buildings. Thirty years ago a mangrove swamp ran along the tracks, at the edge of the harbor. Since then, hundreds of thousands of people have dumped landfill in the swamp to build illegal homes while port officials accepted bribes to look the other way. It is among the most desperately poor parts of the city. When I ventured into this neighborhood called Machar Colony, I visited a shrimp-peeling warehouse. Men shoveled shrimp onto the concrete floor, and children gathered up baskets full of them. I met a girl named Rashida who lined up for her share. She said she was ten. She said she had been attending school until a few months ago, when her family pulled her out so that she could work. She earned less than a dollar a day.

The United Nations noted a sharp decline in urban poverty around the world in the first decade of the twenty-first century. But progress was uneven, and a UN agency described an "urban divide" between haves and have-nots: "a chasm, an open wound." One of the big dividing lines is between the people in the formal economy, like the developers and construction workers at the Icon Tower, and people in the informal economy, like many of those in illegal homes at Machar. The formal economy has higher wages, greater security, and at least some rules.

Rashida.

There are also divides between instant cities. Karachi residents know it, and feel it. It pains them. Mumbai has some of the same problems as Karachi, but is seen as a city on the rise. Karachi has some of the same advantages as Mumbai, but is seen as a city in crisis. The cities of the Persian Gulf have become glittering jewels, relying on legions of laborers imported from more desperate places. Many East Asian cities are on their way to world leadership, leaving other parts of the developing world behind.

Karachi's struggle against extremism was only one of the problems that restrained its progress. In the aftermath of the December 28 bombing and fires, it was up to Karachi's people to bridge Karachi's divides if they could.

MY EFFORT TO TRACK the changing city led me to another crowded neighborhood a short distance from the Wazir Mansion stop. I went there to visit Abdul Sattar Edhi, of the Edhi ambulance service, who had seen the instant city from the beginning. He said to find him at the Edhi Foundation central office, a slapdash little building that served as his headquarters as well as his home.

The building is in Mithidar, the neighborhood Edhi found notable in the 1950s for its "narrow, unpaved allies" and "shakily balanced buildings." His description still applies. The cars that have taken over many city streets do not fit between Mithidar's buildings. So I left my hired car at the edge of the neighborhood, near the little domed shrine of a Muslim saint. Then I started uphill, through crooked streets so narrow that I walked for several blocks without setting foot in sunlight. Men passed me pulling handcarts. The goods of tiny stores spilled out into the streets. This was one of the oldest sections of Karachi, seemingly a self-contained world.

Edhi built his charitable empire out of his base in Mithidar. His ascent started in 1957, when his assets included nothing more than his eight-by-eight-foot pharmacy. That year, when an epidemic known as the Asian flu arrived in Karachi, Edhi rented tents on credit. He stocked the tents with medicines, and treated people whether they could pay or not—signs outside the tents merely asked people to drop what they could into a box. This act of charitable free enterprise paid off: "The people discovered me," he later wrote. "It was the first mass recognition of my work." A grateful businessman donated twenty thousand rupees—the businessman, like Edhi, was a Memon, a subgroup of South Asian Muslims who had converted from Hinduism generations ago, and who prided themselves on their charitable giving. The donation was enough for Edhi to buy a battered old British van, which he converted into an ambulance, the first in the service that would make him a household name. Edhi insisted on driving it himself, ranging farther and farther across the expanding metropolis.

When I came to the Edhi building, the white-bearded old man was sitting behind the receptionist's desk. The phone rang just as I walked in, and he pulled the receiver up to his thick lips. "Hello, Edhi," he sang, and whoever was calling the Edhi Foundation found themselves talking directly to the man himself. It was a bare room except for a few chairs, the usual tangle of electrical wires, and a few papers posted on the walls, including a list of "Rules for Workers," insisting on modest dress: "Must not wear jewelry, thin *dupatta*, or good clothes."

In accordance with his own rules of modest attire, the old man holding the phone was wearing a black Jinnah cap and a black *shalwar kameez* with breast pockets. The practical outfit reminded me, in spirit, of the farmer's coveralls I had seen my grandfather wear in America. His beard stretched down to the pockets.

After finishing the call, Edhi stood and led the way through the doorway where the rules were posted. He loped up a staircase of uneven steps and walked into his windowless office. Two attractive young secretaries, who had been working at a table in the corner, gathered their papers and left as Edhi settled behind his oversized wooden desk.

This former distracted student and seller of *paan* now oversaw ambulances, hospitals, and other charitable services all across Pakistan. He even had a medical evacuation helicopter at his command. Karachi had no centralized emergency numbers like 911 in the United States, but this was no problem; the Edhi Foundation did. In the Edhi office on Jinnah Road, operators waited to answer telephone calls to the foundation's own emergency number, 115. People who called received a subsidized ambulance ride, for which they were typically charged one hundred rupees in Karachi, a little more than a dollar. Edhi ambulances were ubiquitous at the scenes of bombings and other nightmares.

The old man's empire even extended beyond Pakistan. His foundation had branch offices in several countries, including the United States and Britain. British government disclosure forms showed the London branch of the Edhi Foundation collecting well over two million British pounds per year, most of which was sent either directly to Pakistan or else to a bank in Dubai, from which it was pledged to be moved to Pakistan. Hundreds of thousands of American dollars were raised each year at an office in New York. Usually that money, too, was intended for Pakistan, although when Hurricane Katrina struck the United States in 2005, Edhi's New York office wrote a check for $100,000 to the American Red Cross for hurricane relief. The overseas offices commonly raised money by collecting donations from Pakistanis abroad; many of the gifts were described as *zakat,* money that Muslims gave to help the needy as required by their faith. The foundation said it collected most of its money from donations inside Pakistan.

At its center, the foundation's operations were somewhat opaque. It did not disclose, for example, the total amount of its assets in Pakistan. In 2009 an American accounting firm required by law to examine Edhi's New York books said it received no audited financial information from the Pakistan branch. Edhi did not register with the Pakistan Centre for Philanthropy, a nonprofit that certified the governance of charities; an official at the center speculated to me that Edhi's systems might be too old-fashioned to be certified. Yet even that official said flatly, "Edhi does the best development work in Pakistan." Edhi created his own elaborate system of paper receipts to ensure that donations were not skimmed off before they reached him, and people could plainly see the foundation's money at work on many streets. Edhi and his wife Bilquis had been showered with honors by the United Nations and other groups. In the end, the Edhi Foundation's credibility rested on Abdul Sattar Edhi himself. After decades of managing a multimillion-dollar enterprise, the old man and his wife did not even have a house, instead taking spartan rooms inside Edhi's headquarters building. Outside the building, a wooden bench was on the unpaved street; often people would see the old man sitting on the bench in the heat, or even taking a nap like a homeless man.

Edhi's foundation said it refused to accept money from the government, an effort to stay independent of politicians. Of course it was not easy in Pakistan to stay completely free of entanglements. Edhi had accepted donations from the United States, in particular the U.S. Agency for International Development, which provided grants for medical evacuation helicopters. In the early 1990s, American officials were dismayed to learn that Edhi allowed People's Party champion Benazir Bhutto to use one of his American-funded helicopters to fly to political events. (A foundation official later said that Bhutto paid rent for the helicopter, which she requested for travel because she was pregnant). Edhi also waded into political debates, sometimes making jaw-dropping statements, as I would come to learn. In the summer of 2011, during another spasm of violence in Karachi, Edhi held a press conference at which he called for the army to take over the country for three months. He said that politicians were killing thousands of people, and "must be killed in the same way."

At our meeting in 2010, Edhi seemed happy to impress his eccentricity upon me. He showed me a photocopied paper that represented his registration with the province of Sindh as a charity, but having showed this, he advised me that he was required to file other papers, which he had not. He wanted nothing to do with the government. He said he'd never met an honest politician. Nobody but Edhi made decisions about the foundation and its services, which was why he described himself, in English, as a "dictator."

He smiled as he said it—Edhi smiled often—but his family later told me it was true.

He also said, "I am a mentally disturbed person."

I asked him to explain.

"I am psychotic," Edhi said with a wry expression, and then showed me some of the pills that he took each day, one in the morning and one in the evening. They were pills "to relax my mind," he said. The packaging on the pills said Tegral 200. I learned later that the drug was intended for a variety of conditions, including warding off "manic depressive psychosis," although it was also prescribed for severe headaches known as "trigeminal neuralgia."

The patriarch of the ambulance service finally said that headaches were really his problem, not psychosis, and his son Faisal affirmed this.

The elder Edhi also said he suffered from diabetes, as a great many people in Karachi did. He seemed to relish his own frailty, informing me that he was in his late eighties, apparently an overestimate. His family believed the old man was born in 1926, which would have made him about eighty-four when I spoke with him. Some people lowered their age out of vanity; Abdul Sattar Edhi had gone the other direction. Any vanity he possessed was of a sort entirely his own. Because whatever his troubles, he cast them aside and kept working. Edhi attacked Karachi's trouble by following the path of civil society—private people addressing public problems.

Edhi's son Faisal arrived as we talked, and pulled up a chair. Our conversation turned to the Ashura bombing on December 28, 2009, and then to the events forty days later when, on February 5, 2010, a bomb struck Shias assembling for another procession. As we have seen, Edhi ambulances were among those that swarmed the scene and began moving the wounded and the dead toward the Jinnah Postgraduate Medical Centre.

The Edhis maintained a booth outside the glass doors that led into the Jinnah emergency department. It was a simple concrete box. A dispatcher worked in the breeze from a window, and ambulance drivers could pass time out of the sun. I'd spent an hour there myself once, sitting on the edge of a cot while listening to the drivers talk.

The booth was just across the lane from the spot where someone had parked a motorcycle that February day, slipping away unseen.

10 | EMERGENCY NUMBERS

This is where we last encountered Dr. Seemin Jamali, the "Incharge" of the emergency department at Jinnah hospital. On February 5, 2010, an argument was boiling at the emergency department over whether the injured patients should be moved to another hospital.

Dr. Jamali, the woman at the center of that argument, had a big job. She directed about 240 hospital staff in the emergency department, from doctors on down, men and women alike. She also took part in the broader management of the hospital. If women did not enjoy equality with men in Karachi, neither were they denied all opportunity: a woman like Dr. Jamali, coming from an educated family, could choose to cover her hair or not, could choose to pursue a career, and in rare cases could even rise to a position of authority—so long as she could navigate the complexities. "Is it difficult," I asked her once, "as a woman, to be supervising so many people?"

"It is difficult but it makes life easy," she replied. "They don't assault you. It is not easy to be beaten up, not as easily as a man." Conservative men in Pakistan displayed great respect for women in public, and this mattered at the hospital, where patients typically arrived accompanied by crowds of relatives. Some might become extremely emotional. "If there was a man here, they would have assaulted a man very easily; this is a big hospital, things keep happening here. But you know when you look at a face, it's the weaker gender, they don't tend to assault you as much."

The tendency for relatives to accompany patients explained the crowds that filled the emergency department on February 5.

All the hours at the Jinnah hospital that afternoon are captured on video,

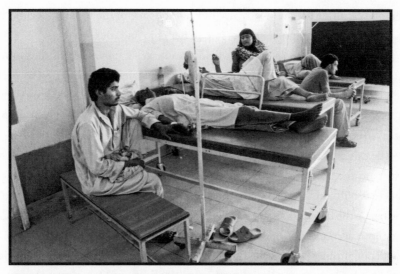

Emergency department, Jinnah Postgraduate Medical Centre.

which Dr. Jamali played for me. Recordings from four security cameras show the scene from slightly overhead—two in the emergency room where initial examinations are made, one in the reception area, and one outdoors, over-looking the front entrance. The first striking thing about the video is the sheer number of people, masses of moving humanity: Shias with white cloths tied around their foreheads, doctors in white coats, policemen, and Scout leaders in gray uniforms with kerchiefs around their necks. Orderlies wheel patients on gurneys into the emergency department and back out into the wards. Every-one seems to be moving somewhere, coming down a hallway, out the doors, back in again. Now and again a sweeper comes through with a mop, working it between the shoes of swiftly moving people. The security camera near the reception desk shows a man holding his own video camera high above the crowd to capture the scene; part of the scene he's recording is a man holding up yet another video camera in front of the first.

An emergency room camera shows orderlies wheeling in a gurney. A doctor in street clothes and latex gloves examines a bleeding man. The doctor makes a decision and orderlies wheel the man away; Dr. Jamali wants patients distrib-uted widely among the operating theaters and hospital wards, making room for new arrivals. This emergency room camera is hard to watch, because it rocks back and forth. It's probably being blown or shaken by the motion of a ceiling fan, although the steady rhythm reminds me of the way that a child in extreme distress will pull her knees up to her chin and rock.

The camera outside the building holds steady. What moves here is the crowd, which grows and wanes like the tide on a beach. The camera is not well focused; all but the closest faces are dots in the late afternoon sunlight, like the impressionistic faces of the crowd in the painting on the office wall of Zulfikar Ali Bhutto. Now and again an ambulance pulls up and the crowd parts for a gurney to be wheeled in.

The camera hangs to the side of the door. From this view the hospital doorway is to the left, and a line of parked ambulances is to the right; the crowd squeezes onto the sidewalk in between. At a few minutes before six o'clock on the tape—the time code is most likely off by one hour; witnesses and contemporary news accounts say it was really approaching five o'clock—something begins happening inside the crowd. Dr. Jamali has just been arguing with a city official and Shia leaders who are insisting the patients be moved to a private hospital. She has reluctantly given her consent and seen off the city official somewhere in the crowd at the door. Now word is spreading that the patients can be moved.

In the foreground, a stray green gurney has been sitting on the sidewalk. A man who's been sitting on it raises himself to get a better look at the crowd. A second man, wearing white, carefully removes his sandals. He stands up on the corner of the same gurney, perching on the edge of this bed on wheels, looking down at the commotion.

Now it is 5:59:33 according to the video time code. Whatever was happening in the crowd seems to have lost its interest. The man on the gurney steps down again and back into his sandals. He is still standing by the gurney when the bomb explodes at 5:59:50.

Smoke shrouds the scene and hangs in the frame for more than thirty seconds. I can make out glass and debris flying. Figures run. The man in the sandals sprints off camera. As the smoke starts clearing, it becomes apparent that the people closest to the door—the people in view of the security camera—have been spared, apparently shielded by the shape of the building and the ambulances from the most direct effects of the bomb. People on the far side of the ambulances were more exposed. One minute and ten seconds after the explosion, men wheel out the first gurneys to collect the wounded. Five seconds after that, two men seize the stray gurney in the foreground and wheel it off camera. One minute and thirty-nine seconds after the explosion the first patient is wheeled back in the door. Less than two minutes after the explosion, a full-scale effort to collect and treat the wounded is under way.

The explosion killed eighteen people.

At the moment of the blast, Dr. Seemin Jamali was just inside the glass doors, talking with an aide. "And I was giving instructions to the staff, and I was just turning my face, and there went the second blast," she remembered. "And it was such a loud sound that I lost my balance and I fell, I suppose it was the shock waves that made us fall. We had all our windowpanes fall off. I couldn't hear anything and I couldn't see anything. I was lost." Then, as she came to her senses, "I could hear shouting and yelling that there was a blast."

"What did it look like?" I asked.

"I want to block my memory," she said. "There was a stampede, somebody passed over me, my shoes were gone." Someone pulled her out of the path of fleeing people, and her fellow doctors checked her for injuries; she had suffered only minor bruises during the attack by religious extremists.

"Thank God for that," she said after a pause.

SEEMIN JAMALI WAS well known in Karachi. Because of her responsibility for the Jinnah hospital emergency department, she informed reporters of casualty figures from the latest atrocity. That was how she came to my attention: I repeatedly saw her name in the news. Before we met, I looked up a string of articles referring to Jamali, which dated as far back as this item in 1999:

> KARACHI: Two men were killed and another 29 people injured on Thursday when a time bomb exploded in a passenger bus near Chand Bibi Bridge . . . leading to widespread panic and chaos in the area. The condition of six injured people was reported to be serious, [said] Dr Seemin Jamali, the Incharge of Emergency Department of JMPC.

More recent items included one from October 2007, when a bomb exploded in the crowd that greeted former prime minister Benazir Bhutto upon her return from exile:

> Dr Seemin Jamali, deputy director of Jinnah hospital's emergency department, said: "We lost count there were so many [casualties] at first. The theatres have been doing operations all day."

Early in 2008, Dr. Jamali was required to testify before a tribunal investigating the attack on Bhutto:

> In reply to a question, she said she had received one severed head
> which was brought in an ambulance, but she could not say exactly
> who had brought it.

When we met, Dr. Jamali informed me that this was not the first time after a bombing that someone had presented her with a severed head. The first came after the bombing of a 2006 ceremony by a Sunni Muslim political faction in Nishtar Park. She also told me about a day when the emergency department held a "mock exercise" to practice for a large number of casualties. As soon as the exercise ended, real casualties began arriving from a bombing at the American consulate.

Jamali was a native of Pakistan. Her father was a senior civil servant, who allowed his daughter to go off to university in Thailand when she received a scholarship. She returned home to work at the Jinnah hospital and married a doctor on staff. Through many years of effort, she was promoted to the position that called upon her to be struck by bombs and handed severed heads.

Dr. Seemin Jamali.

After her staff began recovering casualties from the bombing outside their door, they took stock of the emergency department. Every window was broken. Some in the mob of people had stolen whatever medical supplies they could take away. Dr. Jamali went to find the reporters on the scene, said the hospital was being overrun, and appealed for security. The provincial governor telephoned to promise help.

Police arrived with sniffer dogs, which went through the area searching for any additional explosives. They didn't find anything, although the police told Dr. Jamali that the odds were against the dogs. "They said they had the capacity to smell only in clean areas, and once an explosion has gone off, they would probably not be able to sniff." This may explain why it took so long to find out about the video monitor.

This large and heavy monitor had been left outside the hospital. Dr. Jamali said the police discovered it. "They thought it was a television and that somebody aimed to steal it," she told me. It was carried inside, into the attendants' waiting room. "And then somebody brought it into the ER." And then, having made the rounds of a substantial portion of Dr. Jamali's department, the video monitor was carried back out onto the sidewalk and across the street, where people left it alone for a time, because they were beginning to realize that it might be another bomb.

THE COMPUTER VIDEO MONITOR sat next to the booth used by the drivers of the Edhi ambulance service.

The Edhis had suffered considerable damage from the previous bomb. The explosion injured several drivers, and it could have been worse. Abdul Sattar Edhi, the patriarch, was sitting in one of his ambulances during the explosion.

Not long before the blast, the old man had taken his tour of the emergency department with Dr. Jamali. Then she saw him off at the door, and believed he had left. It was not, however, in his nature to leave. Accompanied by his ten-year-old grandson and two grandnephews, he took a seat in a parked ambulance and watched the chaotic scene unfold. He was sitting close enough to learn of Dr. Jamali's argument with the Shia leaders. "Some people decided to shift some patients to different hospitals," he told me later. "We were getting ready for that when the second bomb blasted." Several Edhi ambulances were shot through with flying metal, but "my ambulance was not touched." Another vehicle, between the bomb and Edhi's ambulance, absorbed the force of the blast.

A few minutes after the explosion, Edhi's son Faisal arrived at the hospital. Faisal checked on his relatives who'd survived the explosion; the ten-year-old boy, Faisal's son, was unhurt, as were Faisal's nephews. Abdul Sattar Edhi, too, was still there. "Everybody was telling my father to leave the scene but he was not willing, and he was resisting," Faisal said. The old man was still present when the television monitor was carried outside and placed next to the Edhi booth.

The last of the sun was gone by the time a bomb disposal expert arrived from the provincial police. He studied the video monitor, and Faisal Edhi sidled up alongside him. The bomb expert was a friend of Faisal's. "He was an old guy," Faisal told me. "He'd had a heart attack, and things like that, and he said please help me. He said, 'I don't have the tools to open the monitor. Can you help me bring the tools?' So I brought tools and he said, 'Can you open it for me?' I opened it. Once it was opened, when I removed the screen from the monitor—I didn't see a picture tube in it. I saw a drum, and there were hundreds of nuts sticking to that drum. The nut which goes with a bolt, right? There were three hundred to four hundred nuts there, sticking to the drum."

Faisal Edhi beheld this device. "Is that a bomb?" he said to the policeman.

But he heard no answer.

"When I looked back, there was nobody behind me."

WHO WAS GRABBING a symbol of modernity—a computer monitor, of all things—and stuffing explosives behind the screen?

The bombs that February 5 bore a strong resemblance to the one that struck the Shia procession on December 28, 2009. I received a description of the explosives from Raja Umer Khattab, senior superintendent of police. He worked in a long stone building left over from British times, where he welcomed me into his air-conditioned office. Umer wore an open-collared shirt and a tightly shaved mustache. He had dark circles under his eyes. The nameplate on his desk included the title Tamga-e-Shujaat, the name of an award he'd received for valor after surviving an attack on a Karachi street a couple of years before.

Here on Umer's computer was a series of photos showing an unexploded bomb that police had recovered in their investigation. The explosives were wrapped inside fabric, forming a cylinder. Heavy white glue coated the outside. Hundreds of steel nuts were stuck to the glue. Someone had neatly distributed the nuts all the way around the cylinder, lovingly pressing them into place one by one. Each bomb was powered by several kilograms of explosives made with potassium chlorate. The detonator was wired to a mobile phone. The bomber called in from a distance, and the ringing phone detonated the device.

Who was making these bombs? I asked.

Umer said the group was called Jundallah. Informants pointed police in their direction, and intercepted mobile phone communications added to the evidence.

"*Jundallah* means 'Soldiers of Allah,'" said Umer. He called them a "jihadi terrorist organization," which was "based in Karachi. But they have a link with an al Qaeda man"—they communicated with a reputed member of Osama bin Laden's organization, an Egyptian last believed to be based in Wana, in South Waziristan, a tribal region on the mountainous border with Afghanistan. On January 24, police arrested four suspects in the Hawkes Bay area of Karachi. They were mostly lower-middle-class men with high school educations. The "al Qaeda man" remained at large, as did another suspect, the Jundallah operative who was believed to have directed the Ashura bombing operation, and who may well have had something to do with the bombings on February 5.

I asked Umer what the suspects in custody had said about their motives.

"Jundallah don't have any history regarding sectarian killing," Umer replied. "But the mastermind of this group likes to disturb the government and destabilize the government. And that occasion of Muharram"—the Ashura event—"is a very highly charged procession." Group members knew a spectacular bombing would cause chaos and discredit the authorities. The bombers might even have been able to forecast that people would set businesses on fire—the bombers "know very well, automatically, the people will do that," Umer said. Karachi mobs had set the city on fire in 2007, when Benazir Bhutto was killed in the northern part of the country. So in Umer's view, killing Shias in the Ashura bombing in 2009 was a means to the extremist group's end—weakening the government—rather than an end in itself.

Jundallah was one of a thicket of Pakistani extremist groups, some linked to each other and all shrouded in mystery. The organizations had grown numerous enough that Jundallah wasn't even the only group called Jundallah. Another "banned outfit," as the newspapers called them, with an identical name operated in Pakistan's far west, and was accused of crossing the border to mount spectacular attacks against the Shia Muslim rulers of Iran.

Karachi's Jundallah had a different objective. According to the terrorism researchers Rohan Gunaratna and Khuram Iqbal, this Jundallah had a link to al Qaeda from its earliest days. Khalid Sheikh Mohammed, a close aide to Osama bin Laden, was involved sometime before 2003 in founding the group, which sought to punish Pakistan's government for its collaboration with the United States. Authorities blamed Jundallah for the bold ambush of a Pakistani military convoy that was carrying an army corps commander in 2004, and a suicide bombing outside the American consulate in 2006. Police claimed to have decimated the group in a shootout in Karachi in 2008, but now apparently believed it was active again.

The 2004 case offered some insight into Jundallah, because after attacking the military convoy, Jundallah fighters were captured. In court records, most of the suspects were described as "students," while one was a leather tannery worker. At least two fixed their names on confessions before all were sentenced to death.

I found the confessions in the office of a longtime Karachi lawyer, Iqtidar Ali Hashmi, who served as a prosecutor in the case. A sign in the lobby of his building said NO SMOKING–CIVIL DEFENSE, but Hashmi smoked through a black cigarette holder as he graciously allowed me to review the files. Partly typed and partly handwritten, the details of the confessions often contained the weirdness of truth—as when a defendant said that one of his fellow militants "started weeping" on the way to the ambush and was allowed to drop out. (For the record, the suspect was formally asked if he had confessed under torture, to which he answered, "No, sir.") One defendant, the group leader, explained that he had committed the offense "in the name of Allah & the Holy Quran (Jahad)." The suspects said they were angry about Pakistan's cooperation with the United States in hunting down militants on Pakistani soil; civilians were being "martyred" in the American-backed operations. They vowed to kill people in the Pakistan government whenever it allowed the Americans to kill or arrest Muslims.

The confessions clarified Jundallah's indentity. Although affiliated with al Qaeda's mostly Arab leadership, Jundallah's men were homegrown—including Atta-ur-Rehman, the group leader. He was born in Karachi in 1970, in a neighborhood near the international airport. He studied at Karachi University, gained a master's degree in statistics, and even joined the student wing of Karachi's dominant political party before drifting into an Islamist student group that had been active in Pakistan for decades. From there he moved into an assortment of radical groups before joining Jundallah. Rather than being foreign interlopers, as they were often described, militants were part of the local fabric.

Pakistan may have been a land of Sufi Muslims and tolerance, a nation founded by an urbane Muslim who liked his scotch, and who urged that as citizens, "Hindus would cease to be Hindus and Muslims would cease to be Muslims," but after 1947 Pakistan was also a laboratory for competing notions of religion and its relation to the state. As we have seen, the newcomers to Pakistan that summer of 1947 included Abul A'la Mawdudi, the founder of the Islamist party Jamaat-e-Islami. Mawdudi was the politician who said Muslim leaders had descended into a new age of *jahiliyya,* or paganism, and whose revolutionary rhetoric called Muslims to a new devotion. While his rhetoric offered up a global vision—which was surely part of his lasting appeal—Mawdudi's quarrel was with straying Muslims as much as with outsiders.

Jamaat-e-Islami's founder died in 1979, but Jamaat lived on, allowed by the military government of Zia-ul-Haq to extend its influence into the government and universities. Islamists redefined Pakistan's ideology, rewriting history as necessary. In 2010 in Lahore I sat down with a leader of a student organization associated with Jamaat; the young man spoke happily of a "clash of civilizations," and said he wanted a nation ruled by Islamic law.

The student told me he was pursuing the same goal as Muhammad Ali Jinnah.

In fairness, Jamaat-e-Islami remained willing to contest democratic elections when Pakistan held them. Its leaders kept the party within the political process even though they rarely won more than a few percent of the nationwide vote. In Karachi in 2010, I visited a Jamaat leader, Assadullah Bhutto, who was cheerful and welcoming. He was a member of the same tribe as Zulfikar Ali Bhutto, the late prime minister; he had the same rhetorical flair and the same intense eyes as his famous clansman, to which he added a full white beard. His conversation tended toward corrosive rhetoric, as when he claimed that America was secretly orchestrating terrorist bombings in Pakistan. But he said it politely while an aide served tea, and even as he denounced American policies, he voiced disappointment that visiting American diplomats did not come to see him. He would have liked to offer advice. He was, in short, a politician.

But during all the decades that Jamaat-e-Islami had been maneuvering for influence in Pakistan, Mawdudi's rhetoric of revolution and *jahiliyya* had metastasized. A scholarly study in the 1960's observed that the largest item in the budget of Mawdudi's party was for publications, and that "his writings have penetrated every corner of Pakistan and many other parts of the world." His vision of political Islam in an age of ignorance was picked up and intensified by an Egyptian scholar, Sayyid Qutb, who endorsed violent struggle to remove unholy leaders. Qutb's writings would influence al Qaeda and other modern groups. With each step the ideology grew more extreme. Modern-day jihadists justified killing civilians by redefining them as combatants, who supported the enemy "in deed, word, or mind." In time, these ideas influenced Pakistani militant groups that enjoyed the sponsorship of the Pakistani military. Many competed with Jamaat-e-Islami for recruits and attention, working in the universities where Jamaat's own ideology had paved the way. As the groups evolved beyond the government's control, Muslims became their targets at least as often as non-Muslims; it was a battle within Islam as much as outside it.

In the early twenty-first century, many Pakistanis had trouble accepting that Muslims would murder Muslims in the name of Islam. Murdering any innocent person was against the faith as they knew it. Some took the mere news of a bombing as an insult to both their religion and their country; some spun out elaborate conspiracy theories to explain the attacks, commonly blaming Indian agents or the American CIA. Although the United States did have embarrassing past links to jihadists, no evidence surfaced that the U. S. was deliberately destabilizing a critical ally that it was simultaneously spending billions to stabilize. This lack of evidence did not stop the conspiracy theories.

One fact remained: the lists of terror victims included the names of people of many faiths, put down on the rolls together. It was on these lists of the dead that equality was finally achieved, so that Hindus would cease to be Hindus and Muslims would cease to be Muslims.

AS FAISAL EDHI STUDIED the unexploded bomb outside the emergency entrance, the police bomb disposal expert moved up close again (he later told me he'd never backed *that* far away from Faisal Edhi, but affirmed that all the rest of the police had long since run away). He studied the bomb in the deepening night. The explosives were connected to the guts of a cellular phone, but somehow had not detonated. Maybe the phone was not properly wired. Maybe the call did not go through.

Or maybe the device lay in perfect working order. Maybe the bomber was still waiting for the best moment to call.

Nobody could discount any possibility until the device was disabled. Slowly, painstakingly—for he really did suffer from a heart condition as Faisal said, and was feeling weak; he would be diagnosed with cancer a few months later—the expert disarmed the bomb with its explosives, its many nuts, and its cell phone detonator. Faisal left him to his job, and finally persuaded Abdul Sattar Edhi to travel safely home.

Inside the hospital, Dr. Jamali was making decisions. News of the day's third bomb forced her to approve the evacuation of the emergency department. The patients were transferred elsewhere and the emergency entrance was closed. It was not an easy decision since hundreds of people arrived at that entrance every day needing help. "Now this is a warlike situation," she told me later. "We are doctors who are trained to doctor patients, and manage patients, and be prepared for disasters, yeah? But not for war. We're not trained to be bombed ourselves like this."

The staff wheeled patients deeper into the hospital or into ambulances waiting at a different entrance. The emergency department drained out. Dr. Jamali stayed at the hospital until after 1:30 in the morning, talking with investigators and officials. Finally she drove back to her house, where she found her two sons waiting up for her, along with other family members who had gathered at the house upon hearing the news. Soon she went to bed, but, she remembered, "I lay awake all night. I lay awake all night, and the first thing that came to my mind is my kids. I thought that if I had died that day, I would have gone away not saying things, anything to my children, and I would have gone away from my family without having said the last word."

She told me of the time she had once attended a presentation by an antiterrorism expert, who said it was now a common strategy to set off a small explosion, wait for emergency responders to arrive, and then set off a larger blast. It appeared that precisely such a disaster had been planned for the hospital itself, and Dr. Jamali was thinking that the bombers might try again someday. That was why she had a talk with her sons. "I wanted to tell them about financial matters, because they're very young, and supposing my husband was also here in the ER." She thought they both could be killed on the job. "I nominated my kids to be legal heirs of any money we get. I said that it can be a risky job, and some things can go wrong sometimes. I've never seen my older child so quiet.

He was sitting there at one-thirty in the morning, and the younger one as well, waiting for me.

"After I talked with them," she said, "my fear of death is less."

Our conversation rambled a little. She told me about the time in January 2008 when police shot it out with militants in a section of Karachi called Shah Latif Town. Police said the militants belonged to Jundallah. They brought several wounded militants to the Jinnah Postgraduate Medical Centre, and the medical staff discovered that one wounded man still had three hand grenades attached to his vest.

"I took it off myself," Dr. Jamali said. She set the vest and the grenades aside, "and then I was really scared. This man was here, and we were here, and we called the bomb disposal squad." The police were "very kind to me," she recalled; she knew nothing about hand grenades, but the police explained that they were safe as long as the pins weren't pulled.

"And I remember the face of that man. And I said to him, 'Why are you doing this?' I couldn't hold myself from asking this. And he kept asking me for water. So we did give him some water on the bed, but I just sat there quietly, 'Why are you doing this?' But he had no answer."

I thought of Karachi doctors I had interviewed in the past. Many had emigrated abroad or at least considered it. I asked Dr. Jamali if she ever thought about moving.

"No," she said. "I have two sisters in America, and they have always asked me to come there and stay there, but I have always told them I want to stay here and do something here. This is my desire now. I have always told my kids I want them to be educated, and that's the only thing I can give them. I have no money, no resources, I earn what I earn. I have risked my life for my work."

She was free-associating now, talking about the importance of education. "And I've learned so much, I'm very happy for what I've learned, I'm very grateful." And then she said one more thing. She didn't say why it was on her mind; she didn't say where she might have heard it before. She said, "I've developed some sense that, you know, I feel that we need to inculcate this: no matter what religion you are, no matter what color you are, what caste you are, what creed you are, you have to treat your fellow human beings like your own.

"And once you have that in you, you have the desire to go ahead. That is what keeps me here. I don't want to go away from my country, because every little drop matters."

After a few hours of rest, Seemin Jamali's staff returned to the ER around eight o'clock on the morning of February 6. They swept up the shattered glass and replaced the medical supplies. The emergency department of the Jinnah Postgraduate Medical Centre reopened at 11:30, less than twenty-four hours after the bombing.

11 | **AIRPORT ROAD**

By then, many developments had grown out of the other events from December 28, 2009—the fires that claimed hundreds of stores at the Bolton Market.

As we have seen, the fires exposed Karachi's obsession with real estate. So many discussions circled back to land: what it cost, who owned it, who occupied it, and who was trying to steal it. No proof showed that a real estate conspiracy motivated the Bolton Market fires, but everyone from angry shopkeepers to urban development professionals believed that someone had destroyed the buildings to clear the land for another purpose.

The fires were still burning on New Year's Day as Karachi returned to life. These were the days when the Nishat Cinema reopened on Jinnah Road, drawing thousands of customers to see *Avatar*. But the Bolton Market fires smoldered in the public imagination. People looked with suspicion on their government. Many conspiracy theories implicated the city's ruling party, the MQM, which included the young mayor Mustafa Kamal. Other conspiracy theories pointed at the People's Party of the Bhuttos, which controlled the province. A number of shopkeepers told me they suspected the fires were set in order to hustle the wholesale markets out of the center city and push them to the periphery. It so happened that the city government actually *did* want to move them, having promoted a plan for several years that would develop new real estate for wholesale markets and other businesses to the outside edge of the city, reducing congestion at the center (and boosting the value of suburban real estate).

In this atmosphere of suspicion, Mustafa Kamal called a New Year's press conference. He endorsed a demand made by shopkeepers: they should be allowed to repair or rebuild their shops in exactly the same locations as before. Kamal even sought to help them. This promise could not have been better designed to assure people of the city's good faith. And even this didn't work. People continued questioning the government. Shopkeepers hung banners with angry slogans on the ruins of their buildings. The mayor was wounded. A few days later he grew so frustrated that he began shouting and cursing during a television interview, denouncing "conspiracy theories" and the people who spread them.

It became another mystery: when Mustafa Kamal spoke, why was it so hard for people to believe him?

THE MAN WHO CALLED the press conference had begun his term intending to restore the people's trust in their government. Kamal told me that when he took power in 2005 he delivered a blunt message to civil servants. "The common citizen on the road, he doesn't feel good about you all," he remembered telling them, "and he doesn't feel good about me as well, because he thinks that we are not good people, that whoever is sitting here is corrupt."

The government's image was so bad that Kamal dismissed a seemingly benign proposal to encourage drivers to follow traffic safety rules. He said people so loathed the government that any campaign to enforce traffic laws would encourage more drivers to ignore them.

Kamal began his battle to improve the city's reputation armed with a marketing degree, a short political résumé, and a talent for seizing the moment. His formal title, *nazim* of the City District Government of Karachi, made him the highest official overseeing the entire metropolitan area; eighteen smaller municipalities were captured within it. One of his official photos showed him wearing a dark suit and tie, as well as a mustache and goatee that gave a little gravitas to his youthful face. His black hair was parted on the side, with a single strand allowed to slip down his forehead in the style of the active politician.

Kamal lived up to his photo when I met him, walking swiftly and speaking in a rapid-fire tenor, as loudly as a man at a crowded party. If he wanted to charm you his bright eyes never left their target. He could have passed for the top salesman at some global tech firm, which was fitting. His previous job had been as information technology minister for the province.

Mustafa Kamal.
The posters show his party
leader, Altaf Hussain.

The leader of the MQM had seen the young man's potential, first placing Kamal in the provincial government and then supporting his election as
nazim. Kamal took office with assurances that he had the power and the money
to change the city, for the MQM was allied with General Pervez Musharraf,
the latest of Pakistan's military rulers. Any discomfort Kamal might have felt
about embracing a coup leader must have been eased by the benefits Musharraf could bestow from the national treasury. Work crews tore up streets and
dug underpasses to disentangle critical intersections. They built overpasses—
flyovers, as people called them in Karachi—to ease congestion on arteries like
the road from Muhammad Ali Jinnah International Airport to the central city.
And if the airport road did not become the Champs-Elysées of Karachi, as
Zulfikar Ali Bhutto and Tufail Shaikh had imagined in the 1970s, it was at least
a "signal-free corridor," a nonstop journey past the gas stations and apartment
buildings and military bases along the way.

The mayor did not usually work out of the old city hall, the British-built
Karachi Municipal Corporation Building with its stone walls and onion domes.
The city council occupied that building now, while Kamal kept an office at the
Civic Centre, the same building in which he installed his video monitoring

center. Hundreds of motorcycles leaned on their kickstands in the parking lot, the commuter vehicles of hundreds of subordinates whom Kamal was aggressively putting to work.

Twice when I went there to meet Kamal he had a motorcade waiting; he took me at high speed across his city, inspecting streetlights and sewers, escorted by black-clad commandos. He was forever in a hurry. At the ribbon-cutting for a renovated community center, he sat down for a slideshow presentation by a center official, but quickly lost patience. "I would just like to interrupt. I know who you are," he said, begging the man to skip the introductory slides. "Please. I know everything. Show us the place where you're sitting right now, and how is it going to be tomorrow."

As I rode with him from stop to stop, I was aware that the mayor's construction projects drew criticism from urban planning professionals. His flyovers, they said, were merely doing what new roads have done the world over: they encouraged more traffic, and shifted tie-ups to new locations instead of addressing the fundamental problems of a city that was growing overly dependent on cars. (By 2007 the city's auto fleet was increasing by an average of 545 cars per day, about two hundred thousand additional cars in a single year.) When the mayor touted a "master plan," a multicolored map showing intended patterns of development, some experts said it was just a pretty map. The planning was not thorough enough, they said, and developers were going to build what and where they wanted.

But nobody doubted Kamal's energy. He won praise from citizens known for speaking independently. Fatima Bhutto, offspring of Pakistan's most famous political family, said Kamal seemed to have the whole city under construction. Ardeshir Cowasjee, the acerbic shipping heir and newspaper columnist who had seen everything in Karachi since before Partition, wrote of "young and energetic Mustafa Kamal, whose intent to do good for Karachi is not in doubt." The mayor was so pleased that he handed me copies of the article on two occasions. (To be sure, Cowasjee had praised Kamal's *intent*; the mayor must have been less thrilled with a column in which Cowasjee "affectionately" referred to Kamal as the man who "digs and digs gutters and roads and moves on without refilling the gaping holes.")

One gaping hole stood next to the Civic Centre. A mayoral aide took me to the edge of this yawning pit. He said it would soon become the basement of a skyscraper on city-owned land, called the "IT Tower"—for information technology. A Malaysian firm planned to attract the kind of back-office jobs and call centers that American firms had lately been locating in India. We walked back inside the Civic Centre, where an oversized artist's rendering of the IT Tower was on display in the mayor's outer office. The same room had a scale model of the proposed Karachi Monorail. It was an office full of dreams.

After a while Kamal burst out to greet me, and took me to visit a newly opened complaint center inside the building. Women were taking calls from across the city. The women were part of the mayor's message—here was a Muslim city where women were not confined to the home—and so was the nature of their duty. "I made my job harder!" the mayor declared to the women. "I brought all these complaints on me that I would never know about before." A man in the corner sidled up to me, introduced himself as an employee of the national government, and gestured toward the mayor. "The Rudy Giuliani of Karachi," he said, which I took to mean that Syed Kamal, like the onetime mayor of New York, was bringing order to a city once considered ungovernable.

It was in many ways a convincing image. The city *was* changing. The improved airport road was symbolic, the face that Karachi wanted to turn to the world. That road, the Shahrah-e-Faisal, was a magnificent ride, where drivers slipped beneath pedestrian bridges and overpasses so swiftly that it was hard to read the graffiti spray-painted on the support beams. Everybody talked about the airport road, not just the international business set. (Once I was visiting Mufti Naim, the deeply conservative principal of a vast Islamic school, who said he loved being able to get to his plane in minutes instead of hours; he used to live in Dallas and flew back on occasion.) Kamal took the road to the airport often, traveling widely outside Pakistan, looking for business opportunities. He told American officials of his country's need to "enlarge the pie." His government produced a promotional booklet full of color photographs entitled "Karachi Calling! Explore the Heaven for Investment." He borrowed ideas from other cities, meeting with the mayors of Washington and Chicago, emulating the storm drains he found in London, and seeking to adapt techniques of garbage collection from Shanghai. "We are cutting and pasting things from different parts of the world," Kamal told me. "What they have done, if that suits to my land, to my environment, I must bring it."

Kamal brought his can-do attitude to his press conference on New Year's

Day 2010. He would demonstrate the truth to those who claimed the city was plotting to steal the Bolton Market land from beneath the shopkeepers' feet. He declared that he had steered plenty of work to city contractors in the past; now he appealed for their help, urging contractors to help rebuild shops right away and worry later about the cost.

And yet his promises did not dissipate the bitter suspicions. Conspiracy theories spooled out day after day, until on January 4 the mayor lost his temper. "I curse all of Pakistan's leaders, and I curse all the political parties who are throwing out such allegations and even the media," he barked on Geo TV. "If we had to clear out those shops, we had many different ways of doing it."

Kamal seemed to know he was losing the argument. "Even though this country has so many disasters," he shouted, "it's only the people of Karachi that are so unfortunate that after these deaths such conspiracy theories are formulated that say they have, with their own hands, ignited their marketplace and let it burn for the sole purpose of getting the business owners to evacuate the premises. . . . If I just wanted to raze it to the ground, why would I be working on restoring it right now? I curse all the heads of Pakistan's political parties, and I curse all the anchors, and all the people of Pakistan that think like that." He went on: "In all of Pakistan, bombs and explosions are commonplace. Nowhere before has anyone accused a city with this conspiracy theory that they themselves did it. My city has burned down, my people have died, and they are blaming us? Son of an owl!" he shouted, using an expression mildly profane in Urdu.

Mayor Kamal's party presented itself as modern, secular, moderate, and a bulwark against Islamist terrorism. The party leader, the man who promoted Kamal to the mayoralty, spoke forcefully against terrorism; American officials often found the MQM to be useful allies. And yet there was another side to the MQM, which made it almost automatic for people to suspect the party when something went wrong. The MQM was the most powerful party in Karachi, and insisted on dominating the streets. It was founded to represent the interests of Mohajirs, the migrants from India who flooded Karachi after 1947, and it did so when necessary by force of arms. Although it had lately tried to broaden its appeal, many people still saw it as an ethnic party at war with competing ethnic groups. Even as the MQM professed to oppose terrorism, many people described the party itself as a group of thugs, or fascists—although some looked about them to check who might be listening before they said things like this.

KARACHI WAS ONE OF many growing cities made turbulent by ethnic politics. In recent years an ethnic political party has controlled Mumbai, India, imposing a regional language on the government of an aspiring world city. In the growing oil city of Port Harcourt, Nigeria, Internet cafés and churches line the commercial streets, while ethnic militias rule the backstreets and set neighborhoods on fire. None of this will surprise people who study the history of American cities. Chicago, for example, grew explosively from the 1830s onward—it was an instant city in its time—and newcomers clustered defensively in their various ethnic neighborhoods. As late as the 1950s, immigrants and their children drew battle lines along major streets or railroad tracks, as described by the newspaper columnist Mike Royko:

> There was . . . good reason to stay close to home and in your own neighborhood-town and ethnic state. Go that way, past the viaduct, and the wops will jump you, or chase you into Jew town. Go the other way, beyond the park, and the Polacks would stomp on you. Cross those streetcar tracks, and the Irish will shower you with confetti from the brickyards. And who can tell what the niggers might do?

Eventually this attitude was built into Chicago. The Dan Ryan Expressway was routed to serve as a wall between black and white neighborhoods, a line to defend against the growing population of black migrants from the South. As Chicagoans spread into the suburbs, so did the racial barrier; in 1998 I followed the Dan Ryan outside the city to where it became Interstate 57, with white suburbs on one side and diverse ones on the other.

In Karachi, too, migration fueled group divisions. The trouble dated back to Karachi's earliest days as an instant city, and related directly to its growth; tension was building from the moment of Pakistan's independence, as we have seen. Sindhis, the historic inhabitants of the province of Sindh, considered Karachi their own, and resented the arriving migrants, or Mohajirs, coming from India. The migrants who flooded the city after 1947 assumed a dominant position for a time, seizing homes that Hindus abandoned and taking many jobs in government. Later the migrants became politically divided, with many attracted to the Islamist party Jamaat-e-Islami. In the 1970s the Sindhis asserted their ethnic nationalism, demanding that education in the province be conducted in their own language, Sindhi, enraging Mohajirs and other groups and sparking unrest that is remembered today as the "language riots." Then, in the 1980s, the MQM mobilized the children and grandchildren of migrants under its banner, alleging that Mohajirs, the "Urdu-speaking people," faced discrimination in everything from housing to government jobs.

As the largest of all ethnic groups in Karachi, the Mohajirs repeatedly swept city elections. They also began changing the landscape of the city. Maybe they didn't have the means to build a Dan Ryan Expressway, but activists put up fortified gates at the edges of neighborhoods they controlled. Riots, general strikes, and gun battles broke out across the city.

And from the 1980s onward the Mohajirs were pitted against another migrant group that also numbered in the millions. These newcomers were ethnic Pashtuns from the war-torn border with Afghanistan. The Pashtuns threatened to swamp Karachi the way the Mohajirs once had.

Many of these new migrants had stories like Mohammad Nader's, a thirtyish man I first met in 2008. Quiet and courteous, with sunburned skin and sad eyes, he dressed in a simple *shalwar kameez*. Of his home province in the far northwest, Nader said simply, "There are no job opportunities and salaries are so low." His father and brothers had moved to Karachi long ago to find work and a better life. Then Nader came to Karachi to attend a wedding, and met a girl so attractive that he proposed to her. "Love marriage," he told me in English, meaning it was not an arranged marriage. He'd come to the city on a train called the Khyber Mail, which rolled down from the mountains near the Khyber Pass from Afghanistan. Nader would hear that train arrive in Karachi many times in the years ahead, because he lived with his bride in an unauthorized settlement by the railroad tracks.

Nader applied for a job with the Edhi Foundation, which hired him as an ambulance driver. We first met at the Edhi dispatch office on Jinnah Road; we sat inside, seeking shade on a blistering day. Nader told me that it took time to get used to the job. Once he drove to a market to respond to reports of a terrible smell and discovered that duty required him to remove a body from a drain.

On May 12, 2007—he remembered the date exactly, as many in Karachi did—Nader came to work and found the city in chaos. Gun battles had broken out along the Shahrah-e-Faisal, the airport road. Nader received word of dead and wounded people and set out alongside Abdul Sattar Edhi's son Faisal, who had decided to drive. Faisal steered toward an overpass called the Baloch Colony Bridge, and continued until gunmen stopped the ambulance. The armed men were communicating with handheld radios. "Their van was parked on the side and it was packed with guns. We didn't argue much with them," Nader said. The men searched the ambulance and were about to let it proceed when one gunman took a closer look at Nader and told him to get out of the vehicle. The gunman could tell that Nader was an ethnic Pashtun.

"Say your holy words," the gunman said, "and remember your God, because you are going to be killed." He put a gun on Nader's temple, just below his mop of black hair.

Faisal Edhi walked around the ambulance to Nader's side. He gently put his hand on the gun and moved it aside. "This is my man," Faisal said. "He works for Edhi. He works for humanity."

Faisal argued until the gunman backed down. Nor was Faisal finished; he wanted to reach the injured people on the airport road. "Forget about the dead bodies," he said, "just let us take the injured people to the hospital." People below were screaming and crying. But the situation was too tense. Somebody fired into the air. Faisal and Nader drove away.

Nader never asked who the gunmen were; it was not the business of Edhi drivers to take sides in political battles. But journalists and other witnesses affirmed that MQM gunmen, as well as their allies in the national government, had taken control of the airport road that day. They were battling against ethnic Pashtuns, among others.

The MQM was blockading the airport road in order to prevent an unwanted visitor to the city. Pakistan's chief justice, Iftikhar Muhammad Chaudry, was scheduled to arrive that day. He planned a speech as part of a growing opposition campaign against Pervez Musharraf, the military ruler who had proved so helpful to the MQM. Opposition parties planned a rally to support the chief justice. Those opposition parties included the MQM's bitter rivals, the People's Party of the Bhuttos as well as the leading party of the ethnic Pashtuns. The MQM saw this as a threat to its own power, and turned out so many of its activists to block the streets that Chaudry could never make it into town.

At two o'clock that morning, an American journalist, freelancer Nicholas Schmidle, arrived at Jinnah International Airport to find that "the MQM had blocked every possible exit and entry point to the airport using shipping containers, buses, and water tankers." Schmidle made it out on foot, meeting a sympathetic police officer who walked him past "two layers of MQM-arranged cordons." On the far side was a city swamped with guns. Battles erupted between the MQM and the chief justice's supporters. By the end of the day, around forty people were killed. One of the dead was an Edhi ambulance driver, and Mohammad Nader went home to his wife that night knowing how easily a second driver could have been killed.

The provincial governor, a distinguished leader of the MQM, later acknowledged that something had gone wrong. Over tea at Governor's House, Governor Ishrat Ul Ebad Khan quietly informed me that he tried before the chief justice's visit to find a compromise that would resolve the explosive situation, but Chaudry and his allies were intransigent. In the end, he said, MQM party workers could not reasonably be expected to stand aside while their political enemies took control of the streets. There remained, however, the awkward fact that the MQM had laid siege to a major international airport and engaged in gun battles across one of the world's largest cities. And the MQM couldn't even save General Musharraf, who was slowly losing his grip on power; he would be forced to call elections within months. Nor could the party easily repair the damage to its reputation. One of Mayor Mustafa Kamal's most notable achievements, the improved airport road, Karachi's smiling face turned toward the world, became a battlefield. The city was portrayed in the global media as a place of inexplicable mayhem. It would be hard for the "Karachi Calling!" brochure to compete.

MUSTAFA KAMAL WAS BORN in 1971, the son of a civil servant who had migrated from India. He was well educated, with a degree from a university in Malaysia, but long before he went abroad he was gaining a political education, serving as an organizer for the MQM in Karachi. He told me that this was the work he loved best, talking with people on the streets and spreading the ideology of his party. He liked to declare, "I'm nobody! Nobody knew me just a few years back," explaining that he came from a family of no special distinction until his political party slated him for advancement. The first time I heard this humble declaration it made him seem familiar and appealing—close to the people, like American politicians who claimed they were born in a log cabin. Later it became clear that Kamal meant something more particular to Karachi.

Unlike an American politico, he was neither celebrating his country's egalitarian political system nor, necessarily, trying to connect with the common man. He was giving homage to his political party, whose wise leader had chosen Kamal for advancement in spite of the young man's relative obscurity.

The mayor argued that in Pakistan's degenerate political system, only the MQM would have allowed a man like Kamal to rise on merit. The other parties were controlled by wealthy landowners or industrialists. It was true that the MQM did not demand that a politician come from wealth, although the party did expect currency of another kind: loyalty.

MQM politicians were fiercely disciplined. They were loyal to their party founder, Altaf Hussain, who was everywhere in Karachi, and nowhere at all. He was in self-imposed exile, having fled long ago to London from his violent hometown. Yet he remained at the center of Karachi's political life. Party leaders, national officials, and even foreign diplomats traveled to see him in London. Newspapers and television stations respectfully chronicled his pronouncements. His face appeared on banners and posters across the city. On the posters Hussain was often speaking, a figure bursting with energy and larger than life—his oversized and mustached mouth wide open, its corners downturned, his bulging eyes looking out through oversized glasses at some distant audience. Sometimes he was wagging a finger; other times he was holding his palms toward heaven.

In 2008 I traveled to see Hussain outside London. The party founder welcomed me into his office suite on a drab suburban strip. Boards on the walls recorded the results of the elections that had just thrown General Musharraf's party out of power. The MQM had done well almost everywhere that Mohajirs were numerous, and badly almost everywhere that Mohajirs were not.

Hussain, jowly and heavyset and wearing a dark suit, ushered me into his private office; we talked about his policies and his career. Many years had passed since his days as an activist at Karachi University. "I formed a student organization in 1978 that was restricted to the Mohajir students," he told me. "They were treated like second- or third-grade citizens in Pakistan." His movement grew out of campus politics—Hussain remembered an early fight to gain Mohajirs space in campus dormitories—but it was an edgy time for campus politics. Universities were dividing along ethnic lines—Sindhis, Bengalis, Baloch, Punjabis, and Pashtuns. Many student political groups were obtaining guns.

Altaf Hussain argued that *his* people, too, were oppressed. Mohajirs had given up their Indian homes to make Pakistan, and now other groups were shoving them aside. On Pakistan's Independence Day in 1979, Hussain went to the steps of Jinnah's tomb and burned a flag in protest. In 1984 he formed the MQM, whose initials stood for the Urdu phrase for "Mohajir National Movement."

MQM activists said their party represented middle-class Mohajirs who were educated and ambitious. There was truth in this, but more was at work than strong minds. Riots broke out between Mohajirs and ethnic Pashtuns. Kidnapping for ransom became common. A study of political violence of the era said the MQM as well as a splinter group known as the MQM Haqiqi, or the "Real MQM," used "blackmailing and coercion for collection of illegal donations." Years later, some MQM activists would tell their stories to a British scholar named Nichola Khan, who had lived in a Mohajir neighborhood during a violent period; the scholar quoted one man who said he was inspired in the 1980s by the speeches of Altaf Hussain: "His words were like magic. They went straight into my heart." The man felt so strongly that he claimed to have committed killings in reprisal for the deaths of Mohajirs, saying that "all those politicians . . . united against MQM and started killing us, so we had no choice. . . . I knew I was in a war situation and so many innocent people had to die. I was convinced killing was the way to make changes. The first time I killed . . . I didn't sleep well that first night but on the second day I had to do it again, and I quickly had to get used to it." Eventually the man fell out with his party, concluding that he was not fighting to change the political system, but only to increase Altaf Hussain's power within it.

While it was impossible to corroborate the activist's story, there was no doubt that he lived in a murderous time. In the 1990s Karachi's violence grew so severe that the army moved in. A report by Amnesty International tracked the urban warfare, noting official figures that 1,770 people were killed in Karachi in 1995 alone, and blaming most of the violence on the two warring factions of the MQM as well as government forces. Altaf Hussain told me the army killed fifteen thousand of his supporters, including members of his family. A diplomat who was in Karachi at the time cast doubt on such a high number, but agreed that many MQM workers were killed. Party leaders fled abroad, including Altaf Hussain, who faced criminal prosecution on charges related to the violence. Later the charges were dropped, and many party leaders were eventually able to return to Karachi. In fact, the balance of power shifted so dramatically that many police officers accused of targeting the MQM in the past were themselves murdered; the MQM denied responsibility. But Altaf Hussain remained in London. He told me his party felt it was unsafe for him to return.

Violence was not part of the MQM's official creed, and the party aggressively rejected specific accusations of murder or thuggery. But party officials rarely swore off what they described as self-defense. "I do not advocate violence," Altaf Hussain told an interviewer in 1999. "But violence breeds violence. When the state itself commits terrorism, when it persistently terrorises its own people, the people will ultimately be forced to retaliate in a similar manner."

As we toured his London offices, Hussain showed me his speakerphone, a key part of his leadership in exile. He chaired political meetings, and even addressed mass rallies, by telephone or video. His voice thundered over a sound system at the park called Jinnah Ground. He told me that he invited the mayor, Mustafa Kamal, to visit him in London, and Kamal went about the streets with a video camera. At Altaf Hussain's direction, the young mayor took images of "bypasses, underpasses, roads, highways," Hussain said, and took the video back home so that he could show Pakistani engineers what he wanted for Karachi.

Hussain's big eyes came alive as he spoke; he wanted to send a message to people who had developed a negative image of Karachi in the past. "I request that they should please visit *now,* and see the difference! See the difference because seeing is *believing*—so they can see what the MQM did." Hussain spoke so expressively that it was easy to understand how he commanded the attention of crowds, and his passion was all the more remarkable because Hussain himself had *not* seen the difference. He had never even traveled the improved airport road.

I bade goodbye to Hussain knowing that I had met the author of a relatively rare accomplishment. Many politicians rallied ethnic groups behind them, but Hussain was distinctive in that he helped to invent his group. That was the view I heard later from Akbar S. Ahmed, the scholar of Islam who came to Karachi as a boy in 1947 and who was, by definition, a Mohajir himself. (Ahmed later migrated again, becoming a civil servant on Pakistan's northwestern frontier before moving to America.) "They're not from one ethnic group," he said of the Mohajirs. They came from many parts of India, and arrived in Karachi with many backgrounds and customs. By the 1980s, most weren't even migrants: Altaf Hussain was the *son* of migrants and a native of Karachi. "What the MQM did," Akbar Ahmed told me, "was they created a new ethnicity which didn't exist, which is the refugee ethnicity, one of the few times in history that an ethnicity has been created out of the air."

Some Pakistanis regarded Mohajirs as a fake ethnicity, which wasn't quite fair. Their identity had been manufactured, but so were other identities. Racial and ethnic groups were defined by blood, culture, and heritage, but of course blood is commonly mixed, and so is culture. Heritage is a matter of the stories we choose to tell about our past, as well as the stories we overlook. Rather than exposing the Mohajirs as fraudulent, a comparison with older ethnic groups illustrated the blurry, overlapping, and strangely plastic nature of collective identities around the world.

So Hussain's was a rare achievement, but not unprecedented. Muhammad Ali Jinnah himself was accused of inventing an ethnic group in the years before 1947, when he argued that South Asia's Muslims were not merely people with a common religion but an entirely separate "nation" that must be led by him. As we have seen, Jinnah clarified his rhetoric once Pakistan was achieved, encouraging everyone to act as equal citizens regardless of whether they were part of the Muslim "nation." But he found it difficult to redirect his people.

THE MQM, too, evolved over time, seeking to broaden its base beyond its original Mohajir supporters. The scholar Nichola Khan believed that was part of the reason for the explosion of city-sponsored construction. Scaling back the emphasis on ethnic nationalism in a city that was becoming more and more diverse, Mustafa Kamal's administration worked to win support through civic improvements. But it was hard work to transcend Karachi's ethnic divisions, as I saw in 2008 when Kamal took me in his black SUV to an area he considered the front line of the city's struggles. His black-clad commandos rode ahead of us on the back of a pickup truck, rifles at the ready and their eyes on the traffic that dashed about us like whitewater.

The mayor directed his driver left and right. Here was a sewer line being dug in an area that had none. Here was a highway that cut travel time to a factory district, and here was a concrete bridge, a little more than half finished, where men worked day and night shifts in hopes of finishing within a month.

But new construction was not all he wanted me to see. He had the driver take us past an Afghan refugee camp, filled with ethnic Pashtuns who'd been living there for years. "You cannot even pass by here in the evening; you will be looted, you will be lucky to come out alive," he said. We were on one of the major highways that led into the city, and he said with dismay that "the entry of Karachi" was in possession of people who were not "civilized."

In the neighborhood called Sohrab Goth—soon to become famous as a reputed hideout for Pakistani Taliban—we rolled through a landscape that seemed exquisitely designed to offend Kamal. Shacks and makeshift storefronts nudged up to the edge of traffic, all of them illegal, he said. Many were flying the flags of the People's Party, which meant that Kamal could not have them evicted without provoking a political fight. Along the highway rose new light poles erected by the mayor's own administration. From each pole hung the blood-red flag of the Pashtun party.

"One might be thinking that I have created this scene or something like that," Kamal said. "No, this is not the case. This side of Karachi is the new area of Karachi, where we have got the expansion of Karachi. Tomorrow they will take over," he said. "They've got the whole area here, and you cannot enter unless you get permission from them." When he said "they" he meant Pashtuns, or extremists—they were the same to him.

When I looked out the window, what I saw were poor people. I asked, "Do you struggle with the question of what you try to offer people like this? So they feel included in some way?"

He said he didn't see poor people. He saw a "mafia."

Kamal pointed to a pedestrian on the road near an Islamic school. "The man who is coming in front of you? Look at him, look at his face. He's the sort of beard you see all over. And you see it's a very strategic location, you can see the superhighway right there. They have a base."

As I listened to Kamal, I thought of his multicolored map of Karachi, the official master plan for the city. "When you say strategic location," I said, "it sounds like you're concerned that somebody on their side has a master plan just like you have a master plan."

"Yes. Yes, they had a master plan before me. And they definitely have a master plan. They definitely have. I do agree. If they want to impose sharia"— Islamic law—"they can do it overnight. All they have to do is impose it and nobody will enter here."

I asked him why he thought Islamists would work up a conspiracy to send millions of ethnic Pashtuns to Karachi. The mayor answered instantly: "They don't want us to control the biggest modern city of Pakistan, and the biggest modern city in the Islamic world." In the battle for civilization, Kamal believed, his constituents would break down along linguistic lines. Kamal's party represented Urdu speakers; that was the main language of the Mohajirs. The Pashtuns, the Pashto speakers, would side with terrorists. "You know Pashtun means like fundamentalist, religiously fundamentalist, religiously extremist, they are coming here," he said. "They are coming. And when it comes to ethnicity they all are, they all are the same." The mayor said his anxiety was part of his motivation for the frantic development of the city. Some of the new roads were intended to open access to land as quickly as possible. This was done in the hope that the public land could be sold to private individuals, reliable men with the resources to defend it against the rising enemy tide.

Later, after his taped remarks were broadcast in a radio story, prompting controversy in Karachi, he wrote me to say he did not mean these words as they came out, but nobody denied the tension between ethnic groups. The terrorist threat in Karachi was very real, as the city saw on December 28, 2009, and Kamal missed no opportunity to remind his city of the threat. But the MQM framed the argument in a way that meshed a little too conveniently with its ethnic rivalries, not to mention its land-use policy. Somehow an ethnic conflict became a religious conflict, which became a conflict over real estate.

Such bitter divisions made it possible to decipher the news dispatches that appeared in Pakistani newspapers, like this item from the *Daily Times* in the spring of 2009:

ALL HELL BREAKS LOOSE IN CITY
AS 23 DIE IN RIOTS

At least 23 people, including political workers, were killed . . . after two MQM workers were allegedly killed by some Pakhtoon members of the land mafia in North Karachi. . . . Riots, clashes and target killings ensued. . . . Miscreants set ablaze over one-and-a-half dozen vehicles, including passenger buses, coaches, loading trucks and dumpers, while several shops were also set on fire. . . . Dr Seemin Jamali, emergency department director of the Jinnah Postgraduate Medical Centre (JPMC), told Daily Times that eight bodies and nine injured were brought to the hospital, while three persons died in the casualty ward.

Here were signs of gunmen competing for turf, as with "two MQM workers" allegedly killed by "Pakhtoon members of the land mafia." Pakhtoons—another spelling of Pashtuns—dominated the transport business, which explained why "passenger buses, coaches, loading trucks and dumpers" would be set on fire in apparent retaliation, as part of a widespread riot that included killing many people and torching "several shops." (Two of the buses set on fire that day can be seen on the cover of this book).

This article also suggested what was really at stake when Mohajirs and Pashtuns went to war: power. Independent observers did not consider the main Pashtun party to be an extremist group. Rather, it was seen as a rival to the MQM, which now claimed to represent millions of Pashtun migrants. Somewhat like the MQM, the Pashtun party was organized on ethnic lines, was accused of links to various criminal land schemes, and nevertheless espoused a moderate political philosophy. The party was called the Awami National Party, or ANP, and it traced its political ancestry to a Pashtun leader from the time of independence, who built a great following on the northwestern frontier and was so devoted to nonviolent politics that he was called the "frontier Gandhi."

Karachi's local leader of the ANP, Shahi Syed, lived in a gated house in an upscale neighborhood. When I visited, the armed guard at the gate wore the distinctive black uniform of Pakistan's Frontier Corps, meaning that he was a Pashtun militiaman imported from the far northwest. Syed wanted a guard he could trust. Inside the compound I shook hands with Syed, a man with bulging eyes, black hair parted on the side, and a black mustache. He spoke in a booming voice that I could have heard from fifty feet away; yet his talk was the banter of the self-made businessman. He told me he'd migrated to Karachi in the 1970s, where he worked in his early years as a laborer. At the end of his workday he would go home in the evening for dinner, then go back out again and drive a rickshaw. Finally he earned enough to buy his own rickshaw, the beginning of a business empire that eventually included a chain of gas stations.

I could not help but think that in a different environment, Shahi Syed might have been able to sit down with Mustafa Kamal and trade stories—two brash and loud and clever men. But that was hardly possible. They were divided in too many ways. The MQM openly questioned how Syed had built his fortune.

Syed cheerfully returned the favor. Although I had brought along an interpreter, he chose to converse in English, saying it would give him a chance to practice. When he got stuck on a word he would consult with my Pakistani colleague and write down what he learned, and such was his description of the MQM that he wrote "extortion" and "gunnysack." Syed showed me voting statistics demonstrating that voter turnout was abnormally high, more than 90 percent, in MQM-dominated districts. He asked if his Mohajir rivals were rigging elections, and worse.

This profound and bitter distrust extended across many ethnic groups in Karachi. It frequently extended down from political leaders to the people at large. And this was the divided city that Mustafa Kamal addressed in January 2010.

Wounded though he may have been by conspiracy theories, the mayor took a step to lower tensions after his angry television appearance. He appeared on the same network a few days later in a calmer mood. The anchor politely asked Kamal to give the names of the politicians and news anchors he had been thinking of when he cursed them in his previous appearance. Kamal declined. "I don't want to start a fight here," he said. Switching between English and Urdu, he apologized instead.

Only time would show if the MQM was sincere about rebuilding the burned shops. As one activist told me afterward, "Everyone was sure the MQM set the fires," but the MQM was able to offer evidence of its innocence each time a shop reopened. Gradually Kamal won over some of his critics, though not all. Some shopkeepers *still* believed the city government had been out to get them all along. A single gesture could not erase decades of mistrust.

12 | PARKS AND RECREATION

During the months that the Bolton Market resounded with the noise of hammers and drills, a different sound was audible in other parts of the city. It was the sound of gunfire.

Karachi's murder rate, very high in 2009, remained high in 2010. Many killings involved members of political parties, still maneuvering for power.

Once I met a woman whose job was to track these killings for the Human Rights Commission. She spread out each day's newspapers and found all stories of murder. She added up the number of dead, then moved on to the next day's harvest. Most killings were quickly forgotten; there were too many deaths to seriously track who was dying or why. But now and again, people refused to let a death be overlooked, and I began to hear about such a case from the fall of 2009. That year a local political activist alleged that the city was trying to allow the construction of houses inside a public park. His fight over the park culminated just a few weeks before the fires of December 28, 2009. The resulting publicity helped to explain why conspiracy theories involving real estate soon swirled around the Bolton Market: the activist's story implicated Karachi's political parties in a deadly competition for real estate.

The activist, Nisar Baloch, was challenging the government in a tangled case, involving years of litigation. But someone preferred an out-of-court settlement. On November 6 the activist publicly denounced the city's most powerful political parties for their complicity in the land grab. By the next morning he was dead.

I HIRED A CAR and driver and went to have a look at the real estate in question. It was in SITE Town—the acronym stood for the Sindh Industrial Trading Estate. This was one of the places where Karachi went through its industrial expansion after World War II, and it remained a manufacturing center, dusty and crowded, blackened with auto pollution and soot. Rude concrete buildings lined Manghopir Road, with improvised upper floors that didn't always match the lower ones, many of the walls not coming together at right angles. I thought of a child's blocks, imperfectly stacked. This was a stonecutting district. The wares of open-fronted workshops spilled out onto the streets. Gray stone slabs leaned against each other side by side, ready to be dealt out like a giant's deck of cards.

Trees appeared along the road behind a high iron fence on the right. They were coconut trees. Walking paths spread across the green lawn below them. Here and there someone lounged on a bench.

This was the entrance to a vast stretch of open space, once larger than New York City's Central Park, though it had grown smaller over time as people built around the edges. Only a few acres had ever been as lovely as the coconut grove. Near the palms I saw gray piles of stone chips, the stonecutters' waste. Beyond them we followed a gravel road past a bare and empty soccer stadium, ending at a vacant lot that truckers used as a parking lot. Beyond the parking lot were vegetable fields, a circular cricket field, and a number of industrial plants.

We returned to the main road and lingered at the front gate, above which hung a giant sign in red, green, and black, the colors of the flag of the Pakistan People's Party. In Urdu script the sign said:

GARDEN OF MARTYR BENAZIR BHUTTO
Also known as
Gutter Baghicha
(480 Acres)

Everything in the sign was a political statement. Since winning power in 2008, People's Party supporters had been renaming almost everything after Benazir Bhutto, their leader who was assassinated during the election campaign. This sign also restated the park's old name, which was a matter of some dispute. Even the acreage was a political statement, since rival political parties disagreed on the size and shape of the park.

We stayed in front of the gate for no more than a minute, long enough to take a few photos. One of them shows a man in white stepping through the gateway and walking toward us.

Amar Guriro, my Pakistani colleague, greeted the man.

"What are you doing here?" the man said. "It's dangerous here, very tense. Why are you taking pictures?"

"Don't worry," Amar said. "We're just photographing historic places of Karachi."

That satisfied the man long enough for us to go. And leave we did, knowing that one of the last outsiders to inspect the property—a court-appointed investigator—had been surrounded by gun-wielding people who said they wouldn't let him escape unless he agreed to support their version of events.

I thought about Nisar Baloch, the man who'd been killed during his fight over Gutter Baghicha. When he died, in November 2009, the neighborhood erupted in protest and mourning. Every business shut down—all the stores and stonecutters along Manghopir Road and beyond. People poured into the streets and blocked traffic. Men brought out guns and fired into the air, disregarding the police who had come out in force. Many people turned up for Nisar's funeral, although none of the men who ran the city or the province could make it. Even the officials of the People's Party, which Nisar Baloch had served for much of his life, concluded that they should be elsewhere.

Nisar Baloch's family and friends said they knew who was behind the killing. In news accounts of the funeral, the group they accused was described, though not actually named. The newspaper *Daily Times* referred to "land grabbers" who were "allegedly backed by an influential political outfit of the city." *Dawn* was a little more specific, referring to "an ethnic party, which is also a coalition partner of the ruling Pakistan People's Party in Sindh." An informed reader could deduce that the MQM was an "ethnic party" that fit the description, though the papers never said that.

Maybe the newspapers' reticence shouldn't have been surprising, since Nisar Baloch was killed less than twenty-four hours after *he* publicly named the MQM.

I LEARNED MORE ABOUT Nisar Baloch in another part of town, in a quiet and slightly ramshackle house that had been turned into an architectural firm.

A portion of the house had been given over to a group of environmental activists. Here I met several times with Mrs. Amber Alibhai, the general secretary of the environmental group, which was called Shehri. Alibhai spoke English with a rich accent, sometimes as rapidly as a machine gun, sometimes as rhythmically as a song. For many years she had been working for Shehri, an organization founded by prominent citizens in 1988. Although several of those citizens had connections to the People's Party, Shehri was registered as a nonpolitical organization, designed to raise public awareness of land-use and environmental issues; *shehri* is the Urdu word for "citizen." Except for a few paid staff, its members were volunteers; the organization raised its modest funds through local donations and occasional grants from overseas—like an annual payment from the National Endowment for Democracy in Washington, D.C.

Shehri had found its calling in preserving any land that was legally defined as an "amenity plot"—a park, a playground, a soccer field, a schoolyard. Many of these properties were scarcely more than wasteland, never having been put to their intended use. In satellite images of the crowded city, such lands appeared here and there like bald spots on an unruly head of hair. But whatever their bedraggled condition, Shehri argued that the parks were irreplaceable; the open space should be preserved for future generations.

The first time I met Alibhai we talked about her effort to preserve a park that the city wanted to use for housing and a hospital. When Shehri sued, saying the parkland was being converted without due process of law, Amber Alibhai received threats.

"What sort of threats?" I asked.

"Well, obviously, to kill us, and this time they even wanted to kill my father, my brother, my son and my husband and the usual."

The usual?

Time and again when I moved about Karachi, I would ask a simple question and a story would tumble out in response, as suddenly as if I had opened an overstuffed closet. Alibhai told me that an anonymous caller reached her husband several times in 2007. "He told my husband that, look, this is your daily routine and these are the names of your children and these are their ages and this is where they study. And this is the name of your father-in-law and this is his age and this is where he goes for a walk in the evening. And I have a photograph of all of them in front of me. And do you want me to fax it to you so that you understand what I'm saying to you?"

Amber Alibhai called the Citizens' Police Liaison Committee, the business group founded to investigate kidnapping; the committee had the technical ability to trace phone calls. Numbers in hand, Alibhai then complained to the provincial governor, a senior official of the MQM, who later affirmed her story to me. The governor arranged for Alibhai's family to receive police protection, and the mysterious threats stopped.

Alibhai did not come away with confidence in the government. She suspected there was a connection between the caller and the authorities—that officials had the ability to "pressurize" her, in the Pakistani expression, and also the ability to call off pressure. "Let me tell you," she said, "my city is run by gangsters. My city is run by the mafia."

The next time I saw Alibhai, we talked about Gutter Baghicha, the park that I was visiting until a local man warned me away. Shehri had been battling over it for years with the help of Nisar Baloch, the activist who lived across the street from the park.

After the protest that arose over his murder, city officials would tell me that Baloch was a gangster who earned his own death, but it was hard for me to reconcile those claims with the descriptions of people who knew him. As a young man, Nisar Baloch became a teacher. He taught at a public elementary school, and organized free computer classes. The area was heavily populated by Nisar's ethnic group—the Baloch people, the descendants of migrants from the western province of Baluchistan (or perhaps not all migrants; some argued that the Baloch had always been here, that Karachi was really a *Baloch* city, not the city of the Sindhis or the Mohajirs, yet another ethnic group that felt the city was stolen from them). Baloch nationalist groups were active in Nisar's area, but it was not toward them that Nisar necessarily leaned. He gravitated to the Pakistan People's Party, which was a national party. The PPP had always been the personal heirloom of the Bhuttos, a collection of feudal landowners and machine politicians, many of whom had been accused over the years of various kinds of corruption; yet Zulfikar Ali Bhutto's old rhetoric of socialism and helping the poor attracted a certain number of left-leaning activists.

Nisar "was a very happy person," Amber Alibhai remembered. "Very forgetful. He was most of the time walking off with other people's reading glasses and leaving his behind. Including my glasses. He would arrive with his files, and there was no structure to them and we would tell him, 'Nisar, you need to file them properly.' But he knew exactly which paper was where, and if you asked him he'd pull it out and give it to you. . . . He would walk in with his papers and he'd drop them here, and sometimes he'd knock off my papers. He was a good soul," she said, remembering that when she was under threat, Nisar brought his nephew to accompany her as she drove about so she would never be alone. "You know, as a woman, I never felt uncomfortable with him.

"And I didn't agree with this silly press conference," she added, and I realized that another story was tumbling out. She was referring to the press conference Nisar called on the day before he died. "You know, he came and wanted to ask me for the money."

What money? I asked. She explained that Nisar wanted to hold the event at the Karachi Press Club, an elegant stone building near the center of town. People typically held media events there, since it was near the offices of news agencies; it was hard to draw a crowd of overworked and underpaid reporters to some remote location. It cost seven thousand rupees to book a room at the Press Club, around eighty dollars.

Nisar didn't have the money, so he asked Amber for it. "When he mentioned this press conference, I guess I was busy and I should've paid more attention. I just shouted at him and said no, you're not doing it because you're exposing yourself and you'll get in trouble. You'll end up saying the wrong thing." She didn't want him getting "personal" or engaging in "vendettas."

She told him goodbye and didn't think of it again. She didn't realize until later that Nisar got the money from another member of Shehri and went ahead.

AMBER ALIBHAI did not see the urgency of holding a press conference because she knew she had to wage a long, slow, careful fight. Shehri had been involved in lawsuits over Gutter Baghicha for most of the organization's existence. The battle went back almost two decades. The story of Gutter Baghicha went back decades before that.

"We received the maps from the British Library in London," she said. In colonial times, "Gutter Baghicha was a forest, and it was a total of about sixteen hundred acres." Later, Shehri activists believed, the land was used as a collection point for the stormwater that flooded Karachi during the monsoon season.

Next the government built a sewage treatment plant, and sewage was used to water crops on a portion of the property. It was called a sewage farm, which explained the land's unappealing name: *Baghicha* meant "garden," so it was a gutter garden. One corner was developed as a proper park, the lovely cluster of coconut trees that I saw during my visit.

Other land was not used at all, and after 1947 it was encroached on all sides. In my research I encountered a city government map from as late as 1962 that pictured the "Karachi Municipal Corporation Sewage Farm" as an enormous green rectangle, a mile and a half by a mile, possibly more than nine hundred acres, but that map may have been out of date even when it was made. Some of the western portion was becoming an industrial park. Some of the eastern area was becoming a settlement for refugees from India.

In more recent years the city approved a plan to build a housing complex on some of the land that remained. The complex was intended for city employees. Shehri sued, and "then we went into the area," Alibhai said, to organize the community. "We knocked on their doors and all, and that's when Nisar Baloch came forward. And we said, 'Hey, this is happening in your backyard, do you know what's going on?'" Nisar agreed to help Shehri, and his family became close friends with Amber Alibhai's family. He founded a neighborhood organization whose name translated as the Movement to Save Gutter Baghicha. "They were the eyes and ears, for so many years, and the case is still pending in the high court."

Even as that slice of the park remained in limbo, it seemed that another slice would be preserved. In 2002 President Pervez Musharraf declared that a portion of Gutter Baghicha would become a national park. In a city map produced in 2005, the national park was shaped something like a scientist's lab beaker, with a broad base and a crooked neck. The government soon began construction of walkways and other amenities. Within a few years, satellite images showed the walkways taking shape; they formed a series of broad and interconnected hexagons, just as projected in the 2005 map.

Then, in 2009, came the event that sent Nisar Baloch over the edge. Work crews began building streets and property walls for houses inside the space for the national park.

NOBODY DOUBTED who would live in the houses or who their political sponsors were. The homes were for Mohajirs, or Urdu-speaking people, as they were often called. They were backed by the MQM. Wanting to understand what happened, I met with Nasreen Jalil. She was a member of the MQM, and was the head of the city council, which publicly endorsed the construction. She defended her party, but was unusually frank about what happened.

Jalil invited me to her home in the upscale area known as Defence. Blue-uniformed guards stood with pump shotguns outside her door. Upon learning that I had an appointment, they ushered me through the gate, across the driveway, and up a lovely set of spiral stairs to the main floor. She greeted me wrapped in a silvery sari and reached out to shake my hand, one of the relatively few women's hands I was offered in Pakistan.

In 2009 Nasreen Jalil had been, in local parlance, the Naib Nazim—essentially the speaker of the city council. She came from a distinguished family. Her husband was an MQM leader. Her sister was Yasmeen Lari, the architect and historic preservationist who is known as the first woman architect of Pakistan. She bade me to sit down in a living room filled with heavy wooden furniture and modernist paintings. When I complimented her on the decor, she waved my words aside. "Everything here is old," she said. Though Nasreen Jalil was suffering from a cough—she sipped herbal medicine through much of our conversation—she sat with me for an hour and a half, and would have stayed longer had I wanted.

Sometime after the tea was delivered I asked about Nisar Baloch. At first she seemed not to remember much about the case. She picked up a telephone and called someone in the city administration to learn more.

She listened for a time, asking follow-up questions, and then turned to me. "What happened was, there are different *katchi abadis* in Karachi. Some of them were being legalized." She went back to the phone, asked a few more questions, explained some more. Sometime after 1947, people had built a settlement on the northeastern section of the sewage farm. In the early 1980s the government legalized that settlement, while also building proper roads through it. "And when they were being organized or developed, the roads were being put up, sewage lines and water were being planned, some people had to be removed." So they needed new homes.

Decades later, in 2009, the MQM-dominated city council remembered its long-ago commitment to find new houses for those long-ago Mohajirs. The council passed a resolution approving the construction of houses on another chunk of the old sewage farm. "And then the Baloch population that was living near Gutter Baghicha, they objected to that," she said.

The Baloch population? I asked if the people getting the new houses were not Baloch.

"No, they were not."

"Were they Urdu-speaking?"

"Yes, they were Urdu-speaking."

"Then it becomes a political or ethnic dispute," I said.

"Yes, yes."

All sides acknowledged that the conflict was ethnic *and* partisan. The neighborhood included many ethnic Baloch, Nisar Baloch among them. Many Baloch supported the People's Party. If Urdu-speaking people moved in with the backing of the MQM, it might shift the neighborhood's political balance.

I reminded Jalil of what happened to Nisar Baloch—that he denounced the MQM, and that the next day he was killed.

She looked surprised. "The very next day?"

"The very next morning."

"By the police?"

"I don't think anyone has been arrested," I said.

NASREEN JALIL SENT ME to meet with men in the old city hall, who were prepared to back up the city's version of events. The employees gave me a pile of documents and maps and let me take them away to study. The city employees also alleged that the murdered activist was a blackmailer and a thug, who had used dubious tactics in the past to bring water service to his neighborhood.

This was a very different impression than I gained when I arranged to meet the widow of Nisar Baloch.

Madiha Baloch was a woman in her late twenties, with striking dark eyes. She wore black clothes in mourning for her husband. I apologized for asking about a difficult subject; she welcomed me to ask whatever I wanted, and smiled often when she spoke of Nisar. She explained that she fell in love with him about eight years before, while taking a computer class. Nisar was the teacher. He was forty and she was nineteen.

"My father and brothers said no because there was too big an age gap," she told me, "but I put my foot down and said I'm going to marry him."

"What did you like about him?"

"He had an inspiring personality." It was not easy for her to explain—who can explain love?—but as I learned more about Nisar I got a sense of the man. He had keen watchful eyes. He was kind: illiterate old ladies went to Nisar when they needed someone to read letters or documents. And he didn't mind if his wife became a teacher like him. Madiha was smitten. She wanted to marry him even though it meant that she would be moving into the house Nisar shared with many relatives.

Later, Nisar would tell a story about how Madiha's family reacted to their plan to marry. In the story, Nisar makes his proposal to marry Madiha. Her mother replies, You? You have nothing! You have no land! How will you support my daughter? Upon hearing of this, *his* mother answers, perhaps ruefully, Not to worry, my son has two pieces of land. He has Jinnah's tomb, which he likes to visit, and the park across the street from our home.

In other words, nothing.

It wasn't so bad. Nisar Baloch had a job and some connections. And he loved the park across the street—which was part of Gutter Baghicha, the little patch with the coconut palms. He liked to climb on his third-floor roof to get a good look. He took Madiha for walks in the park in the cool of an early morning.

The happy couple sat for a photo on their wedding day in 2002. Madiha wears a red dress set off with patterns of gold and assumes the posture expected of the modest Pakistani bride: she's looking down. She's studying her hands, painted with wedding decorations. Nisar sits beside her, smooth-faced and mustached, his eyes flashing with nervous energy as he studies something off camera. It would be natural for his hand to rest on hers, but since they are in public he shifts his right hand away, resting it awkwardly on his left knee. Family and friends surround Madiha and Nisar. Beside Madiha sits one of her disapproving brothers, who slouches on the edge of the couch and looks like he'd rather be anywhere else. Beside Nisar sits a man with a benevolent smile. He's a Pakistani senator who served as a witness at the wedding.

Madiha knew her husband's political work was hazardous. He'd been arrested once, and she'd had to remonstrate with the police to get him out of jail. But it became more dangerous when Nisar led a street protest against the Gutter Baghicha development in 2009. Armed Baloch and Mohajir groups confronted each other. Police said a paramilitary soldier and two passersby were shot. They fired tear gas to restore order, and afterward they filed criminal charges against the organizers of the protest: Nisar Baloch and another activist. Nisar knew that the charges might not be the end of the matter, and knew how cheap human life was in Karachi. Against these realities, he weighed his attachment to Gutter Baghicha, the place he walked through and admired from his roof.

Nisar and Madiha Baloch (center) at their wedding. *[Madiha Baloch/Shehri]*

In the story he told about his mother-in-law, Gutter Baghicha was *his* land, the place that made him wealthy and worthy of a bride.

His calculations finally came down to a single question:

Did he really want to risk his life for a sewer?

IN THE SUMMER of 2009, the environmental group Shehri filed a lawsuit seeking yet another restraining order, this time against the MQM-supported encroachment. Prominent citizens put their names on the complaint, including Abdul Sattar Edhi of the ambulance service, and Ardeshir Cowasjee, the wealthy old Zoroastrian shipping heir and newspaperman.

It was not surprising that Cowasjee would attach his name to the suit. He was a constant presence in the city's debate over land use, and had managed to speak independently in Karachi for years. His eccentric columns in *Dawn* wandered from issues of municipal administration to ruminations on long-dead European kings, interspersed with deadly little descriptions of powerful politicians, like the chief minister of Sindh "with his freshly dyed Cherry Blossom hair and moustache and unchanging facial expression." It was characteristic of Cowasjee's writing style that one of his articles in 2008 *began* with the words, "To digress . . ." But the digression had a sly purpose. He mocked Pakistan's president, Asif Ali Zardari of the People's Party, for "nepotism," giving an aide's niece a government job. Then the columnist completely changed the subject to Gutter Baghicha. He proposed that a park there be named in honor of Zardari's martyred wife, Benazir Bhutto. Judging by the People's Party banner I later saw over the entrance, somebody approved of this suggestion.

In a single column he excoriated and flattered the president of his country. Who could take revenge on Cowasjee after that? Who could even conclude which side he was on? But of course all the way through the column the old man was pursuing the public interest as he saw it. He opposed nepotism, and also wanted to build support for the park.

"I hate hypocrites," he barked at me when he had me over for fish and mangoes. And he went after those he considered hypocrites with carefully worded columns, choosing the targets that he wanted and steering clear of the rest. Whenever we met, he didn't like me taking notes. He didn't want to get in trouble for some stray remark. We ate at the picture window of his old stone house, where he could study his lawn and garden. He claimed that his involvement in preserving open space was purely selfish; he had been fighting for years to stop the city from cutting down a row of trees that we could see from his window. But a different spirit came through in his writing:

> What the few of us battling losers, concerned with open spaces and parklands in this congested overpopulated city, really want is money from those who have money and vocal support from the public, the *awam*, who are the ultimate grand losers when they find themselves with a city in which open spaces, parks and beaches are few and far between.

And it was in this spirit that he put his name on the lawsuit.

The city swiftly answered the lawsuit, in essence: No, no, no, you've got this all wrong. This construction is not in the national park, it is outside the park. And look at the city council resolution—we're just taking care of people from many years ago. (It appeared that the encroachment started *before* the council passed its resolution, but that could be set aside for the moment.) Every fact about the case was disputed, just as every fact about Gutter Baghicha was always disputed, and the judge decided to send an investigator "to ascertain the nature and extent of the various constructions."

The investigator visited Gutter Baghicha on September 26, 2009, and afterward filed a report of his harrowing experience. Although he was escorted by police and the heavily armed Rangers, he faced an ominous sight when he arrived at Gutter Baghicha around four o'clock in the afternoon. "At site approximate one thousand gents and ladies were also gathered of different groups out of them some persons were armed."

The investigator conducted his inspection with difficulty. "There was [a] law and order situation and two groups of the area were armed and created difficulties," he wrote. It appeared that both Mohajirs and Baloch had brought guns. The Mohajirs who'd begun the encroachment were especially insistent. "The ladies and gents were gathered and surrounded [me] and were requesting to allow them to live there as they have constructed and are constructing their houses at the said area by selling their valuable items/articles and they are poor people. Therefore, they have requested [that I] can not leave the place un-less allow/guaranteed them that their houses will not be demolished and forces deployed there may not be asked to leave the area. Therefore, under the heavy forces deployed and found at the time of my site inspection there, I could only be able to come out from the area along with my staff/team by a difficult struggle."

Nevertheless the investigator did find houses under construction in several of the acres that were in dispute. Now it became a matter of dry law, or so it seemed. One of the simpler questions was whether the construction was inside the national park or outside of it.

A map of the national park from 2005 clearly included the land where construction had begun. A map from 2009 clearly *excluded* the land where construction had begun.

Curiously, both maps were produced by the Karachi city government, which seemed to have altered the shape of the national park to accommodate the new settlement. *That* was how the city managed to claim with a straight face that the settlement was outside the park. When I compared the two maps with Google images of the national park under construction, it was clear that Shehri was right: the park's boundaries had moved. The 2005 design of the park could not possibly fit in the remaining land now designated for it.

Defeating the city would take patience; in the fall of 2009, Nisar Baloch seemed to run out of it.

NISAR BALOCH was getting into his late forties. He and his young wife Madiha had never succeeded in having children. Finally she went alone to Mithidar, that crowded neighborhood that was the headquarters of Abdul Sattar Edhi. She knew that the Edhi Foundation left cribs at many of its offices, ready to receive unwanted children. Edhi's wife Bilquis oversaw the adoption service; so it was from the Edhis that Madiha received a newborn girl. When I met her she was a toddler with a head of curly hair, turning her head sideways to study me with a skeptical expression.

Once Nisar was a father, he had even more reason than ever to look after himself, but on Friday, November 6, he called his press conference, paying the rupees he'd borrowed for the room at the Karachi Press Club.

His friend and colleague at Shehri, Amber Alibhai, told me afterward that Nisar was discouraged. "He felt that everything would be lost," she said. Nisar was discouraged not only about the MQM but also about his own Pakistan People's Party. "What had disheartened him was that he was a PPP member, and that his own party—and he knew everybody big in that party, even he's got

Nisar (left) with Asif Ali Zardari (second from right).

a picture of him with [President] Zardari when Zardari was a young man—nobody was prepared to put a stop to the encroachment."

It was true. The PPP and the MQM were in an alliance of convenience, struggling to share power at the federal and provincial levels; the MQM's votes were essential to the coalition that President Zardari's government had assembled in Islamabad. The government had far larger problems, from the struggle to restore democratic rule to the nasty war against extremist groups. This was the explanation I heard when visiting the compound that President Zardari and his party maintained in Karachi. Here I sat with Taj Haider, a gracious elder spokesman of the party. Haider acknowledged that all parties were involved in land grabbing, including elements of his own party.

I asked about Gutter Baghicha. He avoided answering directly, but was informative all the same.

"Gutter Baghicha is one place," he said, "but I think more than one hundred thousand plots have been illegally occupied in Karachi, and political compulsions have forced the government to look the other way." He said both parties were involved, and the People's Party was determined to keep the MQM within the governing coalition. "In order to avoid many problems and come out of anarchy, we had to bend backwards, we had to embark on a course of political reconciliation with the forces that had been with the dictator. I objected to it, but the leadership felt that no, there is an area in which we should avoid all conflict."

The fate of the government was at stake. If Nisar Baloch got into a fight with the MQM, he could not be assured that his friends would protect him.

A NUMBER OF REPORTERS attended the activist's press conference. A photo of the event shows Nisar Baloch sitting in front of a bank of four news-channel microphones. He's reading a document aloud. He's wearing his reading glasses low on his nose; they're attached to a cord around his neck, which perhaps would keep him from losing them.

Baloch denounced one of "the government's coalition partners" for the land grab at Gutter Baghicha. According to a Baloch nationalist newspaper, he said words to the effect that "this is the largest land scam in which Muttahida Qaumi Movement (MQM) is directly involved."

Later his friends said that he forecast his own death at his press conference.

If so, his prediction did not make it into the news accounts that I saw, but his wife, Madiha, told me that he phoned her afterward and said, "They're going to take me now."

The next morning, Saturday, November 7, he rose in his family home. He told his family that he was going out to get some newspapers. He wanted to find what had been written about his press conference. Nisar rolled his motorcycle out onto Manghopir Road, and he could hardly have avoided taking one more look at Gutter Baghicha across the street—the iron fence, the coconut trees, the walking paths, and all those hundreds of acres looming beyond.

Later that day his cousin affixed his name to a statement to police: "I received information that Nisar faced an accident at Love Line Bridge. When I reached there, I saw Nisar's motorcycle down on the road, and I could also see the blood on that spot. I was informed there that some unknown person murdered Nisar with indiscriminate firing and as a result two other pedestrians also got injured." The cousin later saw Nisar's body in the hospital, and said Nisar had been shot in the head. The cousin added, "It was all the result of his press conference on Gutter Baghicha."

Edhi ambulances carried away the wounded and dead.

Columnist Ardeshir Cowasjee, the dead man's ally in the fight over the park, posed a number of questions in print: "Who will be next on the list? Could it be a man of the Rangers? Or could it be a police official? Or a functionary of the City District Government's Revenue Office whose sworn duty it is to protect government and amenity land?"

By and large the MQM was not directly mentioned in the news coverage that followed the killing. Karachi reporters told me that it was common to avoid mentioning the MQM in sensitive dispatches; some said that if they did mention the MQM in an unflattering light, their editors would cut out the references or cancel the stories—killing the stories, as it was called in the news business. One newspaper, the Daily Times, did bring up two major parties in a judiciously worded editorial: "Importantly, Nisar Baloch had criticized both the MQM and PPP in equal measure, the former for complicity in coercion and the latter for its expedient tardiness."

The same editorial made a stark charge against the city administration of Mustafa Kamal, the mayor of Karachi, the man whose constant energy had restored a number of magnificent parks, like the great expanse near the Hindu temple of Shiva. While parks in upscale areas were being restored, the editorial said, "the right of the lesser mortals in the metropolis to public spaces and amenity plots is being flagrantly flouted" in many "working-class neighbourhoods."

When I asked Amber Alibhai, of Shehri, what she thought of Kamal, she said, "I am sure Kamal was a good man if he was born at another time, belonging to another party."

This was not the way that the mayor pictured himself. He described himself as a *victim* of encroachment, not as someone who abetted it. His own dreams for the city were being paved over. The next time we met, he listed his own disappointments. The land on which he planned to expand an amusement park was encroached. The land on which he planned a bus terminal was encroached. "In front of my eyes, my land—my land—I mean the city's land, which was for future plans, have been encroached. I am helpless."

I inquired about the situation at Gutter Baghicha. "What happened to Nisar Baloch?"

"I don't know," he said. "Police will let you know. He was killed."

"I don't think the police will know."

"If the police don't know, then we should be very afraid of them."

"Those killings are never solved," I said.

"Well, definitely, I was not standing there when those killings were taking place."

"I would never suggest that. I'm just wondering what happened."

"He was killed," Kamal said. "He was killed. Even three days back, three people were killed there, you know? Two gangs are fighting there. And they're using the rocket launchers on each other." That was the party's story—that Baloch was killed in some kind of gang warfare.

Later I posed similar questions to Nasreen Jalil, the speaker of the city council at the time of the murder. She, too, dismissed the notion that the MQM was involved.

I asked if someone on the MQM's side might have taken an opportunity to eliminate an annoyance. "I wonder is it possible that there was some person who didn't formally represent the party that was angry about what Nisar Baloch was saying?"

"I don't know," she said. "You must also remember that MQM has worked very hard to create, to remove the label that it had, that it's a terrorist party, and we've worked very hard, so doing anything of the kind would blacken our face again. We have told our people, we have tried to do everything to clean our past. That we'd get involved in this kind of killing directly, or indirectly, that doesn't serve our purpose. You'd still consider us to be the same."

After Nisar Baloch's killing that November, another activist—he was known as Nader Baloch, no relation to Nisar—took over the community organization that was opposing the encroachment. In December came the Ashura bombing, followed by the increase in political tension and political killing. Then came a day in early January when nine people were murdered in separate incidents across the city; the dead were linked with several political parties and included an MQM activist who was beheaded. And on this day, Nader Baloch was also killed, leaving the community organization leaderless again. His supporters soon hung huge photos of him at the gates of Gutter Baghicha; they were still in place on the day I visited the park. In one photo the activist was wearing sunglasses and held a hand on his chin as if in thought. He appeared to be sitting in front of the same iron fence on which his image now hung. The bars in the giant image were aligned to match those of the fence.

AS I RODE away from the park, I realized I knew some of what happened at Gutter Baghicha, even if I didn't know who actually pulled the trigger on Love

Gutter Baghicha.

Line Bridge on November 7. To serve people in the MQM's core constituency, the city approved construction inside land that had been designated for a national park. Whatever legal cover the city council may have provided, the new construction led to an ethnic battle, which the MQM's rivals also failed to restrain. Protests ended in gunfire, criminal charges were filed, an officer of the court was threatened at gunpoint, and activists were eventually killed. Baloch activists as well as Mohajirs brought guns onto the street. Politicians pushed all the buttons of a volatile area, and the situation exploded. Absent more evidence, Karachi's dominant political party could deny responsibility for the assassination of Nisar Baloch and his successor, Nader Baloch. But the MQM could not avoid responsibility for helping to create a deadly situation.

13 | PREMIER LIFESTYLES

In March 2010, gunmen opened fire on a radical Sunni Muslim cleric, wounding him and killing his son. In a separate attack, gunmen on a motorbike killed three other Sunni clerics as they rode in a car. People speculated that the Sunnis might have been killed in retribution for the bombings of Shias that began on December 28 and continued in February. These aftershocks, or perceived aftershocks, of the Ashura bombing gradually blended with other acts in the violent conversation of the city.

The rhythm of death affected the rhythm of life. In May 2010, I arrived in the city at the end of a day when schools and offices were closed for safety during a political killing spree. About forty men were murdered over several days. The killings peaked on Wednesday and continued into Thursday. On Friday the streets seemed quiet, patrolled by the paramilitary Rangers in their pickup trucks. Businesses stayed shut. News arrived of more killings, although the daily toll was dropping. Finally, on Saturday evening, I noticed young people out walking as the sun disappeared. On a major commercial street, shopkeepers opened their metal gates; watches and leather goods gleamed in electric light. The city burst back to life. I thought of the way a desert blooms when it finally rains.

The instant city is resilient, and even after the Ashura bombing, Karachi residents kept trying to make a difference, or at least to do business.

ONE AFTERNOON I HIRED a car to ride to the seashore across the Clifton Bridge. The driver passed a glassy Sofitel hotel under construction, and the spot where Jundallah militants attacked a military convoy in 2004. We glimpsed the gate of 70 Clifton, the walled compound where Zulfikar Ali Bhutto held court until he was overthrown, and where his granddaughter Fatima Bhutto, among other relatives, could be found these days. We swung left in front of the Hindu temple of Shiva, then right at the shrine of Abdullah Shah Ghazi. Ahead, at the seashore, a high-rise glass tower loomed in the sun. The leading edge on the landward side was gleaming white, shaped to resemble a triangular sail, as if some storybook sailboat had just blown ashore off the Arabian Sea. Maybe the boat had just come across the water from Dubai.

This building was part of a complex of towers under construction. It stood on the same property where Karachi's casino had nearly opened more than thirty years before. Tony Tufail, the man who built the casino, gave me the phone number of the man to whom he'd sold the property. The new owner was elusive at first, but eventually an aide said I could come over. The aide was in charge of leasing space in the complex, a self-contained world for the international business set. Four office towers would offer some of the city's finest views, and all were connected on their lower floors by a multilevel shopping mall. The leasing manager gave me no assurance that I would meet his boss, the chief executive of the company, but welcomed me to come for a tour.

A cooling wind blew across the beach as I arrived. A freighter rode out on the Arabian Sea, its outline visible in the haze. In the lobby of the sailboat tower, I waited beside a wall painting at least forty feet long—a vast field of black, a field of blue, and a red ball bouncing into a box. A woman in green stated her business to the receptionist, a man whose dark suit would not look out of place behind the counter of any international hotel.

The leasing manager, Jabir Hussain Dada, emerged after a few minutes. He worked for a firm called Dolmen Builders, and this project was called Dolmen City. Jabir looked to be around forty, his skin unwrinkled though his close-cropped beard was shading toward gray. With much swiping of identity cards we made our way through electronic security gates and walked the cavernous spaces of the future shopping mall, where we talked over the screech of hand-held power saws; workmen were shaving Spanish marble tile. Dada led the way through a series of atriums and future retail spaces.

Dada was lining up foreign companies to anchor the mall, among them a Carrefour—the nearest French equivalent of Wal-Mart. Many of the building materials were imported. The glass and aluminum work came from a contractor in Dubai, and the electrical work from Germany. There was a space for an upscale restaurant overlooking the sea, and room for a children's play area the size of a mansion. It took more than an hour to see the highlights. Jabir said the project totaled 4.2 million square feet, and the mall alone was a million—it would be among the largest malls in Pakistan, and would count as a sizable complex even in America.

We climbed to the roof of the mall, next to the half-finished swimming pool, for a view of the two towers already completed—the Executive Tower, which was already full of tenants, and the Harbourfront Tower, the sailboat-inspired building, which was soon to be occupied. On the way back downstairs and out of the sun, I said I was glad for the ocean breeze. He agreed, then spoke of how he loved Karachi in the evening, when the sun slipped low and the sea breeze blew across the city.

"Are you from Karachi?" I asked.

"Yeah, my father, grandfather, everybody's from Karachi."

"So you're Sindhi then?"

He paused. "Yeah, you can say we are Sindhi, but I don't know much about it. We love to call ourselves Karachiites. Pakistanis."

We continued through the unfinished mall and passed an improvised mosque. Several dozen laborers cast prayer mats across the rough concrete floor and kneeled for the midday prayers. The imam said "Allah Akbar"—God is great— and fell into silence. I lingered, waiting to hear more, but Jabir whispered that in their branch of Islam, "the preacher does not go through the recitation. The recitation is in his heart."

Jabir walked on with the perfect salesman's attitude. He was excited about building a project to international standards. The power, central air, and other systems would be managed by computer. He pointed out the future locations of elevators and ramps suitable for heavily laden shoppers and for the disabled. Nothing about Dolmen City sounded cheap. It was something to see in the spring of 2010, when much of the world was still recovering from a recession, when Pakistan was in the middle of a war, and when Karachi was so explosive; the Ashura bombing had come just a few months before, and it had been just over a week since the attacks on the Sunni clerics.

"How would you describe the timing of this project?" I asked.

"Do you mean this is not a good time to launch this project?"

"I'm asking if it is."

"See, we are very hopeful that there's going to be a turnaround in a year or so," he said. "Though our political stability is not that of other countries, our business entrepreneurs are so confident in this particular country, they are just working."

He showed me the vast room that would become a banquet hall with room for fifteen hundred people to attend a wedding or a conference with a view of the sea.

"We understand the political stability," he emphasized, "but let me just tell you, this city is *definitely* full of opportunity."

Inside the Harbourfront Tower we rode an elevator up to the penthouse office suite, which had twenty-foot ceilings and skylights. Jabir pointed out glass coating on the windows that cut down on the sun's rays; the heat inside was not intolerable, even though the air systems were not yet working. He pointed from the window to the beach below. He said a public park was planned along the edge of the sand, although construction had recently stopped. The only time his boosterish attitude slipped was when he referred to the government. "The people on the top realize, and appreciate, what we are doing, but the people down below, in the bureaucracy, they do not understand," he said.

"Do you have any assurances from the government about the power supply?"

"False assurances? Yes," he said. "Actually we do not rely on them. We have realized we have to do it ourselves, whatever it is." If the power worked, that would be nice; if not, there would be generators.

We rode an elevator down and passed through another security checkpoint, this time with a metal detector, because we were on our way to the Dolmen Builders offices. Jabir ushered me into a cool gray room, ordered up a tray of tea, and asked if I might sit a little while. He would see about getting his boss to give me some time.

I studied Jabir's business card. "Building a Better Future," it said.

MANY DEVELOPERS around the world were struggling in 2010. They included the famous developers of Dubai, which became a Persian Gulf jewel of more than a million people before the money ran short, but the *idea* of Dubai seemed as powerful as ever in Karachi. The sail-shaped tower at the Dolmen City project reminded me of Dubai's enormous sail-shaped Burj Al Arab hotel. And when Jabir Hussain returned to inform me that his boss had agreed to meet me, it soon became apparent that Dubai was, indeed, on the chief executive's mind. His name was Nadeem Riaz, a hefty man with a mustache and shirtsleeves. He seemed comfortable in his office, although it didn't appear like he spent much time there. The bookshelves behind his desk were bare. A black laptop computer lay closed on his clean desk.

Riaz said he came from a trading family and attended St. Patrick's Catholic school in Karachi. His family lived in Dubai in the 1970s, when he was a young man, but in the late 1980s Riaz came home.

"Is Karachi a good place to do business?" I asked.

"Yes," he said. "There's no competition in any business." It was a massive country with a massively underdeveloped economy. Pakistan was more populous than Russia, more populous than Brazil, catching up with Indonesia. Yet its gross domestic product was down around the size of sparsely populated Chile, or tiny Singapore. Riaz chose to see the upside in this. There was room for growth, and he offered office space to international firms that saw the upside too. Executive Tower, the first building to be completed in his interconnected complex, was already home to the Karachi offices of Eli Lilly, Sony Ericsson, American Life, and Bank Islami—pharmaceuticals, cell phones, insurance, and wealth management. The building directory was a summary of the new economy.

It had taken Riaz almost two decades to get this far. Around 1990 he approached Tony Tufail and bought the stillborn casino. His company quickly planned a high-rise development, but, he said, "the government wouldn't allow it."

"Which government?" I asked, but he claimed not to remember. He didn't like to talk about politics. In the 1990s the country swung wildly between the two rival prime ministers Benazir Bhutto and Nawaz Sharif; somewhere in the gyrations, Dolmen was denied permission to build its high-rise project, just as an abrupt change in government prevented Tony Tufail from opening his casino on the same property. Dolmen Builders had to return the money it had collected from investors. The company never even got as far as tearing down the old casino, and so Riaz turned this beached whale of a building into a children's amusement center. The young people who would remember it included Fatima Bhutto, the granddaughter of Zulfikar Ali Bhutto, the prime minister who had planned the casino. A new century would be under way before the political calculus changed enough for Dolmen to proceed with grander plans.

"It's always better to keep politicians from your business," he said, as if passing on a hard-earned lesson. "I mean, I am friendly with them. Some of them are my friends. But I want to keep them out of my business."

By the time the project finally moved forward, Riaz's company had expanded its plans and the Dolmen City complex began to emerge. Provincial environmental officials challenged the beachfront project, asking whether it could survive a tsunami, but they did not stop construction. Riaz said the global financial crisis had slowed him considerably, but he was pushing ahead a little at a time. He still didn't have all the money he needed. He was developing financial instruments in hopes that he could sell them on the Karachi Stock Exchange.

When he needed inspiration, Riaz traveled to his former home in Dubai, wandering its shopping malls, man-made islands, and the world's tallest building. I asked, "Do you find yourself pointing at different spectacular projects and saying, 'I want some of this, I want some of that'?"

"Always you want to do this. This is my goal. This is my dream. Even if I don't make money, I want to do it the best of the best." And not just the glitter—he asked Dubai shopping mall operators to show him "the back of the house"—the out-of-sight places where they received cargo or disposed of garbage. Such a mundane detail, and so important: proper garbage disposal could make the difference between an upscale project and something less.

I recalled that a number of Pakistani businessmen had given up trying to re-create Dubai in Karachi. They had simply moved their money to Dubai, which Riaz, with his history, could surely do. So I asked him what he thought of the security situation in Karachi.

"We are living here and are going to live here. And if I am killed on the street, so what?" he said without emotion. "If I'm living here, I have to work."

He minimized the importance of the killings in the city, as well as the broader terrorist threat to Pakistan. "A small risk is everywhere," he said, suggesting it was an "image" problem. But he knew that others found the image unsettling. "Last year we called in some consultants from Dubai. We needed some help with some things. They agreed to come. And then they called back and said, 'Our families will not allow us to come.' And I said, 'As you like.'" He shrugged his shoulders as he told the story. But it clearly made him sad.

"Do you worry," I asked, "about the future of this country, that things could get a whole lot worse, that there could be a total collapse?"

"No," he said. "No."

Then he thought for a moment.

"Well, not for me," he said. "Maybe for my children, but not for me."

FOR ALL THEIR DELAYS and frustrations, the Dolmen City builders were doing better than some. Dolmen City was well ahead of the IT Tower, the project next to the Civic Centre that was championed by Mustafa Kamal during his time as mayor. In 2008 the Malaysian developers said the economy and the security situation compelled them to put their money elsewhere. No matter, Mayor Kamal's government said cheerfully; the city will finance the building. But by mid-2010 Kamal's government was out of office, and the project was orphaned. When I stopped by the building site, I saw the same vast hole in the ground I'd seen two years before.

Other projects seemed to hover between illusion and reality, like the plan for a luxury neighborhood on the waterfront. It was expected to include forty-five high-rise towers, every one built on reclaimed land—rocks and sand used to extend the beach. The monster project was under the supervision of Steve McCartt, an American who in 2008 gave me a tour of a stylishly furnished model apartment.

"You're going to enter Southern California right now," McCartt said as we crossed the threshold, waving at the plush sofas and hardwood table, informing me that the upscale market in this part of the world loved California style. McCartt himself was a California import, having moved from San Francisco to work for a Dubai-based corporation called Emaar. It billed itself as "one of the world's largest real estate companies" and "a global provider of premier lifestyles." McCartt let me pose him for a photo on a model apartment balcony, which overlooked a floor-to-ceiling artist's rendering of a future beach view. "And where are you in the world?" he asked me, continuing the apartment tour. "You don't know necessarily."

He was only referring to the California décor, but considering that an American executive of a Dubai company was doing business with the Pakistani government at a location that until recently lay under the Arabian Sea, McCartt was saying more than he knew. He represented a global flow of money and ideas from one instant city to another. Just as McCartt was building an entire upscale neighborhood on new land that was largely segregated from the rest of the city, many proposals in other cities seemed to focus less on improving an existing city than on starting fresh. Officials in Mumbai planned to demolish one of the city's famous slums to make room for upscale tow-ers. They were actually building an entire satellite city of the metropolis, called Navi Mumbai, or New Mumbai, which quickly grew to a population of two million. At Inchon, South Korea, the port for the megacity of Seoul, developers were planning a new city on a man-made island; an American firm was leading the project. Chinese officials brought in a Chilean planner attached to a Lon-don firm to help design a satellite city outside the absurdly growing metropolis of Shanghai.

However, the global financial crisis was complicating or choking off such projects, including the forty-five towers planned by Emaar. In the two years after I met McCartt, Emaar insisted it was going ahead with its Karachi devel-opment, but when I dropped by Crescent Bay in early 2010, everything looked about the same as it had in 2008. Ignoring a guard who tried to stop me, I got a glimpse around the edge of a solid boundary wall and saw no sign of new construction.

Steve McCartt was no longer employed by Emaar. The company wouldn't say where he had gone or why, and e-mails to his address bounced back. Where was he in the world? I didn't know necessarily.

THESE DISAPPOINTMENTS brought to mind of an old rumor that swept the city in the 1990s, a terrible period of ethnic violence. The rumor said that Karachi was about to become the new Hong Kong.

People repeating this rumor presumed that when Hong Kong reverted from British to Chinese control in 1996, its corporate executives and bankers would need to relocate rather than do business under a Communist government—and why not Karachi as their alternative? It was a poignant rumor because, on the surface, the stories of these two instant cities were similar. Each port city became a destination for refugees in the shifting political landscape after World War II. Each became a center of textile mills and other industries. Yet the different outcomes were profound. Hong Kong found ways to house its people within the law. Its British overlords managed a working relationship with the giant nation next door. The government maintained order, and the rules did not change every few years. Hong Kong competed against other cities for the business of increasingly mobile firms, and became the home of Asian corporate headquarters. And as the British handover of power approached in the 1990s, Chinese officials promised to preserve Hong Kong's institutions.

Karachi, by contrast, was still struggling with ethnic and religious conflicts. National governments were constantly changing, and they burned resources on conflicts with the giant nation next door. Much of the economy was off the books, and it was only in the barest sense that the government maintained law and order. Instead of fleeing from Hong Kong to Karachi, some people fled the other way. Baseer Naweed was one who did, having arrived in Karachi in 1948, when he was about one year old. Naweed grew up to become a left-wing activist, a journalist, and a radio broadcaster in Karachi. He believed that it was in response to his broadcasts that in 2005 his son was kidnapped, tortured, and killed. The onetime migrant became a migrant again. He moved his surviving family to the safety of Hong Kong, where he took a job at the Asian Human Rights Commission, monitoring human rights abuses in Pakistan.

MANY TIMES IN KARACHI I encountered men and women who took a clear-eyed view of their city's course and cheerfully worked to adjust the tiller. Such a man was Adnan Asdar, a Karachi corporate executive who had a hand in many of Karachi's major building projects, and also had an inclination to public service. We have already glimpsed Adnan in our story; he was the businessman who, at the time of the Ashura bombing, chanced to meet a young Fulbright scholar recently returned from America. The scholar, Zeeshan Usmani, said he had been developing software to analyze suicide bombings, and it was characteristic of Adnan that he did not simply nod his head and say how interesting this was. He started calling contacts within the police department. Soon the Fulbright scholar was standing with top police officials by the banyan tree at the Lighthouse Centre, looking over the bloody street and debris; he later gave a presentation to top law enforcement officials, offering his own analysis of what happened on December 28, 2009.

Adnan took a similarly active approach when he heard that I was coming on one of my visits to Karachi. He'd heard about me through his brother, who had moved to America and become a distinguished academic at the University of Texas. With nothing more to go on than that, Adnan said he would throw open the city to me. And it was thanks to Adnan that I got a look at the Karachi waterfront by sea. He had an architect friend who'd reconditioned an old fishing boat as a pleasure craft, and on this wood-hulled craft the three of us motored past some of Karachi's newest and most expensive towers.

Adnan had bright eyes, a joyous laugh, and hair just long enough that it blew around in the wind. Early in the boat ride he told a story that suggested his eagerness to improve the city, and also suggested that Karachi's physical structure symbolized wider trouble. "My training," he said, "was in forensic engineering—failure investigations." It was the science of understanding why buildings collapsed. Adnan had degrees from the universities of Minnesota and Wisconsin, but when he returned to Pakistan he discovered he couldn't make a living from failure investigations. "Over here, basically, for failures, they want to hush it up. Nobody takes nobody to court. They would rather just quietly put it under the carpet and forget about it, and that's how life is. The idea of forensic engineering, especially in a country like ours, is to somehow be able to educate people not to make the same mistakes," he said, but "buildings are not properly insured, so there's no lawyers. It's always hushed up." Engineers were reluctant to share their experiences, especially if they were embarrassing. And so mistakes *were* repeated, such as the time some years before when a number of buildings collapsed because their flat-slab concrete floors had not been properly reinforced. Adnan said he never made a single rupee from forensic engineering in Karachi. He moved into a different business, although he had on occasion persuaded building owners to allow him to investigate a disaster for free.

As Adnan spoke, we were floating down a broad estuary toward the Arabian Sea. On the left bank we could see the populous and scrambled zone called Korangi, the district where the great planner Doxiadis had tried to create an orderly suburb half a century before, only to be overtaken by events. Today much of the area's pollution flowed into the waters that floated our boat, and although the water was brilliant blue in the afternoon sun, Adnan's architect friend said we were lucky to encounter it at high tide: "At low tide, you can barely breathe because it's so polluted. Untreated tannery water, sewage, feces, chemicals."

The right bank was a different world. We steered parallel to the shoreline of the sandy peninsula that was the focus of so much of Karachi's newest development. We passed a series of condominium towers built by a firm from Singapore. We passed a row of slope-roofed waterfront houses, some of which appeared to have their own swimming pools—fair enough, since the owners wouldn't have been wise to swim in the estuary. Nearby stretched the green fairways of a golf course and the building complex of the exclusive Raffles Club, part of an international chain, which advertised "6-star facilities." If we followed the peninsula around to the far side we would pass the gigantic Emaar development, the location of the forty-five office towers that were planned to rise if the Dubai firm could find the funding.

Adnan explained that the entire peninsula to our right—oceanside real estate roughly the size of midtown Manhattan—was being developed by Pakistan's military. The military was the single most important property owner in the city. "They have a program in the military, which is that every officer, if he retires as a captain or a major, he gets one plot, if he retires as a colonel or a brigadier he gets one residential plot, and one commercial plot. They get it at a very, very minimal price, and they can commercially sell that to anybody outside. And so it's basically they're giving it away to their officers as a pension."

The notion of giving land to retiring soldiers stretched back at least as far as ancient Roman times, but Pakistan was one of a number of modern nations where the military had gradually insinuated itself into the broader economy— Egypt, Iran, and China were others. Pakistan's military-run enterprises produced pharmaceuticals and cereals. "They have cement factories, they have sugar plants," said Adnan. "The military has three construction companies, who do private and government jobs. They buy equipment under the military rules, which is free of any import tax, and come and compete with the private sector." The army controlled vast "cantonment" areas in every city where they could develop land, generating traffic and pollution without any accountability to local governments; this was maddening to Karachi's mayor, Mustafa Kamal, who struggled during his term in office to change the arrangement. The military also sponsored organizations like the Defence Housing Authority of Karachi, which controlled the sandy peninsula. Its president was the commander of the army corps based at Karachi—which made that military officer one of the largest land developers in the country.

Adnan's architect friend, Tariq Alexander Qaiser, gestured toward the golf course. He called my attention to stadium lights along the fairways. "We have electricity outages," he said. "They have night golf."

"Night golf?"

"Night golf. Fully lit."

"Here we have a situation where people are dying," Adnan said, "and people are not able to have electricity for the kids having their exams going on. And over here, when you come back in the evening, you see night golf."

In 2007 a Pakistani researcher, Ayesha Siddiqa, had published a book that detailed the military's chokehold on the economy. The army tried and failed to suppress the book, but it was hard to see why they went to the trouble. Their dominance was obvious to anyone who looked around. When we took our cruise in 2008, Pakistan's military was apparently in retreat as a new democratic government settled into office. Yet my two guides insisted that the army was so firmly in control of the economy that Pakistan's recent elections made no difference. Too much power was concentrated in the hands of generals who would listen to politicians only when it suited their purposes. The men who had much of the money also had the guns.

ADNAN'S SKEPTICISM about the system was striking because he prospered in it. He was chief executive of a communications company, which ran a fiber-optic cable network across the country and wired many Karachi buildings. He worked in a renovated old garment factory—a space designed by his wife, Mahboob Khan, who was a busy architect. Several times I visited their home in the seaside neighborhood of Clifton. It was a clean and modern space with living room windows offering a view of little reflecting pools in their yard. It was an understated house, with little ornamentation, but with fine materials all the way through—stone-tiled floors, artfully designed furniture, the kind of house that made you appreciate the taste of the people in it. The house lacked only one thing that could be found in many upscale Karachi homes, as we discovered when the electricity went out in one of the city's nightly blackouts.

We sat for a moment in pitch dark.

"Kids, bring the generator out," Mahboob called, and the children began feeling their way upstairs.

"We don't have a generator," Adnan explained.

"They're going to bring a flashlight or a candle?" I asked.

"That's the running joke," Mahboob said.

"My wife in particular, she doesn't want a generator in this house because we feel that if the rest of the city is suffering, everybody should learn how it is."

The children returned with candles as we talked.

Mahboob was unhappy with the buildings she designed. Her firm designed hotels and shopping malls for the affluent, for which the owners preferred massive sheets of glass, inappropriate for such a hot and sunny climate. "Unfortunately the bottom line is the money. You know, how much they can earn and what will sell. And it's to the last cent that they count their money. I think this capitalistic fever generates out of your country, you know. And that's where it started, and we've all become part of that global hunger for money."

She started talking about buildings from the colonial era, before air conditioning. They fascinated her as much as they had captivated the planner Constantinos Doxiadis long ago. Thick walls could stay cooler, and buildings could be designed to catch Karachi's sea breeze and channel it through the rooms. This would lower energy and building costs, bringing tolerable housing within range of more people. Cheap homes would have to be small, but could be livable if surrounded by well-designed public spaces.

"I'll tell you one thing," she said. "You've met us at a point where we want to change direction. Okay? I love my work, I love my family, I love my husband, I love my country, I love my city, okay? But right now I want to change directions for the next twenty years of my life, and hopefully God will give me the next twenty years to do it."

Adnan and Mahboob were deciding to go into the low-income housing business. They almost seemed to be deciding as they sat there. She had the skill to design a housing project; he had the energy to get it done.

The next time I saw them, Adnan took me out to see a project his wife had designed in the 1990s. A cooperative of Karachi milkmen built themselves an apartment complex, and since milkmen were not well paid this was a low-income housing project. One of the city's great philanthropies, the Aga Khan Foundation, hired Mahboob to make the plans for a development that covered the equivalent of several city blocks. I walked the streets between apartment buildings. A man passed by, brushing the pavers clean with a straw broom; I saw neither broken pavement nor piles of garbage. Rows of little trees lined the streets, leaves and branches cut into perfect spheres. The tan walls were decorated with bas-relief sculptures of trees. Parks and open spaces were weaved into the design. Here and there I saw a high rectangular water tower; this was one neighborhood where the water pressure would rarely drop off to nothing. Nor would the air conditioning ever go out in these buildings, because there was no air conditioning. The buildings were designed to be tolerable without it, with the rooms angled to catch the prevailing breeze. Stairwells and halls were open to the air, breaking up the façades of the buildings and giving the upper floors a whimsical feel—I thought of the catwalks over a theater stage.

Adnan took me to this project partly out of pride in his wife's work, and partly to illustrate his ambition. "This is what I want to multiply by thousands and thousands," he said. Since I'd last seen him, he had formed a company he called Affordable Housing, Private, Ltd. He wanted to build and sell homes at considerably below the market rate. He had experience and connections in the construction business, and of course he already had an architect whose work he admired. He approached the "People's Housing Cell" of the provincial government, which gave him permission to build on some acreage out near the Northern Bypass, the highway that rounded the edge of the city.

I went to see the civil servant who ran the housing cell, Zia-ul Islam. Adnan was "very idealistic," Islam said. "He wants to prove, and I want to prove with him, that poor people can live in decent housing without spending exorbitant amounts, and we can do it if the government and the private sector get together. Unfortunately the private sector in housing, they've become used to a profit ratio of something like 100 to 150 percent." Housing prices would drop, argued Islam, "if we can bring that down to 10 or 15 percent. And so as far as Adnan is concerned, I know he's not really into making a lot of profits, break even is fine." Zia and I talked over the possibilities in his windowless government office, where he smoked cigarettes as a portrait of Jinnah studied us grimly from the wall. Zia said Adnan was virtually the only developer he'd found in Karachi who was willing to work within the government's constraints. Adnan's goal was to "make a model that others can follow," but it wasn't clear yet who would do so.

Adnan nevertheless worked up detailed plans. His company intended to sell only to people making less than about $175 a month. He intended to prevent politicians from choosing who got a cheap house. ("Whenever you give these as gifts to your party workers," Adnan told me, "they will start selling, they will never live here.") Successful applicants would be chosen through a process overseen by the global civil-society group Transparency International. Homebuyers would be required to stay about five years, but if after that they were able to sell the houses on the free market at a profit, Adnan would heartily approve. The value of the house could help to lift a family out of poverty.

One day Adnan took me to see the property where he expected to begin. His driver, who went by the name James, steered us past the funhouse-mirror

Adnan Asdar.

world that was the outer reaches of Karachi. We passed enormous but shabbily built houses, the local equivalent of McMansions. We passed apartment buildings and sandy lots. Adnan called a halt at a bazaar built on a street median. "You have to see this," he said. Mats on bamboo poles kept sunlight out of the improvised shops. We ducked under a mat into a pool hall, with a magnificent table of carved wood and green velvet sitting on the earthen median. The owner said it was a good business. He had customers before noon, two young men who were paying him ten rupees per game, about twelve cents.

Later, James had to stop the car at a paramilitary checkpoint, where Rangers held Kalashnikov rifles as they questioned each passing driver. This was near the end of the killing spree in May. The checkpoint was part of the government's response. Adnan said a few words through his open window and the gunman waved us on. We passed a massive row of letters, propped up on steel braces like the Hollywood sign, creating a vision in the desert:

DREAMWORLD

I made a note of the sign, meaning to investigate another time. We stayed on course for Adnan's dream, rolling farther into the scrambled suburbs—paved

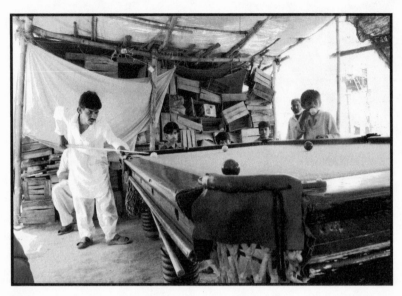

Ten rupees per game.

roads, unpaved roads, half-built roads ending abruptly. We bounced for several hundred yards across bare desert. We came to a thickly populated area, where finished houses alternated with the cinderblock walls of half-built homes under construction. Then we saw a stretch of open desert.

"This is the first lot of fifty acres," Adnan said, as James slowed the car. Adnan pointed out boundary walls and half-built homes along the edges of the property—what was supposed to be *his* property. "All of this is illegal," he said. "They're encroached on the plan. This land is supposed to extend all the way up close to the highway. This is all encroached, so some negotiations are taking place." Adnan was organizing his company and moving swiftly, but the land grabbers had been organized for a very long time, and were moving more swiftly still. He gestured to a tangle of concrete-block walls. "When I came here three months ago, none of the walls were here."

James began pointing out signs that had been painted on the concrete blocks. *Qalat Altaf,* one said—Altaf's Fort. It was a reference to Altaf Hussain, the leader of the MQM. "They put down Altaf over here," James said, "so they know that no other political party will take it."

Adnan read another sign in Urdu. " 'Only Altaf,' " he said. "Which basically gives legitimacy that 'This is an MQM area, don't try to be funny.' "

Part of Adnan's property was still clear desert, in the shape of a trapezoid, wider at one end than the other. One side was defined by the road and an open concrete sewer. The far side was lined by the channel of the Lyari River. Mahboob already had plans to make a green recreation area along the riverside. All they had to do was get the project done before somebody stole what remained of the land.

"This is it, chief," Adnan said as we looked around.

We studied his fifty acres.

There were thousands of illegal homes on all sides.

ADNAN WAS a civic booster, often taking detours in our journeys to show me a free hospital or a trade school, but he proved equally willing to help me find evidence of a dream gone astray. He helped me find the place where, in 1958, Pakistan's military ruler Ayub Khan resolved to fix his city's greatest problem. I wanted to find the spot where the general posed with his shovel at the groundbreaking for the great suburb of Korangi. Even if I could not find the exact place, I was curious to see the suburb he built. The hunt was harder than expected. The suburb wasn't a distinct place anymore. Karachi had exploded outward and swallowed it. People pointed me in the approximate direction, within the two modern areas called Landhi and Korangi, full of factories and bazaars and the homes of more than a million people. But this was roughly the same as if I asked New Yorkers for directions to Levittown, an early mass-produced suburb in America, and people only knew that it must be somewhere out on Long Island.

Then I mentioned the problem to Adnan, whose face brightened. "My office is right near there," he said—right near there approximately. He undertook to find some of the original buildings: "Don't worry about it, chief," he said. "I will take you there on Monday."

Monday came and went without news. Adnan said he had a man who was picking the best spot.

While I never doubted that Adnan would find the location, I began to wonder how much of the original suburb was available to see. I thought of ancient cities I had seen in my travels, like the ruins of Babylon in modern-day Iraq. In that city I stood at a place where archaeologists had dug down to expose ancient archways and rooms. Those structures were many feet below ground level, having sunk under centuries of human refuse and newer construction and sand. That was also the case with ruins in northern Pakistan, where I visited an ancient city called Sirkap. It was actually the ruins of *three* cities, one atop another. My guide pointed out the stone opening of a drainage pipe from more than two thousand years ago, now visible at the bottom of a pit some thirty feet below the current level of the ground.

So I understood that a lot could happen to a city over time. Rarely is anything really built for posterity. But those ancient cities took centuries to grow, flourish, decline, and submerge. Was it possible that Karachi was changing so quickly that thousands of modern houses, parks, and streets went underground in fifty years?

ON WEDNESDAY Adnan called me to his office in Korangi. He didn't know where Ayub had dug his shovel in the ground, but a real estate agent had found him some of the original homes. We climbed in the back of his car and James drove along Korangi's busy roads. Along the way we crashed into a three-wheeled rickshaw, a low-speed collision, no harm done. Then we parked in front of a row of shops and continued on foot, turning onto a street that would have been uncomfortably narrow for the car.

The street was made of packed sand and debris, with high houses crowding it so tightly that it was completely shaded at five o'clock on a late May afternoon. A short distance from the corner we encountered a much smaller house, hardly more than eight feet above the level of the street. The house was set back from the lane, with room for a twisting old tree in front. The house had been white once. Its decorative metal door appeared to be off its hinges.

People were beginning to crowd around us, as commonly happened when a stranger like me appeared in an out-of-the-way neighborhood. "Does somebody live here?" I asked, gesturing toward the tiny house, and an elderly woman came forward. Her strands of gray hair ran in several directions, as did the last of her teeth, and there was a hazy look in her eyes. We established, in a short if rambling conversation, that she had come from India around 1947. She moved into this little house when it was new, sometime soon after 1958.

Now other people stepped forward. They said many families in the neighborhood had come from India after Partition. Until this neighborhood was built, they lived as refugees near the future site of Jinnah's tomb. Mumtaz Ahmed, who had a white cap and deep-set eyes and a goatee peppered with

An original Korangi home with its original resident.

gray, said that around 1960 every house in the neighborhood resembled the old woman's one-story home. "It was a wonderful design," he said, "it was an excellent design, but over the years, people have just encroached here and there."

"What was good about the design?"

"The roads were wide, there were a lot of parks, and there were other amenities, school facilities." But over the years the parks were covered over—mainly with wedding halls. The streets narrowed as people replaced their tiny houses with larger ones, capturing public space to make more private space. The old woman's original house was set at least twenty feet farther back from the street than the newer houses on either side of it. This explained why the generous lane laid out by the planner Constantinos Doxiadis was now a shadowy gulley.

Something else happened. The street began to rise, built up by decades of accumulated garbage and sediment from monsoon floods. Years ago, an open sewer drained off stormwater. Later, the sewer was covered—seemingly an improvement—but the city never cleared it when it clogged. "When it was an open drain," Mumtaz said, as others in the crowd agreed, "at least once a year, we could clear it out with a shovel or something." Instead, as the sewer became useless and the street level rose, houses began to flood in monsoon season. The old woman's house from Ayub's time was built two feet above the ground; now it was two feet *below,* which explained why it seemed so short. The house was gradually going underground.

Some people reacted to this by building higher houses, with higher first floors. But the street kept rising.

We walked down the street to see Mumtaz Ahmed's house, which was one of the newer ones, handsome and brick-fronted and bay-windowed. He sat on his smooth concrete front porch, which was a little less than two feet above ground level; his feet rested on the ground.

The porch was three and a half feet high when he built it.

Before many years passed, Mumtaz's house would be as worthless as the old woman's.

On that street I finally understood what happened to those ancient cities I had seen; this must have been roughly the way that Babylon went underground, and the way that cities were layered on top of cities at Sirkap. Great empires and grand dreams were buried by simple entropy. Bad drainage. Failure to clean the sewers. Failure to pick up the garbage. Failure to look after the neighbors. Failure to respect the greater good. Failure to govern. Failure, in short, to find workable solutions to chronic problems.

Mumtaz Ahmed's short history of his neighborhood offered evidence of a law of the instant city. When a growing city maintained public services and protected the public interest, then private interests had a chance to prosper.

But when the public interest was neglected and the environment was debased, then private interests, too, would be steadily and inexorably destroyed.

14 | DREAMWORLD

Once in the dusty industrial zone known as SITE Town, I walked into a warren of buildings and climbed the wrong stairway by mistake. At the top of the stairs I encountered the kind of people whose desire shaped and reshaped Karachi from 1947, and helped to build the city as we saw it on December 28, 2009.

I stood in a concrete hallway lined by storage lockers, each with a roll-down metal gate. Young men were folding blankets and sheets, packing them in plastic. It was a fabric wholesaler, and everybody who worked there had come to Karachi within the last ten years.

A young man named Afridi ran the business from a glass-topped table shoved into one of the storage lockers. He wore trendy glasses with black rectangular frames. He had a tightly shaved goatee, and his gray *shalwar kameez* was a cut fancier than normal, with a yellow design stitched into the cuffs and the collar. Afridi said he was only twenty, but had his name written in Arabic script on the business sign at the bottom of the stairs. He told me he was born in the Swat Valley in Pakistan's far northwest, lately famous for battles between the army and Taliban insurgents. In his village Afridi became consumed with the idea of getting an education. He told his parents he could do it if they would only send him to stay with relatives in Karachi. "I forced them," he said. He was disappointed with the quality of the government-run secondary school where he finally enrolled in Karachi, but he learned enough to converse with me in English. Village elders were impressed with him and gave him money to start this firm in Karachi. It was an investment for the elders. When they needed a little money, they called Afridi and asked him to send some back to the village.

Afridi.

Afridi managed the other young men, who had come from the same village in Swat. They stayed with relations or other people from their village while earning three hundred to four hundred rupees per day—four or five dollars at that time. "It's better than Swat," one said.

The young men maintained ties with their distant village, which wasn't hard. Around the corner from Afridi's business, a man sat behind a wooden table on the sidewalk, selling bus tickets for five daily departures to the far northwest. Each bus went to Peshawar, at the edge of the mountains, then onward to the next valley over from Swat. The ride cost about fourteen dollars, or sixteen for passengers who preferred an air-conditioned bus.

Many companies served similar routes, which underlined a reality of the city. A metropolitan area is commonly defined as a city and all the settlements around it that are linked to the city by commuting. By that definition, far northwestern Pakistan would count as part of the Karachi metropolitan area. People regularly commute a thousand miles home to their villages. The bus manager at the desk told me the peak travel time came soon after men collected their paychecks at the end of each month; they bought tickets home, intending to return many days later.

This commuting pattern meant that the migrant flow could change quickly. If conditions grew worse in the northwest, the commuters could draw friends and relatives southward. If jobs dried up in Karachi, the commuters could go home permanently. This was called reverse migration, and many instant cities experienced it. Shanghai, for example, breathed in millions of migrants when times were good, then breathed them out during the economic crisis of 2008 and 2009. Waitresses and factory workers reluctantly returned to farms and villages.

Afridi, the fabric wholesaler, said the recent pattern from the Swat Valley was clear. "In the last two years, there are more people coming," he said. Those two years had been an especially hard time of fighting in Swat; at one point the army required all civilians to temporarily leave their homes. "So they are migrating to Karachi. Everybody knows the reason behind it. First one person from a family comes here, and then they call to the others, 'We have got opportunity for earning money or the peaceful life,' so they also come here."

"Is it a peaceful life in Karachi?"

"Yes," he answered, and then reconsidered. "In Pakistan, there isn't any city which is peaceful." Of Karachi he said, "I cannot say it's peaceful, but it may be better."

Afridi and his employees lived a provisional existence. They served as social and economic barometers, moving north or south depending on conditions. Migration like theirs is not a single act. It's a process.

AFRIDI WASN'T MARRIED YET. "I'm going to, *inshallah*," he said—using the Arabic word that means "God willing." If God willed it he would settle down, and then his life would change. He would put down roots. He would become more like Mohammad Nader of the Edhi ambulance service, who had made his choice to settle down some years ago.

From time to time I talked with Nader, the migrant who had a gun pointed at his head during the political disturbances in 2007. When I reached out to him in early 2010, he welcomed me to visit his apartment. He came out to the edge of his unauthorized neighborhood to meet the car, walking down the busy street in a pale blue *shalwar kameez*, his mop of black hair the same as I remembered, his smooth-shaven face friendly and open. He settled into the car and directed the driver down narrow streets. There wasn't any traffic. There couldn't be on streets like this. The car scraped against steps and protruding pipes on either side of the lane. We crept past children burning trash. Finally the street came to a T, where we disembarked and climbed dimly lit stairs.

Nader bid me to sit in a slot of a room, lit by a single high window. We talked by the light that filtered through a perforated concrete screen in front of the window, which cut down on the glare and heat from the sun. There was a bed along one wall, and an ornate gold-accented bench along another. A ceiling fan hung overhead. A barrel of water stood out in the hallway. Nader introduced me to his father, who wore his beard dyed orange in the style of many Pashtuns.

This was the last time I had seen Nader since the Ashura bombing, and he told me how he had carried away some of the dead and injured who were strewn on Jinnah Road that day. He handed me an Urdu-language newspaper he had been saving. The entire front page was bordered in black and covered with photos of mutilated bodies, as well as the vivid orange flames of buildings on fire.

Nader had missed the follow-up bombings on February 5, 2010; he told me he'd had a premonition about the day and stayed home. Otherwise he might have been passing the time between ambulance runs in the little booth the Edhis maintained just outside the Jinnah hospital emergency room, near the spot where the bomb exploded that day, and where the wandering video monitor with the unexploded bomb was finally placed.

"So do you still like this work?" I asked.

"What else can I do?" he replied. "There is no option. I don't like this business, because of my daughters, but there is no option. I can't switch anywhere, so I am just doing this."

Looking at his words on this page, it seems obvious that I should have expected such an answer. But I was surprised. I'd assumed he enjoyed moving about the city and helping people in distress. I'd assumed he did the job because he liked it. I asked him to remind me how much he earned; he said fifty-five hundred rupees per month. It seemed like a good salary a few years ago, but inflation had lately increased his rent—to fifty-five hundred rupees per month.

"All my salary goes to the rent," he said, "and my wife, she sews clothes as a tailor. So she is managing the food."

I remembered his romantic story of how he'd come to Karachi—riding the train called the Khyber Mail from the northwestern hills, attending a wedding, meeting a girl, falling in love. "Is living in Karachi as good as you had hoped it would be?"

"It is not a place to live. I just got trapped."

There was an awkward pause. The ceiling fan spun.

"So you want to leave?"

"I will not leave now. I will wait until conditions are better. I will save some money, and then I will leave."

"How are you going to save money?"

"I don't know."

I had come to Nader's home with my Pakistani colleague Amar Guriro, who interpreted our talk. Now Amar had a question. Amar, too, was a young man from the countryside, the son of a poor tailor. Karachi did not always treat Amar well, but he loved it. He loved working as a newspaper reporter, even though his employer failed to make the payroll for months at a time. Amar so loved the city's buildings and their history that we could hardly go anywhere without his suggesting that we stop to admire some old building or shrine. He liked to tell friends back in his village, "If you come to Karachi for a few days you will hate it, but if you come to Karachi for forty days, you will love it and never want to leave," and his enthusiasm for the city informed the question he asked of Mohammad Nader: "Is it possible to leave Karachi after living here for so long?"

Nader answered instantly. "My heart says every day to leave this place."

Later Nader added that because his wife came from Karachi, it would be hard to persuade her to move to his home village. She was a city girl. But he ached to go.

His words brought to mind a conversation I'd had with a Karachi psychiatrist, who'd been living in Karachi since he migrated to the city in 1948. The elderly psychiatrist said that massive numbers of people in Karachi were suffering from post-traumatic stress, or PTS, the kind of mental anguish popularly associated with survivors from a war. It usually went untreated. Many people responded to Karachi's trouble by living in a lower gear, limiting their ambitions and moving about like "the living dead." They'd lost hope, he said.

Nader seemed to have lost hope for himself, though he still hoped for the next generation. His two daughters wandered in the room, two and three years old, both with their hair cropped short. They were curious, quiet, well-behaved. Both seemed to be dressed in their finest clothes for my visit, one with a faux-fur collar and the other in a red shirt bordered with gold. "I want to send them to an English school," Nader said. "It is the modern language. I spend my life in a bad way. I don't want my children to be the same."

His wife Shaheen arrived next, walking in from an adjoining room where several women of the extended family had been keeping away from the male visitors. Shaheen, as a Karachi woman, felt confident enough to come out and say hello. She had a beautiful red-and-gold *dupatta* wrapped around her head.

The family sat for a photograph on the ornate bench. Nader's father sat stiffly with his glasses and orange-tinted beard. Shaheen folded her hands on her lap and looked down in a traditional pose of modesty. The children gazed at the camera, and Mohammad Nader sat in the middle, head tilted to one side as he studied the camera, the face of a man who was trying not to look sad.

Mohammed Nader (center) and family.

NADER'S BOSS, Abdul Sattar Edhi, was also thinking of the future. "The next generation will not be like this," the old man said when I visited him, and our conversation turned to the city's violence.

This migrant who'd seen everything in Karachi since 1947 was sitting in his windowless office, thinking of children now being born. "They will think differently," Edhi said. "People are changing a lot now; they are thinking of the mistakes that were done earlier; so it will not go like this forever. It will change." Someday, people would look beyond their ethnic and religious differences.

At another point, the old man said that crime would stop if only Islamic law could be imposed. Chop off a few hands, he said, and people would behave.

I pondered this. "Is this country becoming more religious?" I asked.

"Not particularly," he answered mildly, and his remark about chopping hands began to seem like an old man's frustration rather than a serious position, like an American who said crime would decrease if the cops shot a few robbers on sight. A moment later he spoke thoughtfully. He said Islam could never be imposed by the government. People would have to adopt it freely or not at all. "We always talk about humanity, and tolerating each other. And it will happen," he said. The people "will understand later on that they were being used by bad politicians."

We were sitting with Edhi's son Faisal, who had cleared bodies after the Ashura blast and helped to disarm the bomb at the Jinnah hospital. Edhi expected his son to see better times. "My family will continue my foundation. My daughter; my daughter's son; my own son; my wife; they are going to keep this going."

Knowing that Edhi's wife was deeply involved in his charitable work, I asked if I could meet her. He said I could. She was right there in the Edhi headquarters.

We walked up another flight of uneven stairs. If there is one consistent difference between the architecture of the West and that of the developing world, it is in the small but revealing matter of stairs. Studies show that people are less likely to trip when each step is the same height and depth. American building codes enforce this idea, but improvisation prevails in Pakistan—it's normal to pick your way up steps of several heights and depths. So it is that Americans make a smooth and ordered climb in a world that was designed for their comfort and safety in ways they may not even realize, while Pakistanis must adjust and learn the feel of every step. Edhi climbed swiftly on the steps. The stairway turned, and he was out of sight; I hurried to keep up. Finally we came to a sparse room painted a sort of pale hospital blue. Two cots, a wooden bench, a plastic-framed mirror hanging on the wall: other than a few end tables, that was all the furniture in the apartment.

Bilquis Edhi stood to greet me and then sat cross-legged on a bed. She must have been at least twenty years younger than her husband, with a smooth and handsome face. She draped a patterned orange *dupatta* over her hair, a cloth that matched her long shirt. Abdul Sattar took a chair in the corner. Faisal brought in a chair for himself.

I was just settling in to ask a few questions, but Bilquis required no questioning. Instead she launched into a diatribe. It seemed as if she had been sitting there waiting to vent to the next person who came in the door. "Anywhere in the world a woman is a slave," she announced.

The remark was so unexpected that I assumed she was saying it to be humorous. "Are you a slave?" I asked.

"Yes, I am a kind of slave," she said with a gesture toward the old man sitting contentedly in the corner. "I am living with him because my children would have suffered if I left. When a man grows old he is no good to women."

She repeated this point several different ways. Abdul Sattar Edhi had a hint of a smile on his face as he listened, and finally offered a salvo of his own. "There should be four wives," he said.

Bilquis did not take the bait. "He is married to the foundation," she said. "He has never spent a full day with me. He is married to the foundation first. He is eighty-five," she added, saying that he failed to take care of himself. "If some emergency happens he becomes twenty."

She was beginning a performance that would continue for at least half an hour, and the conversation grew more involved as Bilquis began to speak of Abdul Sattar's history with women. It emerged that he had a thing for the nurses and secretaries who worked in Edhi Tower. Long before Bilquis met him, he was in love with a nurse for a dozen years, but in the end she left him. "Women would not marry him because he was a strict man, and a beggar," Bilquis said. "Back then all he had was his dispensary and one ambulance, he was making four or five thousand rupees per month." Finally the nurse that Edhi loved abandoned him and "married a moneylender."

Next, Bilquis came to work for Edhi as a very young woman in 1964. She studied to become a midwife in a course that Edhi sponsored, and she caught Edhi's eye. They married, had four children, and adopted a fifth. Bilquis said she stayed with him even though he paid no attention to her and abused his own health. He was diabetic. He'd had bypass surgery. Still he went riding around in ambulances.

"Do you ever tell him to take care of himself?"

"He never listens to me!" she shouted. "He has never given us a gift or even a penny. As for vacations, he has always taken us in an ambulance when he had a body to shift somewhere. He takes us out a couple hours into some rural area, and we would never stay in a hotel."

Abdul Sattar Edhi sat with his hands folded on his lap, still with a wry smile on his face. "This is very good entertainment," he said.

Her stream of complaints went on. It was like listening to an angry stand-up comedian. Faisal Edhi was laughing; I was laughing. I began to sense that it was an act, and maybe one she had performed before, although that didn't mean her anger was staged. Maybe her humorous approach also allowed her to vent a little truth.

Bilquis Edhi and Abdul Sattar Edhi.

She went on for so long that I finally asked, "What do you like about this guy?"

"He's a good man," she said. "My mother used to say he is *only* a good man, but he will not provide enough for you. I had a dream to have a nice house, but he never would allow it," she said, with a look around their single bare room.

She went on to reveal that in 1980, after more than a decade of marriage to Bilquis, Abdul Sattar took a second wife. Again it was a woman who worked for him. Bilquis waited; the latest young item eventually left.

"What did you think of him having a second wife?" I asked.

"I don't think anymore. My heart is already broken. I don't think anymore." Later she added, "I have given my whole life to him but he has never given me a house." She said that she believed a woman should not accept a divorce. "Remarriage is the worst thing in life," she said. "It's better to tolerate the first husband."

She began lecturing her son Faisal, one of the next generation of Edhis who would be called to carry on the Edhi enterprises. Bilquis complained that Faisal, too, didn't spend enough time with his wife. She said Faisal should do better. Then she turned back to her husband, the man who, with her help, had for decades done as much as anyone to get the city of Karachi through one day and into the next. "You'll never do anything," she said. "You put your hand in your pocket and thread comes out."

Later, I thought of the young migrant that Abdul Sattar Edhi had been in the 1940s, dreamy and impatient, struggling to pay attention to a movie, wondering what he would be. Finally he embraced an ambition, and it was a soaring ambition, though it involved no outward sign of material success. He held on to that ambition year after year. Along the way, the Edhis had come to represent the character of Karachi—passionate, witty, resilient, and gloriously strange.

And for all of Bilquis's angry words, I sensed that she still loved him. How could she have gone on so bitterly, and at such length, if she did not?

I STILL HAD in my mind the words "Dream World," which I had seen on a giant sign on the edge of the city. I finally looked it up on a website.

> *Welcome to Dreamworld*
> *Dreamworld Resort is the outcome of The*
> *Almighty's Benevolence, Magnificence and*
> *Magnanimity, for which we will remain*
> *indebted, forever.*

Dreamworld appeared to be a combination water park, golf course, and weekend getaway. On its colorful website, the most common word was "Alhamdulillah," which translated as "Praise to God," or "All praise to Allah." The word appeared to be part of Dreamworld's business model. "The BIGGEST Spring Festival of Pakistan was celebrated with its traditional Zest Alhamdulillah!" the website announced. "Dreamworld Treasure Hunt Family Car Rally 2010 went smoothly Alhamdulillah!"

Elsewhere on the site, I read that "the biggest beverage brand of Pakistan, Pepsi, is now the Official Carbonated Drink of Dreamworld resort." Two days later, I stood at a concession stand in the center of the Dreamworld complex and ordered a Pepsi.

Dreamworld was built on a hill, seventy or eighty feet high, overlooking the plains where housing developments were going up in the northeastern part of the city. The hilltop was a launching pad for water slides that twisted down the slope, some hundreds of feet long, with names like Crazy River and Kamikaze. Safety rules were posted in English. Teenagers were plunging down the slides on tubes at 10:30 in the morning. More people were prancing in the beach surf of a giant wave pool, boys in swimsuits, girls modestly attired in pants and T-shirts.

A restaurant overlooked the slides from a little peak on the hill. A higher peak was occupied by a series of "chalets," rooms available for an overnight escape.

The park had opened in the early 1990s. In those days it would have been in the countryside—the jungle, as people sometimes called it. Now the city was spreading around the base of this hill like a flood. "When I came," said the employee at the top of a waterslide, "there were just a few homes over there, but now there are many." I'd seen the houses on the way in, big and boxy and spread out, many surrounded by boundary walls. Here and there stood a half-built apartment building or a corner barbecue restaurant. Some of the roads were fully paved and split by medians; others were gravel. Some city blocks were filled, and others were waiting for new buildings, like unoccupied squares on a chessboard. It was an entire world under construction. We stood at the top of the waterslide, looking out at the suburbs in the haze.

Dreamworld was a membership club, at which members were required to pay a one-time lifetime membership fee of 400,000 rupees, which for most people in Karachi was the equivalent of many years' earnings. There were also monthly maintenance fees. A Dreamworld manager told me there were more than ten thousand members of the club.

That manager, a Karachi native named Michael Shahzad, ushered me into an indoor lounge for a chat. "How has business been the last couple of years?"

Dreamworld. *[Amar Guriro]*

I asked. "Alhamdulillah, good," he said, adding that, "alhamdulillah," this upscale business had hardly been affected by the economic trouble of recent years. Karachi was such a vast city that somebody was always making money. Michael described Dreamworld as a family park, with children's movie nights and games and dances on Sunday nights. "It's a really amazing and romantic facility," he said, and "we have, alhamdulillah, an eighteen-hole golf club." I had seen the fairways, with grass watered just enough to stay alive, stretching across the countryside to one side of the hill.

"What is your competition?" I asked.

"There is no competition. Because the number of activities which we are offering to the members, nobody has. We have a bowling alley, the water rides, indoor activities . . . Alhamdulillah, there are lots of good places. But there's no competition, alhamdulillah."

He said that when he came to work here seven years ago, Dreamworld was surrounded by vacant land and lonely roads and "street dogs. Alhamdulillah, now you see there are lots of houses, and it's very populated."

I didn't comment on Michael's use of the word "alhamdulillah" six times in ten minutes, nor did I mention the word's repeated display on the Dreamworld homepage. For all I knew he was devout and thoroughly grateful to God, and so were the owners who employed him. There was no reason to doubt his sincerity. Still I wondered if, on some level, it was a defense mechanism. Michael was managing a park where people could take a room for the weekend, and where girls and boys were allowed to swim together. The girls did nothing racy, and during my visit most took seats in the shade, but it was an utterly different environment than I had seen in more conservative zones farther north. Once near Peshawar I encountered a pond at the edge of the ruined garden of an ancient Mughal emperor, where scores of boys and young men plunged joyously in the water; when I asked a few dripping boys where the girls were swimming, they shrugged. Girls just had to find somewhere else. Dreamworld reflected the more open ethos of Karachi, but I wondered if the habitual references to God served as an inoculation, reassuring conservatives that people weren't running some kind of sex club up here.

I thanked Michael for his information, and stood up.

"Thank you very much," he said, shaking my hand. "God bless you."

Talking with people around the waterslides and the wave pool, I learned that the park had been opened that morning for a corporate outing. Only for events like this did nonmembers gain admission into Dreamworld. The event was a "Mango Party," sponsored by Engro, a fertilizer company. Engro employees could bring their families, which was how Azeira Channa gained admittance past the uniformed guards at the front gate. She was from the countryside, she said, from a village in northern Sindh. Not long ago her son got a job with the fertilizer company, and when the company transferred him to Karachi he brought his relatives. "I really love Karachi," Azeira said with feeling. "It has lots of opportunities." She loved to go to the Bagh Ibne Qasim, the restored seaside park near the Hindu temple and the shrine of Abdullah Shah Ghazi. Today was her first visit to Dreamworld, and she was delighted to be sitting on a plastic chair in the shade, watching people splash in the wave pool. She sat with her two teenage daughters, who were perfectly confident in speaking with a foreigner. Both the girls had brown skin and beautiful smiles. Both told me they were attending school. Both spoke English, which the mother did not; she spoke Sindhi, the language of the province in which she'd grown up.

The younger daughter, Jamila, was thirteen. She said she wanted to be a pilot when she grew up. "A big airplane," she specified, not a small one.

Later, I went to find my driver. He would normally have waited with the car, but had taken the opportunity to wander the park a little while, snapping pictures with his pocket camera. He'd never been anywhere like Dreamworld. He likely never would again.

PART FOUR

RENEW KARACHI

15 | BIRDS

In the spring of 2010 I traveled to Sau Quarter, another of the neighborhoods built half a century ago during the days of Ayub Khan. This one included a Shia Muslim community, and I went there with two members of a Shia political group who acted as my guides. Walking down a narrow lane, we came to the gate of a house. We removed our shoes as we stepped into the visiting room—many households had such a room, with a separate entrance so outsiders could meet the men without any risk of encountering the women—and here I came face-to-face with Mohammad Raza Zaidi, the man who had talked his way past a policeman to participate in the Ashura procession the previous December.

Zaidi was killed in the bombing, but his family had a photograph of him, staring droopy-eyed at the camera. He must have been somewhere cold; a blue checked jacket was zipped up to his beard. The family had the photo enlarged so that the image of his head and shoulders was at least six feet high, and having made him much larger than life, they propped him in a corner of the visiting room. Zaidi's father and brother greeted me, and we sat on the floor in front of the photo, talking while Zaidi's gigantic face loomed over us.

I asked them who they thought was responsible for the bombing.

"America," said Zaidi's much younger brother Iqbal. "Everywhere there are agents of America. They are either in the shape of the Taliban, or al Qaeda, in another shape. But they are working for American agencies," meaning intelligence agencies, the CIA. "So I believe that they did this blast."

Zaidi's father didn't accept his son's view. "*Nahi, nahi,*" said Mustafa Hussain Zaidi. No, no. America wasn't responsible, that made no sense. He switched briefly to English, and nominated a suspect of his own: "The Pakistan government. Yes," he said, then back to Urdu: "The place was filled with explosive materials, but nobody checked it. I was really surprised that nobody checked. They checked all the way along the route, but not that particular place." Neither the father nor the son said he was satisfied with the police investigation of the bombing. Neither man seemed aware that the police had arrested four members of the extremist group Jundallah.

These arrests should have given the authorities some credit, but in hindsight it was probably better if the family didn't pay attention.

Mustafa Hussain Zaidi with an image of his murdered son.

A few weeks after my visit to Zaidi's family, the Jundallah suspects were taken to the city court in Karachi. At about 3:15 in the afternoon, just after a hearing, police escorted the suspects back to the ground floor, where they stopped a moment to rest. Exactly two policemen were guarding the four terror suspects who were blamed for one of the more awful crimes in the history of the city.

Several gunmen approached, having somehow learned where to find the prisoners. The gunmen hurled hand grenades, killed a constable, and managed to free all four of their Jundallah comrades. The suspects fled in several different directions. Police said they gave chase, killing one of the four suspects, but the other three disappeared along with the men who freed them. The police chief later acknowledged that the posting of two guards was well below the security level that was called for in such a high-profile case. But he added that the police who oversaw the security arrangements deployed whatever resources they had available. He promised to deliver punishment "if we find anyone guilty of negligence."

EVEN AS THE accused bombers slipped away, the consequences of their actions were slowly being erased. The shopkeepers whose businesses had been destroyed on the day of the bombing were beginning to revive their operations.

Construction crews were pouring new concrete foundations for buildings that had been completely destroyed. Burned-out shops were refitted and refilled with balloons, cookware, or home appliances. Now and again I went back to visit Khalid Rashid, the seller of plastic goods who told me how he fruitlessly begged the police to let him defend his burning store on December 28. By March his shop walls were replastered, and an electrician was about to finish wiring the new outlets. By July he was fully restocked. Across the street a building was under construction.

Many shopkeepers did not carry insurance, leaving such matters in the hands of Allah—"God will provide," as several told me. Their faith was rewarded when rich people and taxpayers provided. The government produced compensation checks. Pakistani businesses donated money through the local chamber of commerce. Still more money came from the U.S. Agency for International Development and from the American Business Council, an organization of U.S. firms that were active in Karachi. The United States was not popular in Pakistan, but swiftly made friends at the Bolton Market; everywhere I went among the scorched and broken shops I heard good wishes for America.

Near the spot where the Ashura bomb exploded, the box of wayward scripture had not been replaced. In its place the city had built a white concrete memorial. Its Urdu inscription read:

FOUNDATION STONE
In Memory of the Martyrs of the Day of Ashura
By the Holy Hands of Syed Mustafa Kamal
City Nazim

Motorbike riders crowded Jinnah Road, contending with buses painted circus reds and greens. Shopkeepers on all sides sold curtains, clothes, and ceiling fans. A restaurant served plates of *biryani*, a spiced rice dish commonly topped with meat; the restaurant is called the Delhi Darbar, in honor of the owners' ancestors from nearby India. The used-shoe salesmen in the park hung some of their selection from a rod like prized fish.

Other than the memorial, it was as if nothing had ever happened.

The building of the memorial proved to be one of the last acts of Mustafa Kamal's term as *nazim* of the City District Government of Karachi. The provincial law authorizing the creation of local governments had expired; the leading parties, the People's Party and the MQM, could not agree on a new law. Kamal's office ceased to exist. The mayor and all the other elected officials in Karachi had to clean out their desks and walk away from the Civic Centre and the Karachi Municipal Corporation Building, the old city hall. They were replaced by a caretaker administration of civil servants.

There was no elected government in the city of Karachi. The political impasse continued for many months.

Violence intensified. On August 2, 2010, an MQM politician was murdered. It was an especially brazen killing. The victim was a member of the provincial assembly, and was shot down at a mosque while attending a funeral. The killers raced away on motorcycles. Since the lawmaker was a politician, and also a Shia, whose killing was almost sure to spark chaos and unrest, there was a long list of plausible suspects, but in the absence of evidence the MQM chose to focus on ethnic Pashtuns and their main political party, the ANP. A senior MQM parliamentarian declared that "it doesn't matter" who the killers were; "the fact is the terrorists are enjoying the patronage of the ANP and they are now jointly targeting the MQM." Another senior MQM leader declared, "Every MQM activist will now be looking to pay back the people involved in this heinous act." That night gunmen spread through the city, shooting people and setting Pashtun-run buses on fire.

Edhi ambulances brought casualties to the Jinnah Postgraduate Medical Centre, where a newspaper reporter contacted Dr. Seemin Jamali for information on casualties. "We have received 10 bodies with gunshot wounds," she said. "Currently, we have thirty-eight gunshot wounded with some of them having multiple wounds." Within days, the citywide death toll exceeded one hundred. The entire city shut down for days. Businesses lost billions of rupees in revenue.

Pakistan's situation was deteriorating in many ways. I sent a note of sympathy to Arif Hasan, the urban planner. "Big changes are in the offing in Pakistan and the region," he replied. "The changes are so big that they cannot take place without conflict and disruption of civic life and institutions."

SO THIS IS the instant city in the early twenty-first century. The United Nations estimated Karachi's 2010 population at 13.1 million. City officials believed that the population was several million higher. Nobody really knew. Pakistani law called for a census in 2008, but it was delayed.

If the last known trends were to continue, according to the United Nations, Karachi's population would grow to 16.7 million in 2020, and 18.7 million in 2025. In the space of fifteen years, then, Karachi would add something like 5.6 million people, an amount *greater than the entire current population of the Washington, D.C., metropolitan area, which has accumulated for more than two hundred years.*

Karachi's change reflects a lifetime of change across our urban world. In the summer of 1947, New York was the largest city in history, with a metropolitan area of around twelve million people. The United Nations building was soon to rise on New York's skyline, with banks of tinted glass windows reflecting a world in transition. European cities were barely starting to repair the devastation of the Second World War. Tokyo was rubble. Other cities had been spared, but did not loom large. Lagos, Nigeria, had fewer than three hundred thousand people. Dubai was a speck on a map.

Today Tokyo is the largest urban area the world has ever seen, encompassing around 36 million people. (Metropolitan New York fell behind despite growing to nineteen million.) Tokyo is part of a complex of manufacturing and financial centers along the Pacific Rim—Los Angeles, San Jose, Seattle, Seoul, Shanghai, and Hong Kong, among others. Some are megacities, commonly described as urban areas of ten million or more.

Lagos, São Paulo, and Mexico City are also megacities, and vast as they are, such giants do not encompass most of the world's urban growth. Small cities and even small towns have exploded in size—half a million here, three million there. These smaller cities will encompass most of the world's urban growth between now and the year 2030.

In many cities, migration has brought disparate ethnic, racial, and religious groups into uneasy contact. It happens in Europe (North Africans in Paris, Pakistanis in London) as well as the United States. Is it any wonder that Arizona would become the epicenter for the American debate over illegal immigration? The political and population center is an instant city, metropolitan Phoenix, roughly sixteen times larger than it was in 1950. Anglo migrants from the north arrived along with migrants from Latin America, making an urban area that's almost entirely new, where the rules are still being written.

The resulting social conflicts challenge the very nature of a city, where people come together to do business or share ideas. In his famous speech of August 11, 1947, when he urged citizens to overlook "color, caste or creed," Muhammad Ali Jinnah might well have been stating the creed of urban life. Jinnah said his countrymen should follow the example of Great Britain, which had long ago outgrown its centuries-old conflicts between Protestants and Catholics. Setting aside the exception of Northern Ireland, Jinnah was correct. But if Jinnah's London seemed like the highest example of secular politics, modern-day London seems tense and unsettled. The bombings of London subways and a double-decker bus in 2005 prompted years-long debates about security, as well as broader debates over Muslim immigration. Fear of militants has affected attitudes and even architecture: major buildings are now designed with a view toward defense. In 2010, nothing symbolized this anxiety better than the unveiling of the design for a new U.S. embassy planned for London. It was to be separated from the neighborhood, surrounded by a pond and a trench that brought to mind a castle moat.

WHEN WE BUILD a city, we take our grandest dreams as well as our deepest anxieties and set them in concrete for the next generation. We have reason to be horrified by some aspects of the cities we have built so quickly since 1945, but I am optimistic about what the next generation will do with the cities we bequeath them. I have said that the most powerful force in the instant city is the desire of millions of people to improve their lives, however slightly. Their desire need not forever be thwarted. And with that in mind, we may consider a handful of modest steps that could improve the prospects of our chosen instant city, Karachi.

The first necessity is for Karachi to embrace its tradition of religious diversity. It will surprise many Westerners, and maybe even some Pakistanis, to learn that any part of Pakistan might *have* a tradition of religious diversity. In early 2011, the world was stunned when a Pakistani provincial governor, Salman Taseer, was murdered in Islamabad by one of his own bodyguards, simply because he wanted to modify a blasphemy law that had been used to persecute Christians. Even more stunning news came in May 2011, when the world discovered that Osama bin Laden was able to hide in a Pakistani town for years, apparently able to find enough support within Pakistan to safely sustain himself until he was finally killed in a U.S. military raid. We find different ways of thinking, however, in the history of Karachi. The city was highly diverse and somewhat tolerant before 1947. Even after the disastrous departure of most Hindus, Karachi was more diverse than it seemed. A few Hindus stayed, along with Zoroastrians such as Ardeshir Cowasjee, not to mention varieties of Muslims who have lately been drummed out of the mainstream. Shias have held significant political positions, starting with Muhammad Ali Jinnah himself. There are even Christians in Karachi, who maintain old cathedrals and institutions like St. Patrick's high school.

Many minorities live quietly, blending into their surroundings, but they burst into the headlines on February 5, 2010. When the bomb exploded at the Jinnah Postgraduate Medical Centre, it killed six members of a Christian family who'd come to visit a mother and her newborn child. We can draw a lesson from their sacrifice. If a man plants a bomb in a crowd intending to kill members of one religious minority, and manages at random to kill members of a different one, maybe minorities are more numerous than they seem.

Karachi's diversity is an asset in a world that is fractured along religious lines. If, for example, Karachi's Christians and Hindus were more fully and openly welcomed into public and commercial life, they would effectively become ambassadors for Pakistan. They could explain their country to its detractors, providing a bridge to non-Muslims in India and the West. If religious minorities could say convincingly that they lived in freedom and security, they would compel the world to think differently of Pakistan.

To accomplish this, no Muslim would need to do anything except follow the advice of the founder of Pakistan. Jinnah was right in 1947. He remains right today.

Jinnah's example also demands that Karachi embrace its *ethnic* diversity. Political parties based on ethnicity have been a disaster. Changing will pose a challenge for the Pashtuns' ANP, for the Baloch and Sindhi nationalist groups based in the city, and for the most powerful ethnic party of all, the MQM. In fairness, the MQM has lately tried to broaden its appeal, even changing what its initials stand for, so that instead of "Mohajir National Movement," its name translates as "United National Movement." However, many of the people who must share Karachi with the MQM are unconvinced.

Karachi's failure to embrace its diversity serves as a cautionary tale. But the city can find the antidote within its own history, and in the words of the Karachi native whose portrait hangs on so many walls.

KARACHI WOULD ALSO improve its political situation by protecting a free press. Here, some of the work is already done. Scores of newspapers and television channels are available across Pakistan today, and carry on a rambunctious debate. But it's a selective debate. Even courageous reporters must choose their battles; the wrong detail can bring a threatening phone call or worse. Journalists sometimes truncate their stories to the point that they make no sense unless the reader already knows what is going on. People should not be forced to censor themselves out of fear for their own safety.

It goes without saying that Karachi needs more law and order, but as in many instant cities, the economy has evolved so far outside the law that this is not a straightforward matter. By one estimate, more than half the city lives in unauthorized housing. Every proposal to deal with this situation is fraught with trouble, because millions of people have to live somewhere. The government formed an "anti-encroachment cell" that began to target and tear down illegal housing in 2010. This instantly became a partisan issue when the Pashtuns' ANP contended that Pashtuns' homes were singled out. The program had to be put on hold after gunfights left two dead. Months later, a group of police officers arrested some alleged land grabbers, only to be "suspended, demoted or transferred" soon afterward.

A People's Party spokesman, Taj Haider, told me that the government should become a land dealer itself, selling thousands of plots at low prices. This would help people find cheap homes, and undercut the prices of illegal land suppliers. His argument reminds me of the case for legalizing drugs. It could work—but given Pakistan's corruption, it's hard to imagine politicians selling land at below-market rates without someone finding a way to rake off profits at the expense of the state.

In recent years Karachi did have one advantage. Planning for the entire metropolitan area was brought within the jurisdiction of a single city government, headed for four years by Mustafa Kamal, which could make coordinated efforts to direct development into useful areas. It was an intriguing reform, one that is only a dream for many American metropolitan areas, which usually sprawl awkwardly across city, county, or state borders. Unfortunately, Karachi's advantage was at least temporarily thrown away when the local government law expired. The People's Party and the MQM could not agree on modifications to it.

It was a setback for democracy when elected officials had to leave their offices. Whatever flaws the old law may have had, it would have been better for Karachi if the provincial government had simply renewed the law unchanged and moved on. Doing this would address another necessity for Karachi: stable, predictable governance.

Once I was talking with a senior civil servant who came to the verge of tears. He acknowledged all the problems with Pakistan's national government—yet he wanted that government to finish its five-year term. He didn't want a snap election, a military coup, or a savior. "Let the system work," he begged. Let the five years expire, then let the people vote on another government. People could make more progress than if they were forever starting over from scratch. That was true of Pakistan in general, and Karachi in particular.

It would be better if the government were also efficient and inspired. But it would be an improvement to have any government that maintained order without constantly changing the rules. Business owners and entrepreneurs could know that they had a few years of stability ahead of them. Communities would have breathing space to solve basic problems, as people already do when they dig their own sewers in Orangi. Planners might even have the opportunity to channel growth in ways that would make the city cleaner, greener, and more energy-efficient.

Since 1947, Karachi has suffered an overdose of history. Too much has happened there. History will likely inflict itself on the city again, as Pakistan struggles with its demons. It is not necessary for any politician to add to the uncertainty. If I were allowed to wish only one thing for my friends and acquaintances in Karachi, I would wish for them to have a steady, respectable, boring government.

On the way home from school, Machar Colony.

TOWARD THE END of one of my trips to Karachi, I decided to buy a bird. I'd seen the bird sellers in traffic, holding up their wares in plastic nets. These were the birds that young men collected so that drivers could pay to set them free. We stopped the car on a street corner and rolled down the window to signal a young man with netted birds in both hands. We stepped out of the car to talk, and he led the way over to the side of the street, where he kept a cage full of extra sparrows with feathers shaded brown.

The seller gave his name as Shamo. His *shalwar kameez* was the color of auto pollution. He had deep brown skin and deep-set eyes and a mop of black hair. He might have been twenty, but said he didn't know his age.

I asked him why people bought the birds and set them free. I suspected that the answers differed, having heard that people of different faiths had all found meanings for the practice within the context of their beliefs. My devout Muslim driver bought birds because it "eased the mind," as he said with a tap of his finger to his head, although many of the bird sellers were Hindu. But when I inquired of Shamo, he said he didn't know why anybody bought birds. People just did. Shamo accommodated them. He purchased the birds in the market for fifteen rupees each and sold them all day for whatever he could get.

I asked Shamo what he would sell me for the hundred-rupee note in my hand, which showed Muhammad Ali Jinnah tinted red. He said for that price I could have all four of the birds in his cage. When he dug into the cage the sparrows scrambled away from his fingers, but he skillfully gathered up the first bird and it went still in his cupped hands. Then he placed the bird in my open palm.

The sky was gray that afternoon, as it was almost every day in that week in July. It was the leading edge of the monsoon season. Within four days the skies would open, flooding street after street in Karachi. Then the rains would move inland with devastating force, the worst monsoon in decades, killing more than a thousand people. The Indus River would soon overflow its banks and spread as many as fifteen miles wide. Twenty million people would be forced to higher ground, a substantial percentage of the entire country. It was the kind of extreme weather event that scientists were beginning to link to global climate change, which was connected in turn to the exploding rates of energy use that powered the commerce and the cars of the instant city.

Soon Karachi would face another wave of refugees, people inbound from the countryside needing shelter and food, just as the Mohajirs had come starting in 1947. But during this week in July, the deluge was still in the future, its scale unsuspected. The city was quiet. The sky looked like rain, but it rarely rained; I thought of storms in the desert, where the parched air absorbs rain that never quite reaches the ground. That was the kind of gray sky we saw overhead, and toward which the bird turned its head when Shamo placed it in my palm. With the beat of soft feathers on my hand, the bird raced away in the direction of the clouds.

Shamo dug out a second bird, and then a third. Along the way, he gave me a look that suggested he was unimpressed with my style. Maybe I should have grasped the sparrows for a moment, said a prayer, or given them a shove into the sky. Instead I was just holding my palm open, and each of the first three birds did no more than bounce on my hand, like a diver hopping on the board before going airborne.

Then Shamo fished the final bird from the cage, and this one settled down in my palm. It stayed in place. It didn't seem to know it was free, didn't know what to do any more than I did. Finally I gave the sparrow a push upward and the little bird took wing, soaring over traffic and out of sight.

A NOTE ON SOURCES

I was gathering material for this book when Romana Kishwar helped me to crystallize the reason that I felt so strongly about writing it. We met while boarding a plane from Doha, Qatar, to Karachi. A man struck up a conversation as we walked up the aisle, and someone in the crowd recognized my voice. I felt a tap on my shoulder and turned to see a teenaged girl in glasses and jeans, who asked, "Are you that guy from NPR?"

I was that guy. The teenager introduced me to her mother, who said without further preamble, "Why are you going back to Karachi? Didn't you just report from there two years ago?" This was Romana Kishwar, who said she had heard every one of a series of reports I'd done from the city. It was flattering, of course, but Ms. Kishwar was not done with me. As we flew beyond the Persian Gulf and over the Arabian Sea, her daughter Maryam came up the aisle to tap my shoulder again. Her mother wanted me to come back and talk some more.

The older Ms. Kishwar wore black-rimmed glasses and kept her hair pulled back, a severe look eased by her warm smile. She said she had grown up in Karachi, and moved to America twenty years ago. She lived in Connecticut until her husband changed jobs. Now she lived outside Austin, Texas. "I miss Connecticut," she said.

"Do you miss Karachi?"

She paused. "Not really." The city was getting very dangerous, she said. She was on her way to Karachi to collect a relative and bring her to America.

Then she started talking about my radio stories from Karachi, and it became apparent that even though she had left Karachi, Karachi never left her. She listened to my reports with the special sensitivity of anyone hearing a stranger blather on about her hometown. "I prayed to God that I would have a chance to help you," she said. "You needed to go deeper. I mean, you got the news. But there is so much more. I felt like you needed to learn more."

She was right. That was the answer to her earlier question, when she asked why I was returning to her city.

If Romana Kishwar concludes that I learned a little more about Karachi, and began to make sense of news headlines that would otherwise seem senseless, the credit belongs to the people of her hometown. They are the principal sources for this book. The vast majority of my interviews were conducted in the city, on the record, and on tape. Many interviews were conducted in English, and many others with the aid of interpreters in Urdu, Pashto, or Sindhi.

Four Pakistanis served me as interpreters at various times: Amar Guriro, Razzak Abro, Riaz Sohail, and Junaid Khan. All were veteran journalists whose suggestions and insights helped me understand Karachi's culture, politics, and streetscape. I also had an interpreter in the United States: Zuleqa Husain, who patiently taught me as much Urdu as I could absorb.

When researching Karachi's history since 1947, I was fortunate to find a range of sources. Some people who remember past times are still alive; others left behind vivid memoirs or oral histories. Several Karachi residents, including Irfan Khan and Hamida Khuhro, directed me to additional books and papers. Between visits to the city, I explored the incomparable collection of the Library of Congress in Washington, D.C. "I thought you guys just did your research on the Internet now," a taxi driver once said while driving me to the library, but so much remains beyond the electronic cloud, like the defunct Karachi newspapers that the librarians brought me in great bound volumes. More documents came from the Ford Foundation archive in New York and the archive of the urban planner Constantinos Doxiadis in Athens, Greece. American diplomatic papers are reproduced in *Foreign Relations of the United States,* a series of thick volumes that are available in print and have also been placed online by the University of Wisconsin. Experts on the region, such as Akbar Ahmed and Steve Coll, were extremely generous with their time.

Of the many histories and biographies I consulted, two books by Stanley Wolpert—biographies of Jinnah and Zulfikar Ali Bhutto—were particularly valuable, as were *The Sole Spokesman,* Ayesha Jalal's rigorous study of Jinnah, and *Life After Partition,* Sarah Ansari's examination of Sindh after 1947. Many Karachi writers contributed to a book of vivid essays called *Karachi: Mega-*

city of Our Times. Several United Nations reports were troves of information about scattered cities around the world. A fuller list of useful works is in the bibliography.

There is another kind of source for this book: sources of support and inspiration. My wife Carolee held our lives together while I was overseas. My daughter Ava put up with my absences, as well as the times when I was busy writing at home—right beside her but still very far away. Of course Ava had no choice but to live with me; I have no idea why Carolee has stuck with me all these years. It would be hard to overstate the value of living with someone who loves you and believes in you.

The book had been on my mind for some time when my friend and colleague Michele Norris encouraged me to actually write it. Tracy Wahl, who had accompanied me on a memorable trip to Karachi, went on to serve as a trusted sounding board and advisor. Tom Gjelten made sure that I met the literary agent Gail Ross; Gail and her collaborator Howard Yoon stuck with this project even though, when I described my schedule for completion, Gail said in her cheerful way, "Everybody thinks you're crazy." Given a choice of publishers, I chose The Penguin Press even though the publisher, Ann Godoff, and the editor, Laura Stickney, had different ideas than I did of what the book should be. I liked that they had different ideas, and also that they did not insist that I must follow them; our free discussions made for a better book than any of us conceived at the start. At NPR, Ellen McDonnell saw the value of this work and fought for it; Madhulika Sikka was a tireless advocate for this project, as she is for all my work, and a wise counselor to whatever talent I may possess. Bruce Auster, a gifted editor, offered clear-eyed advice. Renee Montagne, my co-host at *Morning Edition,* made many adjustments in her own life to cover me during my time off for writing and reporting, and never said a word about it except that I should do whatever I needed to do.

A number of specialists, residents of Karachi, and trusted friends gave of their time to read drafts of various chapters of this book, comment on what they found there, and in many instances identify mistakes or omissions. In addition to several of the people mentioned above, these readers include Deborah Amos, Ayesha Jalal, Nichola Khan, Irfan Khan, Kamran Asdar Ali, Jack Gill, Asma Khalid, Nicole Beemsterboer, and Erum Haider. Of course any mistakes in the final product are my own.

As I sifted all my sources, I knew that I would gain one perspective on this city. There are other perspectives—Romana Kishwar's, for starters, not to mention all the current denizens of Karachi. The city has at least 140 residents for every word in this book. While Karachi means many things to many people, I believe an essential personality comes through. If you were a jet-lagged traveler, I don't think you could ever wake up in Karachi and need a moment to remember what city you're in today. You feel it; you know. If this book succeeds at all, it lets the city speak for itself and be judged on its own terms.

POPULATION OF SELECTED INSTANT CITIES

	1950	1980	2010
UNITED STATES			
Phoenix	221,000	1.4 million	3.7 million
Houston	709,000	2.4 million	4.6 million
Los Angeles	4 million	9.5 million	12.7 million
LATIN AMERICA			
Brasília	36,000	1.3 million	3.9 million
Medellín	376,000	1.7 million	3.6 million
Mexico City	2.9 million	13 million	19.4 million
São Paulo	2.3 million	12 million	20.2 million
EAST ASIA			
Ürümqi	102,000	881,000	2.4 million
Hong Kong	1.7 million	4.6 million	7 million
Shanghai	4.3 million	5.9 million	16.6 million
Tokyo	11.2 million	28.5 million	36.6 million
INDIA			
Chandigarh	40,000	406,000	1 million
Delhi	1.3 million	5.5 million	22.1 million
Mumbai	2.8 million	8.6 million	20 million
PAKISTAN			
Faisalabad	168,000	1 million	2.8 million
Karachi	1 million	5 million	13.1 million
PERSIAN GULF			
Dubai	20,000	254,000	1.5 million

	1950	1980	2010
AFRICA			
Port Harcourt	60,000	482,000	1.1 million
Nairobi	137,000	862,000	3.5 million
Lagos	325,000	2.5 million	10.5 million
STABILIZING CITIES (Instant cities of an earlier age, now expanding more slowly)			
Chicago	5 million	7.2 million	9.2 million
Paris	6.5 million	8.6 million	10.1 million
London	8.3 million	7.6 million	8.6 million
New York	12.3 million	15.6 million	19.4 million

Urban areas (cities and contiguous suburbs) estimated by UN Population Division.

A NOTE ON POPULATION FIGURES

Cities in this book are usually discussed in terms of their metropolitan areas—
the central city plus suburbs and other outlying areas linked by commuting.
New York, for example, is not described as a city of 8.2 million (the approximate number within the city's legal boundaries) but as a city of about nineteen
million. The metropolitan area is the best definition of a city in the age of the
automobile. The United Nations Population Division measures each city as an
"urban agglomeration," which is more compact than a metropolitan area, but
both terms encompass the great bulk of a modern city and are used almost
interchangeably in this book. When comparing cities, I rely on UN estimates,
because they are compiled by the same people using the same methods. UN
estimates, however, are ultimately based on national census figures that vary in
their quality and timing. Thus the reader should take all population figures as
useful approximations. Even if a census of an instant city was exactly correct,
the city is growing quickly enough that the figure was likely out of date by the
time of its publication.

NOTES

NORTH OF NORTH KARACHI

1 *Karachi's population was around four hundred thousand:* The 1941 census showed 359,492 and a pattern of steady growth. "Report on an Enquiry into the Family Budgets of Industrial Workers in Karachi," S. R. Deshpande, Government of India, 1946.

1 *Today it's at least thirteen million:* In general, population estimates after 1950 are taken from the calculations of the United Nations Population Division, *World Urbanization Prospects: The 2009 Revision Population Database,* http://esa.un.org/wup2009/unup/index.asp?panel=2. See "A Note on Population Figures."

3 *the urban population has grown by close to three billion people:* The UN estimated about 730 million urban dwellers, or 28.8 percent of the world population, in 1950; and 3.4 billion, or 50.5 percent of the world population, in 2010—an increase of about 2.7 billion. *World Urbanization Prospects.*

3 *This trend has produced... at the war's end:* United Nations Population Division, *World Urbanization Prospects: The 2009 Revision Population Database,* http://esa.un.org/wup2009/unup/index.asp?panel=2.

3 *Modern cities also add population by sprawling into rural areas:* The three main drivers of urbanization are natural increase, migration, and rural areas "reclassified" as urban. UN-HABITAT, *State of the World's Cities 2010/2011: Bridging the Urban Divide* (London and Sterling, VA: Earthscan, 2008).

3 *Karachi swallowed hundreds of villages:* The Orangi Pilot Project–Research and Training Institute has documented this process in recent years through a dramatic series of satellite photos, showing the city washing up and around villages like a flood.

3 *the most significant movements to cities have come in Africa and Asia:* UN-HABITAT, *State of the World's Cities 2010/2011,* 22. The report says that migration accounts for about 25 percent of worldwide urban growth, and that migration is more pronounced in South Asia, East Asia, Africa, and the Middle East.

CHAPTER 1: PROMENADE

10 *living better than people almost anywhere else in Pakistan:* According to the United Nations Human Development Index. United Nations Development Program, "Pakistan National Human Development Report," 2003. http://www.un.org.pk/nhdr/htm_pages/cp_1.htm.

10 *"We're not a poor country":* From conversation in Karachi, March 2010.

11 *1,747, by one count, in the year 2009:* Figures compiled by Human Rights Commission of Pakistan, Karachi office, 2010.

11 *Taliban fighters are believed to visit Karachi:* "Taliban Find Safe Haven in Pakistan's Karachi," Reuters, May 14, 2010.

11 *a base for attacks outside Pakistan:* Rohan Gunaratna and Khuram Iqbal detail several such attacks, and argue that "Al Qaeda could not have operated globally without a forward operational base in Karachi." *Pakistan: Terrorism Ground Zero* (London, Reaktion, 2011), 121.

12 *he moved from Karachi to New York City:* Interviews with Faisal Edhi, May 2008 and March 2010.

13 *two blood banks and a home for poor children:* Edhi Foundation. www.edhifoundation.com.

13 *"obsessed with self-imposed discomfort":* Abdul Sattar Edhi and Tehmina Durrani, *A Mirror to the Blind* (Karachi: Edhi Foundation, 1996), 51.

CHAPTER 2: LIGHTHOUSE

15 *"You need someplace to sit with a boy":* Interview, June 2010.

15 *"a landmark of the city":* Interview with Bobby Memon, March 2010.

15 *"I am not a Shia":* Ibid.

16 *"It's like a small country":* Ibid.

16 *police officers collecting money from the driver of a stopped car:* Kamal performed this demonstration for me in May 2008.

17 *Pakistani presidents, prime ministers, and a military coup leader:* St. Patrick's high school's long list of "Old Patricians," its distinguished graduates, includes Asif Ali Zardari, the current president, as well as General Pervez Musharraf, who conducted a coup in 1999. http://theoldpatricians.org/illustrious.htm.

17 *men on motorcycles were following Shia professionals:* "Killing Doctors," by Steve Inskeep, NPR News, March 19, 2002.

17 *In 2006 a gathering of Sunnis was bombed:* "Bomb Carnage at Karachi Prayers," BBC Online, April 11, 2006. Special Coverage, Jang Newspapers, Karachi, April 12, 2006.

17 *"There's a lot of terrorism in this country":* Interview with Abbas Kumeli, March 2010.

18 *police blamed one of the explosions on gas from an open sewer line:* "Second Blast in Karachi in Two Days," *Dawn,* December 28, 2009.

19–21 *Mohammad Raza Zaidi:* Details from interview with Syed Mustafa Hussain Zaidi and Syed Iqbal Haider Zaidi, May 2010.

21 *fundamentalist movements had gained strength in recent decades:* A vivid and detailed summary of Sunni-Shia cooperation and rifts is contained in chapter 3 of Vali Nasr's *The Shia Revival* (New York: W. W. Norton, 2004).

22 *the worldwide Scouting movement:* Robert Baden-Powell published his best seller *Scouting for Boys* in 1908. It was republished, with Elleke Boehmer's illuminating introduction detailing Baden-Powell's motivations, as *Scouting for Boys: The Original 1908 Edition* (New York: Oxford University Press, 2004).

22 *Pakistan's chief Scout:* Pakistan Scouts, 2010.

22 *issue a statement urging young Scouts to help battle terrorism:* "Zardari Urges Scouts to Help Fight Terrorism," *Daily Times,* February 22, 2010.

22 *"America is a developed country":* Interview with Najeeb Ilyas, March 2010.

22–23 *The organization claimed seventy thousand members in Karachi:* Pakistan Scouts' estimate, 2010.

24 *"Start passing out the sweet water":* Interview with Najeeb Ilyas, March 2010.

24 *inside that box:* Interview with Raja Umer Khattab, special superintendent of police, Karachi, May 2010. Interviews with Zeeshan Usmani, independent analyst, June–July 2010.

24 *shrapnel and smoke:* Reviewed in Karachi, March 2010.

24 *"I am an unlucky man":* Interview with Najeeb Ilyas, March 2010.

26 *"One of the bodies I shifted":* Interview with Faisal Edhi, March 2010.

26 *They called the marchers' mobile phones:* Hasnian Abbas, for example, had this experience when searching for his brother Murtaza. Interview, May 2010.

CHAPTER 3: NATIONAL ARMS

27 *Early media reports … "suicide bomber":* "Suicide Attack on Ashura Procession," *Dawn,* December 28, 2009.

27 *The Taliban soon claimed responsibility:* "Taliban Claim Responsibility for 'Suicide Attack,'" *Dawn,* December 30, 2009.

27 *the discriminating suicide bomber would prefer lightweight ball bearings:* "Cameras Didn't Record How Bomb Was Planted," *Dawn,* January 5, 2010.

27 *the "casualty pattern" didn't fit with a suicide attack:* The scholar's name was Zeeshan Usmani. Interview, June 2010.

28 *The explosion could only have come from inside it:* Interviews with Raja Umer Khattab, May 2010, and Zeeshan Usmani, June 2010.

30 *"There was fire all around":* Interview with Faisal Edhi, March 2010.

30 *"If something happened, what were they going to do?":* Interview with Bobby Memon, March 2010.

30 *the situation would escalate and the whole city would explode:* News International, January 2, 2010.

30 *made off with Chinese- and Turkish-made handguns:* Interview with shop owner, May 2010.

31 *"saying they couldn't do anything":* Interview with Khalid Rashid, March 2010.

33 *"One is the blast, and the second is after the blast":* Interview with Raja Umer Khattab, May 2010.

34 *"the burning and looting was pre-planned":* "Karachi-Brief Report on Aushora Incident on 28th December 2009," Human Rights Commission of Pakistan, January 9, 2010, 3.

34 *"Everybody knows, but nobody will tell you":* Interview with Abdul Hai, May 2010.

34 *"I think it was a conspiracy to cause a clash between Shias and Sunnis":* Interview with Faisal Edhi, March 2010.

35 *"There is no evidence we can get about chemicals":* Interview with Raja Umer Khattab, May 2010.

36 *"I have no doubt in my mind there was a great conspiracy":* Interview with Yasmeen Lari, March 2010.

36 *"Within an hour of the Ashura blast":* Shaheen Sehbai, *News International,* Saturday, January 2, 2010.

37 *The caller bid Hasan a courteous goodbye:* Interview with Arif Hasan, July 2010.

38 *"targeted killing,"... "political workers killed":* "Murders in Karachi January to April 2010," Human Rights Commission of Pakistan, May 2010.

38 *a political worker who was beheaded in early January:* "9 More Die as Karachi Bleeds," *The Nation,* January 8, 2010.

38 *"And I just knew that it was the sound of a blast":* Interview with Seemin Jamali, March 2010.

40 *Edhi told me later that he took a seat inside one of the Edhi ambulances:* Interview with Abdul Sattar Edhi, March 2010. His son Faisal affirmed that Abdul Sattar Edhi was present when he arrived after the bombing.

CHAPTER 4: JINNAH'S TOMB

44 *December 25, 1876:* Stanley Wolpert, *Jinnah of Pakistan* (New York: Oxford University Press, 1984), 5.

45 *he briefly aspired to be an actor:* Ibid., 14.

45 *"a feeling of space and ease":* Speech in Karachi, August 25, 1947, quoted in *Daily Gazette,* August 26, 1947.

46 *"racketing":* "Sind Government Issues Ordinance to Control Hotel Rates," *Sind Observer,* August 9, 1947, 7.

46 *"Swamped Over By Outsiders":* Sind Observer, July 1, 1947, 1.

46 *"JUBILEE":* Advertisement, *Sind Observer,* August 10, 1947, 7.

46 *"only ideal & exclusive restaurant":* Advertisement, *Sind Observer,* August 15, 1947, 1.

46 *Factories turned out chemicals, paper, and glass:* S. R. Deshpande, "Report on an Enquiry into the Family Budgets of Industrial Workers in Karachi" (Rawalpindi: Government of India, 1946).

46 *People drove Chrysler sedans, and could order:* Advertisement, *Sind Observer,* July 2, 1947, 1.

46 *"The Birth of the Blues":* "Today's Radio," *Sind Observer,* August 17, 1947, 9.

46 *Pan Am Clippers arrived several times a week:* Advertisement, *Sind Observer,* July 2, 1947, 3.

48 *"Mr. M.A. Jinnah... landed at 5-38 p.m.":* "Jinnah Arrives in Karachi," *Daily Gazette,* August 8, 1947, 1.

48 *a newsreel crew took footage of the Great Leader:* Albert Grobe, "Pakistan New Dominion As India Splits," 1947. Republished by Harappa Bazaar, www.harappa.com.

49 *like 1729 . . . or 1843:* Arif Hasan, *Understanding Karachi* (Karachi: City Press, 1999), 15–16. Also Yasmeen Lari and Mihail S. Lari, *The Dual City: Karachi During the Raj* (Karachi: Oxford University Press), 8, 43.

50 *most Indians lived beyond the reach of All India Radio:* From allindiaradio.org/about1.html: "When India attained Independence in 1947, AIR had a network of six stations and a complement of 18 transmitters. The coverage was 2.5% of the area and just 11% of the population."

50 *they could hope for jobs:* Sarah Ansari, *Life After Partition: Migration, Community and Strife in Sindh, 1947–1962* (New York: Oxford University Press, 2005), 49. The government was expected to attract seven thousand civil servants and their families.

50 *"there to carve out careers unimpeded by competition from Hindus":* Ramachandra Guha, *India After Gandhi: The History of the World's Largest Democracy* (New York: HarperCollins, 2007), 375.

50 *51 percent of the city was Hindu, and other religions were practiced as well:* The 1941 census counted 183,883 Hindus, or 51.15 percent of the population. Muslims were 152,385, or 42.39 percent. "Non-European Christians" were 8,393 (2.34 percent), Jains were 3,214 (0.89 percent), Sikhs 4,794 (1.33 percent), and "Other" 6,825 (1.9 percent). Cited in Deshpande, "Report on an Enquiry into the Family Budgets of Industrial Workers in Karachi."

50 *"Apologists of the partition of India":* "Profession and Practice," *Sind Observer,* July 1, 1947, 1.

51 *"it was said that she knew half of the population of Karachi":* P. Rajeswar Rao, *The Great Indian Patriots,* vol. 2 (New Delhi: Mittal Publications, 1991), 221.

51 *"Caste, Idolatry":* Ibid., 219–20.

51 *Hindus in the province of Sindh were far more likely to be literate:* Ansari, *Life After Partition,* 69.

51 *became the local language of business:* Ibid., 34.

51 *"Super Ten Saloon Cars":* Sind Observer, July 1, 1947, 1.

51 *"Hindus lived for centuries on good terms with their Muslim neighbours":* K. Punniah, "One Year After Partition," *Triveni,* September 1948.

52 *his family was Shia:* Wolpert, *Jinnah of Pakistan,* 4.

52 *His doctors, his steward, and even his late wife were non-Muslim:* Akbar S. Ahmed, *Jinnah, Pakistan and Islamic Identity: The Search for Saladin* (London and New York: Routledge, 1997).

52 *asked for help in forming a national shipping line:* The magnate was the father of Ardeshir Cowasjee. Interview with Ardeshir Cowasjee, Karachi, July 2010.

52 *"were not divided," . . . get an education:* Ritu Menon and Kamla Bhasin, *Borders and Boundaries: Women in India's Partition* (New Brunswick, NJ: Rutgers University Press, 1998), 210.

52 *Her Hindu neighbors refused to touch the doorway of her home:* Ibid., 210.

52 *"Muslim Typist . . . Christian preferable":* Classified advertisements, *Sind Observer,* August 3, 1947, 6.

53 *"the protection of Hindu religion":* As reported by D. F. Karaka, *Betrayal in India* (London: Victor Gollancz, 1950), 50.

53 *"common for Hindus to pay homage":* L. K. Advani, *My Country My Life* (New Delhi: Rupa & Co., 2008), 31.

53 *a friend persuaded Advani to join the RSS:* Ibid., p. 38. Karaka, *Betrayal in India,* contains a concise contemporary description of the RSS, 48–51.

53 *some Hindus began to leave Karachi:* The *Daily Gazette* reported that Hindus began leaving soon after Pakistan was announced on June 3, and reported "continued migration" weeks later; July 15, 1947, 2.

53 *"'Do stay on in Karachi'":* M. S. M. Sharma, *Peeps into Pakistan* (Patna: Pustak Bhandar, 1954), 134.

54 *"The minorities . . . will be safeguarded":* "Jinnah's Assurance to Minorities," *Daily Gazette,* July 14, 1947, 1–2.

54 *"I do not know what a theocratic State means":* Ibid.

54 *"Hindus of 'Pak' Should Not Feel Panicky":* Sind Observer, August 9, 1947, 7.

54 *Seven people were killed:* "Communal Frenzy Flares Up," *Sind Observer,* August 10, 1947, 4.

54 *"Violence must be met with violence":* "Tandonji Accuses Muslims of Intimidating Minorities," *Sind Observer,* August 10, 1947.

54 *"repercussions":* "Liaquat Ali Charges Kripalan with Inciting Hindus," *Sind Observer,* August 11, 1947, 1.

54 *"One Thousand Shots Exchanged in Peshawar"*: *Sind Observer,* August 10, 1947, 4.

54 *"by a gang of about 37 Muslims"*: *Sind Observer,* August 10, 1947.

55 *"There is nothing wrong with me"*: Letter from Jinnah to M. A. H. Ispahani, quoted in Ispahani, *Qaid-e Azam As I Knew Him* (Karachi: Forward Publications, 1966), 231.

55 *"There is no Government of Pakistan"*: Shahid Hamid, *Disastrous Twilight: A Personal Record of the Partition of India* (London: Cooper, 1986), 227.

55 *a flag with a small British Union Jack in one corner:* Mountbatten to Jinnah, June 24, 1947. Printed in *Jinnah-Mountbatten Correspondence, 22 March–9 August 1947* (Research Society of Pakistan, 1998), 115.

55 *"any flags and buntings for decoration"*: *Sind Observer,* August 10, 1947.

55 *"You Mussulmans"*: Hamid, *Disastrous Twilight,* 218–19.

55 *"As the time for Partition gets closer"*: Ibid., 223.

55 *"obsolete"*: *Sind Observer,* August 10, 1947, 1.

55 *"Rioting by the Sikhs has started"*: Hamid, *Disastrous Twilight,* 223.

56 *killings at a rate of more than two hundred per day:* Ibid., 223–24.

56 *"Lahore and Amritsar are scorched-earth cities"*: *Sind Observer,* August 11, 1947, 2.

56 *the alleged manufacturing of bombs:* Ibid., 5.

56 *A lawmaker proposed rethinking the Islam-accented national flag:* *Sind Observer,* August 12, 1947, 1.

56 *the old man's words were just a buzz to people in the galleries:* The *Sind Observer,* August 12, 1947, notes that "Mr. Jinnah made a 40-minute speech which was inaudible in the press and other galleries owing to the failure of electric current."

57 *Winston Churchill, a contemporary he admired:* Arthur Herman, *Gandhi and Churchill: The Epic Rivalry That Destroyed an Empire and Forged Our Age* (New York: Bantam, 2008), 568.

57 *"Now what shall we do?"*: Newspapers recorded Jinnah's words slightly differently—usually the same words but in some cases a different order; all text here is from *Dawn,* August 14, 1947.

58 *"dispelled the fears of those who were told to expect a theocratic State"*: *Sind Observer,* August 14, 1947, 2.

58 *"deserves to be written in letters of gold"*: *Daily Gazette,* August 13, 1947, 2.

58 *forty people killed and thirty injured:* *Sind Observer,* August 12, 1947, 1.

58 *"Several houses were burning in Amritsar City"*: Hamid, *Disastrous Twilight,* 225–26.

58 *"The atmosphere was tense"*: Ibid., 227.

58 *finally preferred to shove Jinnah to the margins:* One of the many distinguished histories of Partition, Ayesha Jalal's *The Sole Spokesman* (Cambridge University Press, 1985), argues that Jinnah was outmaneuvered in negotiations. Jinnah held out the demand for Pakistan to solidify Muslims behind his leadership, but failed to define what Pakistan should be and even left doubt that he truly wanted the state that emerged. Finally it was forced upon him with borders and terms that many Muslims considered ruinous.

58 *hurry up and leave:* Hamid, *Disastrous Twilight,* 227.

59 *"a peaceful aspect"*: Albert Grobe, "Pakistan New Dominion As India Splits," 1947. Republished by Harappa Bazaar, www.harappa.com.

59 *Jinnah's Hindu friend M. S. M. Sharma posed a question:* Sharma identifies himself as the person who asked this question in *Peeps into Pakistan,* 134–37.

59 *Few leaders imagined:* Yasmin Khan, *The Great Partition* (New Haven, CT: Yale University Press, 2007), 122.

59 *"I remember quite vividly"*: Interviews with Arif Hasan, May 2008 and July 2010.

60 *"there would be a good chance of domination in the new country"*: E-mail exchange with Baseer Naweed, November 2009.

60 *"The 2,000-odd bodies of the dead"*: Karaka, *Betrayal in India,* 52–53.

60 *"People have gone mad"*: Hamid, *Disastrous Twilight,* 237.

60 *There was nowhere beyond Karachi but the sea:* The southwestward flow of "overspill" refugees is analyzed by Sarah Ansari in *Life After Partition,* 60–68.

60 *climbing in a decade from 600,000 people to 2.5 million:* Steve Tsang, *A Modern History of Hong Kong* (London: I. B. Tauris, 2004), 167.

60 *"instability, civil war and repression"*: UN-HABITAT, *The Challenge of Slums: Case Studies for the Global Report on Human Settlements 2003* (London and Sterling, VA: Earthscan, 2003), 25.

60-61 *half million people who fled the war in nearby Iraq*: UN-HABITAT, *State of the World's Cities 2010/2011: Bridging the Urban Divide* (London and Sterling, VA: Earthscan, 2008), 134.

61 *Refugees from other conflicts*: Ibid., 134.

61 *Kabul . . . climbed by more than a million*: United Nations Population Division, *World Urbanization Prospects: The 2009 Revision Population Database*, http://esa.un.org/wup2009/unup/index .asp?panel=2.

61 *"What will I be?"*: Abdul Sattar Edhi and Tehmina Durrani, *A Mirror to the Blind* (Karachi: Edhi Foundation, 1996), 33.

61 *"the heavy smell of fish"*: Ibid., 40.

61 *Soon Edhi switched to selling* paan: As recounted in ibid., 43–45.

62 *"intensity in the eyes" . . . "like a ferocious tiger"*: Ibid., 43.

62 *a constable fired twenty-three shots, killing five*: "No Need for Panic in City," *Daily Gazette,* September 5, 1947, 2.

62 *Authorities raced to tamp down rumors*: Ibid.

62 *"stabbed to death"*: Ibid.

62 *James Joyce and H. G. Wells*: "Twentieth Century English Novelists," *Daily Gazette,* August 30, 1947, 3.

62 *Afghan Snow*: Advertisement, *Daily Gazette,* September 1, 1947, 4.

62 *Sinbad the Sailor*: Advertisement, *Daily Gazette,* August 30, 1947, 6.

62 *"by moral and intellectual force"*: "Appeal to Muslims to Protect Minorities," *Daily Gazette,* September 2, 1947, 3.

63 *"attacked a passenger bus with fist blows"*: "Pakistan Staff in Frenzy," *Daily Gazette,* September 8, 1947, 2.

63 *"goondas," . . . killed Sikhs and Hindus with knife thrusts*: "Section 144 in Karachi," *Daily Gazette,* September 10, 1947, 3.

63 *were anxious about the potential power of the new arrivals*: Sarah Ansari, in *Life After Partition,* 77, writes that the central government was concerned for years about whether opposition politicians would mobilize discontented new arrivals.

63 *"who have suffered in Hindu dominated areas"*: "Sind Can Only Take In Limited Number," *Daily Gazette,* August 7, 1947, 8.

64 *Muhammad Ali Jinnah visited a refugee camp*: Khan, *The Great Partition,* 176.

64 *"NO MORE REFUGEES FOR KARACHI"*: *Daily Gazette,* September 18, 1947, 1.

64 *half a million in Karachi by May 1948*: Ansari, *Life After Partition,* 64.

64 *"heart failure"*: *Sind Observer,* September 12, 1948, 1.

64 *six hundred thousand people turned out*: "Over Six Lakh People Offer Funeral Prayers," *Sind Observer,* September 13, 1948, 1.

66 *a division so profound*: Stanley Wolpert, quoting this speech in *Jinnah of Pakistan,* 339–40, asks, "What was he talking about? Had he simply forgotten where he was? Had the cyclone of events so disoriented him that he was arguing the opposition's brief?"

65 *"Gettysburg Address"*: Ahmed makes this case in detail in *Jinnah, Pakistan and Islamic Identity* (London: Routledge, 1997).

66 *"orphans"*: *Sind Observer,* September 12, 1948.

CHAPTER 5: SHRINE AND TEMPLE

68 *He felt better already*: Interview, March 2010.

69 *"We come in peace"*: Interview, March 2010.

70 *Hindus went from 51 percent of Karachi's population to about 2 percent*: From 1941 census figures compared with 1951 census figures. Arif Hasan and Masooma Mohib, "The Case of Karachi, Pakistan," p. 3, from *The Challenge of Slums: Case Studies for the Global Report on Human Settlements 2003* (London and Sterling, VA: Earthscan, 2003).

70 wanted to avoid police questioning: Advani tells this story in *My Country, My Life* (Kolkata: Rupa & Co. 2008), 51.

71 much of the skill and education of the city's elite was disappearing with them: Sarah Ansari, in *Life After Partition: Migration, Community and Strife in Sindh, 1947–1962* (New York: Oxford University Press, 2005), writes that the departure of the first Hindus "was regarded as scarcely a lesser crisis than the arrival of so many destitute Muslim refugees from India," 54.

71 not even 5 percent of Muslim men could read, and fewer than 1 percent of women: Ansari, *Life After Partition,* 69.

71 "could not reconcile himself to the idea": *Daily Gazette,* September 25, 1947, 1.

71 "will give the fairest deal to all minority communities": "Minorities Assured of Fairest Deal through Nazimuddin's Broadcast," *Dawn,* January 4, 1948.

71 "KARACHI'S SUDDEN OUTBREAK OF VIOLENCE NOW WELL IN HAND": Headline from *Dawn,* January 7, 1948, 1.

72 "There was a sudden flare up": Ibid.

72 a mob attacked a convoy of refugees from the north: Sarah Ansari reconstructs the events in *Life After Partition,* 56–57.

72 "taken to safe places": *Dawn,* January 8, 1948, 1.

72 some 180 people were killed: The *Daily Gazette* printed this figure a week after the incident, on January 13, 1948, 1. Sarah Ansari, in *Life After Partition,* estimates two hundred. The day after its initial reference to "some deaths," *Dawn* gave a figure of fifty-one dead, including a number of Muslims.

72 "saw a number of people engaged in looting houses": *Dawn,* January 7, 1948, 1.

72 "We had never really thought of leaving": Ritu Menon and Kamla Bhasin, *Borders and Boundaries: Women in India's Partition* (New Brunswick, NJ: Rutgers University Press, 1998), 209.

73 "cotton sheets, shirts, beddings": "Muslims Surrender Looted Property," *Daily Gazette,* January 11, 1948, 1–2.

73 moved to India after the riots: M. S. M. Sharma, *Peeps into Pakistan* (Patna: Pustak Bhandar, 1954), 173.

73 "evolving into a Fascist State": Shri K. Punniah, *Triveni,* September 1948.

73 The former editor of the Sind Observer *was found lying dead in the street:* P. Rajeswar Rao, *The Great Indian Patriots,* vol. 2 (New Delhi: Mittal Publications, 1991), 223.

74 "Jinnah told my father": Interview with Ardeshir Cowasjee, July 2010.

74 The 1951 census: Hasan and Mohib, "The Case of Karachi, Pakistan," 3.

75 People followed the money . . . Lagos exploded: Leslie Green and Vincent Malone, "Urbanization in Nigeria: A Planning Commentary," in *International Urban Survey* (New York: Ford Foundation, 1972 or 1973 [date unclear]), 5.

75 "derelict . . . mills, empty houses": Ibid., 15.

75 "urban revolution": Ibid., 5.

75 The government began a massive housing program: Steve Tsang, *A Modern History of Hong Kong* (London: I. B. Tauris, 2004), 204–5.

75 two hundred thousand spindles . . . 1.3 million: Stephen Philip Cohen, *The Idea of Pakistan* (Washington, D.C.: Brookings Institution Press, 2004), 66. Ansari, in *Life After Partition,* 76, notes that many of these were allocated to Karachi.

75 "Foreign, particularly American, speculators": "Building Boom in Karachi," *Dawn,* July 28, 1950, 4.

76 "There were many people living with us" . . . "little more than shacks": Interview with Akbar S. Ahmed, January 2010.

76 "What was left at night . . . washed away the next day": "Rain Brings Suffering for Refugees," *Dawn,* July 28, 1950, 9.

76 to shelter somewhere in the "suburbs": Ansari, *Life After Partition,* 134.

76 "pulled out chairs, tables, and cycles": "Mob Raids KMC," *Dawn,* August 17, 1950, 1.

77 "For goodness sake": "Jinnah's Assurance to Minorities," *Daily Gazette,* July 14, 1947, 1–2.

78 Conservative Muslims had railed for a century: Quentin Wiktorowicz, "A Genealogy of Radical Islam," *Studies in Conflict and Terrorism* 28 (2005): 76.

78 *"not just a portion, but the whole planet"*: Abul A'La Maududi, "Jihad in Islam," 1939 speech reprinted by International Islamic Federation of Student Organizations, Salimiah, Kuwait, 6.

78 *"Islam is not the name of a 'Religion'"*: Ibid., 5.

79 *The twentieth century was a new age of jahiliyya*: Wiktorowicz, "A Genealogy of Radical Islam," 78.

79 *His was a narrow and rigid Islam*: Seyyed Vali Reza Nasr, *The Vanguard of the Islamic Revolution* (Berkeley: University of California Press, 1994), 7.

79 *put him in jail for a time in 1948 . . . sentenced to death*: Charles J. Adams, "The Ideology of Mawlana Mawdudi," in *South Asian Politics and Religion,* ed. Donald E. Smith (Princeton, NJ: Princeton University Press, 1966), 377.

79 *their relative freedom from corruption*: Ibid., 380.

79 *Jamaat-e-Islami held a conference*: Ansari, *Life After Partition,* 175.

79 *Secularists painted slogans in English*: Ibid.

79 *Jamaat candidates won the Karachi municipal elections*: Ansari, *Life After Partition,* 173; Adams, "The Ideology of Mawlana Mawdudi," 378.

79 *Sunni Muslim refugees began agitating*: Ansari, *Life After Partition,* 175.

79 *meetings of a Muslim minority known as Ahmadis were disrupted*: Ibid., 109.

79 *one of Mawdudi's arrests came after his publication of an attack on Ahmadis*: Ibid., 111.

CHAPTER 6: GROUNDBREAKING

81 *He couldn't pay attention*: Abdul Sattar Edhi and Tehmina Durrani, *A Mirror to the Blind* (Karachi: Edhi Foundation, 1996), 45.

81 *"narrow, unpaved allies"*: Ibid., 63.

81 *"Assassination . . . Infighting"*: Azhar Hassan Nadeem, *Pakistan: The Political Economy of Lawlessness* (Oxford University Press, 2002), 328.

82 *He built neighborhoods such as Sau Quarter*: "Muharram in Sau Quarter," *Dawn,* January 5, 2009.

82–83 *The photo is from December 1958*: *Times of Karachi,* December 6, 1958, 1.

83 *"humid and unhealthy"*: M. Ayub Khan, *Friends Not Masters* (Oxford University Press, 1967), 85.

83 *"an enervating climate" . . . "bear on the government"*: Ibid., 96.

83 *"sat there on these great big horses"*: Dennis Kux, *The United States and Pakistan, 1947–2000: Disenchanted Allies* (Washington, D.C.: Woodrow Wilson Center Press / Baltimore: Johns Hopkins University Press, 2001), 56.

84 *"I believe those fellows are going to fight any communist invasion"*: Ibid.

84 *"a hoax"*: Letter from the ambassador in Pakistan (Langley) to the assistant secretary of state for Near Eastern, South Asian, and African Affairs (Rountree), *Foreign Relations of the United States, 1955–57,* vol. VIII, *South Asia* (Washington, DC: U.S. Government Printing Office, 1987), 488.

84 *exceeded $500 million in a single year*: Kux, *The United States and Pakistan,* 84.

84 *"doing practically nothing for Pakistan"*: Memorandum of Discussion at the 308th Meeting of the National Security Council, Washington, D.C., January 3, 1957, *Foreign Relations of the United States, 1955–57,* vol. VIII, *South Asia,* 25–26.

84 *"Now we seem hopelessly involved in it"*: Ibid.

84 *"The hour had struck"*: Khan, *Friends Not Masters,* 70.

84 *"Pakistan's elected government will be that of civilians"*: Shahid Hamid, *Disastrous Twilight: A Personal Record of the Partition of India* (London: Cooper, 1986), 219.

85 *Abdul Sattar Edhi had purchased his first vehicle in 1957*: Edhi and Durrani, *A Mirror to the Blind,* 70.

85 *feared that he would lose*: Kux, *The United States and Pakistan,* 97.

85 *threatening civil disobedience in Karachi*: "Civil Disobedience if Polls Delayed," *Dawn,* October 5, 1958.

85 *the new leader of the Muslim League, too, urged greater emphasis on Islam*: Kux, *The United States and Pakistan,* 99.

85 *"The ruthless struggle for power"*: *Dawn,* October 8, 1958, 1.

85 *"the free world"*: Eisenhower's reply to Mirza, from October 11, 1958, is in *Foreign Relations of the United States, 1958–60*, vol. XV, *South and Southeast Asia* (Washington, DC: U.S. Government Printing Office, 1992), 673.

85 *"danger"* . . . *"if only by implication"*: Telegram from the Department of State to the embassy in Pakistan, October 6, 1958, *Foreign Relations of the United States, 1958–60*, vol. XV, *South and Southeast Asia*, 666. Dennis Kux, in his distinguished history of the period, interprets this telegram somewhat differently, concluding that the United States wanted to head off the coup. I read the United States as finding the coup distasteful, but weighing its options and deciding to acquiesce. Subsequent events showed the United States swiftly embracing its anticommunist ally.

86 *"my dear President Mirza"*: Letter from Secretary of State Dulles to President Mirza, October 17, 1958, *Foreign Relations of the United States, 1958–60*, vol. XV, *South and Southeast Asia,* 677.

86 The Man Who Knew Too Much: *Dawn,* October 8, 1958, 3.

86 *"uneasiness and nascent fear"* . . . *"the absence of any checks on the police"*: Telegram from the embassy in Pakistan to the Department of State, October 15, 1958, *Foreign Relations of the United States, 1958–60*, vol. XV, *South and Southeast Asia,* 676.

86 *waiting to arrest him . . . the sale of an unregistered 1958 Chevrolet:* "Khuhro Arrested on Blackmarket Charge," *Dawn,* October 10, 1958, 1.

86 *"I am a man in a hurry"* . . . *"so little time to do them"*: Khan, *Friends Not Masters,* 76.

86 *"The capital must be moved out of Karachi"*: Ibid., 85.

87 *"I mentioned in the Cabinet"*: Ibid., 83.

87 *"The resettlement"* . . . *"It was essential"*: Ibid., 82.

87 *"The ultimate shape of this colony"*: "Gen. Ayub Lays Foundation of Korangi Satellite Town," *Times of Karachi,* December 6, 1958, 1, 5.

88 *"rely on their wits to thrive"*: Jean Gottmann, *Megalopolis: The Urbanized Northeastern Seaboard of the United States* (Cambridge, MA: MIT Press, 1961), 46.

88 *"migration and employment growth . . . thereby drawing more migrants"*: Peter Morrison, "Migration from Distressed Areas: Its Meaning for Regional Policy" (New York: Ford Foundation, 1973), 17–18.

88 *four million people in 1950 to 6.5 million in 1960:* United Nations Population Division, *World Urbanization Prospects: The 2009 Revision Population Database,* http://esa.un.org/wup2009/unup/index.asp?panel=2.

88 *"furnaces, sliding doors, mechanical saws"*: Jane Jacobs, *The Economy of Cities* (New York: Random House, 1969), 152.

88 *"an entirely new urban form"* . . . *"broad tree-lined boulevards"*: Andrei Sorensen, *The Making of Urban Japan: Cities and Planning from Edo to the Twenty-first Century* (New York: Routledge, 2002), 162.

89 *Constantinos Doxiadis caught the midnight flight:* Doxiadis's diary, December 15, 1958.

89 *Ford had been assisting with planning and development:* Doxiadis's diary, December 15, 1958; also "Design for Pakistan: A Report on Assistance to the Pakistan Planning Commission by the Ford Foundation and Harvard University" (New York: Ford Foundation, February 1965).

89 *Doxiadis snapped photos of arid land:* Doxiadis's diary, December 17, 1958.

89 *The philosopher Plato spoke to him:* Constantinos Doxiadis, *Between Dystopia and Utopia* (Hartford, CT: Trinity College Press, 1966), x–xi.

90 *They worked everywhere from Baghdad to Rio de Janeiro:* Doxiadis Associates archive, archive .doxiadis.org; also *Between Dystopia and Utopia.*

90 *"helped resettle 10 million humans in 15 countries"*: *Time,* November 4, 1966.

90 *"Several aspects of the problem begin to worry me,"* . . . *"I wonder if they can"*: Doxiadis's diary, December 15, 1958.

90 *"During this flight I am impressed"*: Ibid., December 17, 1958.

90 *"It is the pet scheme of the Government"*: Ibid., December 15, 1958.

91 *"in a self-contained community rationally planned"*: Ghulam Farid Khan, "Identification of Attitudes of Juggi-Dwellers Living in Jacob Lines Towards Korangi Township," Thesis, Graduate School of Ekistics, Karachi, October 1970, 13.

91 *"It was a grand plan"*: Interview with Arif Hasan, March 2010.

92 *He left spaces for gardens:* Chaudry Salimullah, "A Study of the Various House Types Constructed for the Low Income People at Korangi," Thesis, Graduate School of Ekistics, Karachi, 1962, 55.

93 *Better to build houses with sun-dried bricks:* Doxiadis's diary, December 17, 1958.

93 *resettled 13,079 families in new homes:* Ghulam Farid Khan, "Identification of Attitudes of Juggi-Dwellers," 9.

93 *In between a formal lunch and a formal dinner:* Chronology assembled by the Dwight D. Eisenhower Memorial Commission, http://www.eisenhowermemorial.org/presidential-papers/second-term/chronology/1959-12.htm.

93 *"I Like Ike":* Markus Daechsel, "Sovereignty, Governmentality and Development in Ayub's Pakistan: The Case of Korangi Township," *Modern Asian Studies* 45 (2011): 152.

93 *they included government workers:* Khan, "Identification of Attitudes of Juggi-Dwellers," 41.

94 *"the residents not paying their nominal rent":* Dawn, November 2, 1960, reprinted within ibid., 13.

94 *a "serious setback":* "450 Families Evicted from Korangi," *Dawn,* January 11, 1961, reprinted in ibid., 14.

95 *there was "great reluctance":* Ibid.

95 *"gradual integration" . . . "higher income-classes":* Doxiadis Associates, "Islamabad the Capital of Pakistan," undated, 9.

95 *according to a confidential report by Doxiadis's firm:* The 1961 report is titled "Confidential: Greater Karachi Resettlement Programme, Weaknesses and Problems," and says on page 7, "Only displaced persons were shifted to Korangi, although the programme was calling for mixing of population, to avoid social problems in the future." Ford Foundation archives.

95 *"The people living there became poorer":* Interview with Arif Hasan, March 2010.

95 *"On trucks you take cattle, not people":* Interview with Mumtaz Ahmed, May 2010.

95 *they abandoned their new homes and moved back to the center city:* Daechsel, "Sovereignty, Governmentality and Development in Ayub's Pakistan," 140.

96 *before more properties were "spoilt":* Doxiadis's diary, November 29, 1963.

96 *"We did not have the institutions and expertise":* Interview with Arif Hasan, March 2010.

96 *not enough experienced engineers:* Doxiadis Associates, "Confidential: Greater Karachi Resettlement Programme, weaknesses and problems," 1961, 6. Ford Foundation archives.

96 *"There is no control or guidance whatsoever," . . . "not maintained at all":* Memorandum from Papageorgiou to Doxiadis, "Korangi and North Karachi—October 1971," Doxiadis archives.

96–97 *"They started dividing up the land":* Interview with Arif Hasan, March 2010.

97 *"It is very interesting":* Lt. Col. N. Ahmed, "Report on Urban Construction Survey in Karachi 1963," 1964. Library of Congress, Washington, DC.

98 *"One-fourth of the people of Karachi are still shelterless":* Investment Advisory Centre of Pakistan, "Socio-economic Survey of Karachi, Part I" (Karachi-Dacca, August 1971), 49.

98 *"big cattle-breeding area," . . . "ruined," . . . "everyone does as they please":* Memorandum from Papageorgiou to Doxiadis, "Korangi and North Karachi—October 1971," Doxiadis archives.

99 *"dystopias," . . . "why don't they lead anywhere?":* Doxiadis, *Between Utopia and Dystopia,* xi.

99 *"It is true that man is lost":* Ibid., 19–21.

99 *By 1971, Karachi's population was estimated at 3.5 million:* Investment Advisory Centre of Pakistan, "Socio-economic Survey of Karachi, Part I," 46.

CHAPTER 7: SELF-SERVICE LEVITTOWN

100 *people like Nawaz Khan:* He was interviewed by researchers who recounted his story: Azmat Ali Budhani, Haris Gazdar, Sobia Ahmad Kaker, and Hussain Bux Mallah, "The Open City: Social Networks and Violence in Karachi" (Collective for Social Science Research, 2010), 22.

100 *Nawaz told Karachi researchers his story:* Ibid., 22.

101 *developed a master plan for the city:* Arif Hasan, *Understanding Karachi* (Karachi: City Press, 1999), 28.

101 *a population of 5.4 million by 1981:* Arif Hasan and Masooma Mohib, "The Case of Karachi, Pakistan," p. 3, from *The Challenge of Slums: Case Studies for the Global Report on Human Settlements 2003* (London and Sterling, VA: Earthscan, 2003).

102 *539 irregular neighborhoods ... 2.5 million people:* Interview with Rafique Engineer, March 2010.

103 *Doxiadis ... had proposed to demolish:* Constantinos Doxiadis, *Between Utopia and Dystopia* (Hartford, CT: Trinity College Press, 1966), 63.

103 *"had no tangible results":* Leslie Green and Vincent Malone, "Urbanization in Nigeria: A Planning Commentary" (New York: Ford Foundation, 1972–73), 31.

103 *"Chaotic traffic conditions":* Ibid., 14–15.

103 *A more recent study:* Edward Glaeser, *Triumph of the City* (New York: Penguin, 2011), 73.

105 *"Everybody says land mafia":* Interview with Perween Rahman, March 2010.

105 *"Now everybody is a land supplier":* Ibid.

106 *"I was designing a hotel":* Interview with Perween Rahman, May 2008.

106 *"It was the start of a land grab":* Interview with Perween Rahman, July 2010.

107 *"He was a man who would say":* Interview with Perween Rahman, May 2008.

107 *grants from the Bank of Credit and Commerce International:* Akhtar Hameed Khan, *Orangi Pilot Project: Reminiscences and Reflections* (Karachi: Oxford University Press, 1996), 49.

107 *"I became a state within a state":* Interview with Shamsuddin, March 2010.

108 *"They are redundant":* Interview with Perween Rahman, March 2010.

109 *"What we do":* Interview with Wahab Khan, May 2008. See "Karachi's Growth Fuels Demand for Illegal Housing," by Steve Inskeep, NPR News, June 5, 2008.

110 *"Of course we all understand":* Interview with Muhammad Shoaib Suddle, June 2008. See "Karachi's Growth Fuels Demand for Illegal Housing."

112 *"Don't you think they're underfed?"* Interview with Shinaz and Razia, May 2008. See "Karachi's Growth Fuels Demand for Illegal Housing."

CHAPTER 8: CASINO

114 *"was covered with cobwebs":* Anjum Niaz, "Why Dubai Chalo, Why Not Karachi?" *News International*, August 26, 2008.

115 *"You should come to my house":* Interview with Tony Tufail, March 2010.

115 *the building dated back to 1886:* This is also affirmed in Hamida Khuhro and Anwer Mooraj, *Karachi: Megacity of Our Times* (Karachi: Oxford University Press, 1997), 315.

116 *"No Dogs or Natives Allowed":* Interview with Yasmeen Lari, May 2010.

117 *In 2002, a bomb blew up a bus outside the Sheraton:* "Suicide Bomber Kills 11 French Engineers at Karachi Hotel," *Guardian* (London), May 9, 2002.

117 *In 2002, 2003, 2004, and 2006, attackers struck the American consulate:* NPR News, June 14, 2002; CNN, February 28, 2003; www.Pakistandefence.com, March 15, 2004; NPR News, March 2, 2006.

119 *"constant talk within my household":* Kamran Asdar Ali, "Men and Their 'Problems': Notes on Contemporary Karachi," in *Comparing Cities: The Middle East and South Asia*, ed. Kamran Asdar Ali and Martina Rieker (New York: Oxford University Press, 2009), 49.

119 *Indian movies were banned:* Interview with Masih ul Hassan, May 2010.

120 *"As the booze flowed":* Anwer Mooraj, "Karachi Before Prohibition," in Khuhro and Mooraj, *Karachi: Megacity of Our Times*, 321.

121 *a volunteer in a 1950 United States Senate campaign:* Stanley Wolpert, *Zulfi Bhutto of Pakistan: His Life and Times* (New York: Oxford University Press, 1993), 34.

121 *Bhutto's dubious advice played a role in Ayub's decision to go to war:* Wolpert, *Zulfi Bhutto of Pakistan*, 91.

122 *Bhutto seemed to encourage the breakup of the country:* Having won in West Pakistan but not in East Pakistan, Bhutto raised a divisive slogan of "Us here, you there!" and then pushed to delay the start of a parliament that he would not control. East Pakistan ultimately declared independence. Wolpert, *Zulfi Bhutto of Pakistan,* 146–49.

123 *"very small pieces":* Ibid., 172.

123 *"wild rumors":* Ibid., 228.

123 *Bhutto also took over the ships run by his neighbor Ardeshir Cowasjee:* Interview with Ardeshir Cowasjee, May 2008; e-mail exchange, April 2011.

123 *"I might have called him a damn fool"* ... *"'Just tell me what I have done'"*: Interviews with Ardeshir Cowasjee, May 2008 and July 2010.

126 *Scores were killed in twin bombings in Lahore in 2010*: BBC, May 28, 2010.

126 *"deteriorated over decades"*: Abul A'La Maududi, "System of Government Under the Holy Prophet (with discussion of the method of implementing it in Pakistan today)" (Lahore: Islamic Publications, 1978), 27.

126 *blamed the country's troubles on "wine"*: Vali Nasr, *The Vanguard of the Islamic Revolution* (Berkeley: University of California Press, 1994), 171.

128 *"General Mohammad Zia-ul Haq, who was talking to newsmen"*: "Zia Reiterates Stand on Elections," *Dawn*, December 5, 1977, 1.

128 *"Pakistan, which was created in the name of Islam"*: "Zia Praises People's Islamic Sentiment," *Dawn*, July 6, 1977, 8.

128 *"AMPUTATION OF HAND FOR THEFT"*: *Dawn*, July 11, 1977, 1.

128 *"moral criminal and a murderer"*: Nasr, *The Vanguard of the Islamic Revolution*, 190.

128 *a Carrier air-conditioning system*: "White Paper on the Performance of the Bhutto Regime, Vol. I" (Islamabad: Government of Pakistan, 1979), 11.

129 *"We will meet one day"*: Wolpert, *Zulfi Bhutto of Pakistan*, 325.

129 *"The people said, 'Forget Bhutto'"*: Interview with Masih ul Hassan, May 2010.

129 *Eli Wallach in an old spaghetti western called* Ace High: Advertisement, *Dawn*, April 3, 1979, 3.

129–30 *"Even after dusk and before dawn"*: Linda K. Richter, *The Politics of Tourism in Asia* (Honolulu: University of Hawaii Press, 1989), 141.

131 *the organization was still patiently working toward its original goals*: Interview with Dr. Mohammad Fiaz, March 2010.

131 *an "infrastructure" of extremist groups*: Interview with Ikram Sehgal, February 2010.

134 *one such establishment . . . was bombed*: "Gambling Den Blast Death Toll Rises to 19," *Daily Times*, April 23, 2011. Also "Club Where Bomb Exploded," *Dawn*, April 22, 2011.

CHAPTER 9: ICON

139 *"It's like the wind"*: Interview, March 2010.

140 *"We're building Pakistan's tallest building"*: Interview with Zain Malik of Bahria Town, May 2010.

141 *when bombers struck the shrine of Abdullah Shah Ghazi*: "Twin Suicide Attacks at Abdullah Shah Ghazi Shrine," Pakistan *Express Tribune*, October 7, 2010; "High Grade 'Military Explosives' Used in Blast at Karachi Shrine," *Dawn*, December 6, 2010.

141 *far better than rural areas of Pakistan*: United Nations Development Program, "Pakistan National Human Development Report 2003," http://www.un.org.pk/nhdr/htm_pages/cp_1.htm.

141 *Karachi's literacy far surpassed that of the surrounding countryside*: In 2007 the government gave urban Karachi's literacy rate as 79 percent. Rural areas of Sindh recorded a literacy rate of 36 percent, mainly because literacy for rural women was only 16 percent: http://www.statpak.gov .pk/fbs/sites/default/files/social_statistics/publications/pslm_prov2006-07/2.14a.pdf. The census in 1998 found 64 percent literacy in urban Sindh, and 25 percent in rural areas: http://www .census.gov.pk/Literacy.htm.

141 *experts saw them as a useful alternative to inadequate government schools*: Two such experts are Rebecca Winthrop and Corinne Graf, authors of "Beyond Madrasas: Assessing the Links Between Education and Militancy in Pakistan" (Washington, D.C.: Center for Universal Education, Brookings Institution, 2010), 17.

142 *attracted the interest of a Japanese firm*: "JICA Offers Soft Loan, Cooperation to KCR," *Daily Times*, July 24, 2011.

142 *dumped landfill in the swamp*: Azmat Ali Budhani, Haris Gazdar, Sobia Ahmad Kaker, and Hussin Bux Mallah, "The Open City: Social Networks and Violence in Karachi" (Collective for Social Science Research, 2010), 23.

142 *a sharp decline in urban poverty around the world*: UN-HABITAT, *State of the World's Cities 2010/ 2011: Bridging the Urban Divide* (London and Sterling, VA: Earthscan, 2008), x.

142 *"urban divide"* . . . *"a chasm, an open wound"*: Ibid., viii.

144 *"The people discovered me"*: Abdul Sattar Edhi and Tehmina Durrani, *A Mirror to the Blind* (Karachi: Edhi Foundation, 1996), 70.

145 *the London branch of the Edhi Foundation collecting well over two million British pounds per year*: Disclosure forms filed with Britain's Charity Commission on October 29, 2010, showed an income for 2009 of £2,626,300, and expenditures of £1,804,850, with the remainder being saved. Nearly all the reported expenditures represented money sent to Pakistan; a strikingly small amount was spent on staff and fund-raising. www.charitycommission.gov.uk.

145 *Hundreds of thousands of American dollars*: $888,540 was raised in 2009, according to disclosures required by New York State. The overwhelming majority was banked in the United States. New York State Office of the Attorney General, www.charitiesnys.com.

145 *$100,000 to the American Red Cross*: The money was given in September 2005 to the Greater New York branch of the Red Cross, which passed it on to the national headquarters for Katrina assistance. Confirmed by e-mail from Sam Kille, NY Red Cross spokesman, May 5, 2011.

145 *many of the gifts were described as* zakat: Disclosure forms filed with Britain's Charity Commission on October 29, 2010. www.charitycommission.gov.uk.

145 *it collected most of its money from donations inside Pakistan*: www.edhifoundation.com.

145 *did not disclose . . . the total amount*: Interview with Faisal Edhi, April 2011.

145 *it received no audited financial information*: 2009 disclosures to New York State Office of the Attorney General, www.charitiesnys.com.

145 *"Edhi does the best development work in Pakistan"*: Interview, April 2011.

146 *had been showered with honors*: Among them Asia's Magsaysay Prize in the 1980s, and the UNESCO-Madanjeet Singh Prize for the Promotion of Tolerance and Non-Violence. http://www.unesco.org/new/en/media-services/single-view/news/francois_houtart_belgium_and_abdul_sattar_edhi_pakistan_to_share_2009_unesco_madanjeet_singh_pr/.

146 *Agency for International Development, which provided grants*: One such grant was $1,050,000. Letter from Frederick A. Will, USAID, to Abdul Sattar Edhi, July 31, 1988. Published at: http://pdf.usaid.gov/pdf_docs/PDAAY301.pdf.

146 *American officials were dismayed*: According to U.S. official who served in Pakistan in the 1990s, interviewed July 2011.

146 *Bhutto paid rent for the helicopter, which she requested for travel because she was pregnant*: Interview by Amar Guriro with Anwar Kazmi of the Edhi Foundation, July 2011.

146 *"must be killed in the same way"*: from notes of Amar Guriro, one of the reporters at the press conference.

146 *a "dictator"*: All of Edhi's comments from interview, March 2010.

CHAPTER 10: EMERGENCY NUMBERS

148 *She directed about 240 hospital staff*: Interview with Seemin Jamali, March 2010.

148 *"It is difficult but it makes life easy"*: All Jamali's comments from interview, March 2010.

151 *The explosion killed eighteen people*: The Jinnah Postgraduate Medical Centre released a list of thirty dead, of whom twelve were believed to have been killed in the explosion at the march. "Unfazed Doctors Return to Jinnah Hospital," *Dawn*, February 6, 2010.

151 *"Two men were killed"*: *Dawn/News International*, www.karachipage.com/news/Oct_99/100899.html.

151 *"Dr Seemin Jamali, deputy director"*: *The Scotsman*, October 20, 2007.

152 *"In reply to a question"*: *Dawn*, January 29, 2008.

153 *"Some people decided" . . . "my ambulance was not touched"*: Interview with Abdul Sattar Edhi, March 2010.

154 *"Everybody was telling my father to leave the scene"*: Interview with Faisal Edhi, March 2010.

154 *"He was an old guy," . . . "When I looked back"*: Ibid.

154 *Raja Umer Khattab, senior superintendant of police*: Interview, May 2010.

156 *Khalid Sheikh Mohammed, . . . was involved*: Rohan Gunaratna and Khuram Iqbal, *Pakistan: Terrorism Ground Zero* (London: Reaktion, 2011), 179.

156 *sentenced to death*: "Death Penalty Awarded to 11 Activists of Jundullah Group in Corps Commander Attack Case," *Pakistan Tribune*, February 22, 2006.

156 *"started weeping"*: Trial record, 241.

156 *"in the name of Allah & the Holy Quran (Jahad)"*: Confession of Atta ur-Rehman, June 30, 2004.

156 *He was born in Karachi . . . radical groups:* Gunaratna and Iqbal, *Pakistan: Terrorism Ground Zero,* 181.

157 *"clash of civilizations"*: Interview, May 2010.

157 *He was, in short, a politician:* Interview with Assadullah Bhutto, May 2010.

158 *"his writings have penetrated every corner of Pakistan"*: Charles J. Adams, "The Ideology of Mawlana Mawdudi," in *South Asian Politics and Religion,* ed. Donald E. Smith (Princeton, NJ: Princeton University Press, 1966), 381.

158 *was picked up and intensified by . . . Sayyid Qutb:* Quentin Wiktorowicz, "A Genealogy of Radical Islam," *Studies in Conflict and Terrorism* 28 (2005): 78–79.

158 *"in deed, word, or mind"*: Ibid., 89.

158 *he later told me he'd never backed* that *far away:* Interview, July 2010.

159 *really did suffer from a heart condition . . . would be diagnosed with cancer:* Visit to Munir Ahmed Sheikh in a Karachi hospital, July 2010.

CHAPTER 11: AIRPORT ROAD

162 *the city government actually* did *want to move them:* An update on the long-standing plan to move the wholesale markets appears in a press release from the office of the governor of Sindh, Ishrat Ul Ebad Khan, an MQM leader, on January 6, 2011. http://www.governorsindh.gov.pk/pressrelease/news.asp?id=2558.

163 *He endorsed a demand:* E-mail exchange with Mustafa Kamal, March 18, 2010; also *Dawn,* January 2, 2010.

163 *"conspiracy theories"*: Geo TV, January 4, 2010.

163 *"The common citizen on the road"*: Interview with Mustafa Kamal, March 2008.

163 *marketing degree:* Ibid.

165 *"I would just like to interrupt"*: "Karachi Mayor Tries to Clean Up City, Politics," NPR News, June 3, 2008.

165 *By 2007 . . . 545 cars per day:* Urban Resource Centre, "Total no. of vehicles in Karachi up to 2007," www.urckarachi.org.

165 *Fatima Bhutto . . . said:* Interview with Fatima Bhutto, March 2008.

165 *"young and energetic Mustafa Kamal"*: Ardeshir Cowasjee, "To the Rescue of Kidney Hill," *Dawn,* January 13, 2008.

165 *"digs and digs gutters and roads"*: Ardeshir Cowasjee, "Karachi and Its Parks," *Dawn,* March 4, 2007.

166 *"I made my job harder!"*: Interview with Mustafa Kamal, May 2008.

166 *Mufti Naim . . . in minutes instead of hours:* Interview with Mufti Naim, March 2010.

166 *"enlarge the pie"*: Interview with U.S. government official, 2010.

166 *"We are cutting and pasting things"*: "Karachi Mayor Tries to Clean Up City, Politics," NPR News, June 3, 2008.

167 *"I curse all of Pakistan's leaders,"* . . . *"Son of an owl!"*: Geo TV, January 4, 2010.

168 *"There was . . . good reason to stay close to home"*: Mike Royko, *Boss: Richard J. Daley of Chicago* (New York: Penguin, 1971), 32.

168 *The Dan Ryan Expressway was routed to serve as a wall:* Adam Cohen and Elizabeth Taylor, *American Pharaoh: Mayor Richard J. Daley: His Battle for Chicago and the Nation* (New York: Warner, 2000), chapter 5.

168 *white suburbs on one side and diverse ones on the other:* "Chicago Segregation Increasing," NPR News, April 20, 1998.

169 *"language riots"*: Suhail Zaheer Lari, *An Illustrated History of Sindh* (Karachi: Heritage Foundation, 2002), 323–25.

169 *put up fortified gates at the edges of neighborhoods they controlled:* Azhar Hassan Nadeem, *Pakistan: The Political Economy of Lawlessness* (New York: Oxford University Press, 2002), 124.

169 *"There are no job opportunities"*: Interview with Mohammad Nader, May 2008.

170 *"Say your holy words,"* . . . *"He works for humanity":* As quoted by Mohammad Nader, interview, May 2008.

170–71 *"the MQM had blocked every possible exit"* . . . *"two layers of MQM-arranged cordons": Slate,* May 17, 2007.

171 *around forty people were killed:* The *New York Times,* May 13, 2007, reported thirty-nine killed; wire services said "more than 39"; in Karachi the figure is commonly given as forty-one.

171 *One of the dead was an Edhi ambulance driver:* "Edhi Driver Gunned Down in Malir," *Dawn,* May 13, 2007; also "Karachi Ambulance Driver Risks Life to Save Others," NPR News, June 2, 2008.

171 *MQM party workers could not reasonably be expected to stand aside:* Interview with Ishrat Ul Ebad Khan, May 2008.

171 *"I'm nobody!":* He said this frequently as I followed him in 2008.

172 *"I formed a student organization in 1978":* Interview with Altaf Hussain, May 2008.

173 *On Pakistan's Independence Day in 1979:* Oscar Verkaaik, *People of Migrants: Ethnicity, State and Religion in Karachi* (Nashville: Vanderbilt University Press, 1994), 1.

173 *"blackmailing and coercion":* Nadeem, *Pakistan: The Political Economy of Lawlessness,* 124.

173 *"His words were like magic"* . . . *"all those politicians":* The scholar withheld the activist's name for his safety; in her book she gives him the pseudonym Arshad. Nichola Khan, *Mohajir Militancy in Pakistan: Violence and Transformation in the Karachi Conflict* (London and New York: Routledge, 2010), chapter 1.

173 *A report by Amnesty International tracked the urban warfare:* Amnesty International, "Pakistan: Human Rights Crisis in Karachi," February 1, 1996. http://www.amnesty.org/en/library/info/ASA33/001/1996.

173 *agreed that many MQM workers were killed:* Interview with diplomat, 2008.

174 *police officers accused of targeting the MQM . . . were themselves murdered:* The *News International* published the text of an interior ministry report saying eighty-three officers involved in operations against the MQM were later murdered, and that "political parties, specially the MQM," had armed wings. The MQM said the report had no link with reality. *News International,* May 23, 2010.

174 *"I do not advocate violence":* Nichola Khan, "Violence, Anti-Convention and Desires for Transformation Amongst Pakistan's Mohajirs in Karachi," *Cultural Dynamics* 22, no. 3, (November 2010): 229.

174 *"They're not from one ethnic group":* Interview with Akbar S. Ahmed, January 2010.

177 *"ALL HELL BREAKS LOOSE IN CITY": Daily Times,* April 30, 2009.

179 *"extortion" and "gunnysack":* Interview with Shahi Syed, May 2010.

179 *"I don't want to start a fight here":* Geo TV, January 2010.

179 *"Everyone was sure the MQM set the fires":* Interview, July 2010.

CHAPTER 12: PARKS AND RECREATION

180 *She added up the number of dead:* Interview, May 2010.

182 *neighborhood erupted . . . Every business shut down:* "Gutter Baghicha Bachao Tehreek President's Murder: Baloch-Dominated Areas Remain Tense," *Daily Times,* November 9, 2009.

182 *People poured into the streets and blocked traffic:* Ibid.

182 *Men brought out guns and fired into the air:* Ibid.

182 *none of the men who ran the city or the province could make it:* Ibid.

182 *concluded that they should be elsewhere:* Ibid.

182 *"land grabbers"* . . . *"backed by an influential political outfit of the city":* Ibid.

182 *"an ethnic party":* " 'Ethnic Party' Blamed for Nisar Baloch Murder," *Dawn,* November 15, 2009.

183 *Except for a few paid staff, its members were volunteers:* Source: Shehri, 2008–10.

183 *an annual payment from the National Endowment for Democracy:* Interviews with officials from Shehri and National Endowment for Democracy. http://aiddata.org/project/show/34016464.

183 *"Well, obviously, to kill us":* Interview with Amber Alibhai, May 2008. "Amid Threats, Activist Fights Karachi Development," NPR News, June 4, 2008.

183 *"He told my husband"*: Ibid.

184 *the provincial governor . . . who later affirmed the story to me*: Interview with Governor Ishrat Ul Ebad Khan, May 2008.

184 *"Let me tell you"*: Interview with Amber Alibhai, May 2008. "Amid Threats, Activist Fights Karachi Development," NPR News, June 4, 2008.

184 *He taught at a public elementary school, and organized free computer classes*: Interviews with Amber Alibhai and Madiha Baloch, March 2010.

184 *some argued that the Baloch had always been here*: I heard this argument from a Baloch journalist in May 2008.

184 *"was a very happy person," . . . "saying the wrong thing" . . . "personal" . . . "vendettas"*: Interview with Amber Alibhai, March 2010.

185 *"We received the maps from the British Library"*: Ibid.

186 *"Karachi Municipal Corporation Sewage Farm"*: The 1962 map was in a city-produced pamphlet, "Municipal Corporation of the City of Karachi: Gateway to Pakistan." Library of Congress.

186 *"then we went into the area"*: Interview with Amber Alibhai, March 2010.

186 *"They were the eyes and ears"*: Ibid.

186 *In 2002 President Pervez Musharraf declared*: "Citizens Slam Delay in Work on Park: Gutter Baghicha," *Dawn*, October 19, 2003. Musharraf made the announcement on April 28, 2002.

186 *In a city map produced in 2005*: "History of Court Cases Against KMC Officers' Co-operative Housing Society, Karachi, C.D.G.K., Govt of Sindh & Others." Document produced by the City District Government of Karachi and given to the author in July 2010.

186 *satellite images showed the walkways taking shape*: Google images taken in 2010.

187 *"What happened was"*: All quotes from interview with Nasreen Jalil, July 2010.

188 *"I put my foot down and said I'm going to marry him"*: Interview with Madiha Baloch, March 2010.

189 *afterward they filed criminal charges*: "NGO Activists Booked for Violence," *Dawn*, August 27, 2009.

190 *In the summer of 2009, the environmental group Shehri filed a lawsuit*: Ahmed, Moinuddin, Nazir, "Report in Compliance of Court's Order," High Court of Sindh at Karachi, Suit No. 1484 of 2008, Ardeshir Cowasjee and 5 Others, Plaintiffs, C.D.G.K. and 4 Others, Defendants, September 2009.

190 *"with his freshly dyed Cherry Blossom hair"*: Ardeshir Cowasjee, "A Date Etched in Memory," *Dawn*, September 14, 2008.

190 *"To digress . . . "*: Ardeshir Cowasjee, "Bagh-i-Benazir & Diversions," *Dawn*, November 2, 2008.

191 *"I hate hypocrites"*: Interview with Ardeshir Cowasjee, July 2010.

191 *"What the few of us battling losers"*: Cowasjee, "A Date Etched in Memory."

192 *"At site approximate one thousand gents and ladies"*: Ahmed, Moinuddin, Nazir, "Report in Compliance of Court's Order," September 2009, 2.

192 *"There was [a] law and order situation"*: Ibid., 3.

192 *A map of the national park from 2005 . . . from 2009*: All sides, including the city, provided me with materials that included both maps. When I compared the two maps with a Google satellite image showing the national park under construction, it was evident that the national park design shown in the 2005 map could not possibly fit into the space that was designated for the park in 2009. The park had been made smaller.

193 *it was from the Edhis that Madiha received a newborn girl*: Interview with Madiha Baloch, March 2010.

193 *"He felt that everything would be lost"*: Interview with Amber Alibhai, March 2010.

194 *Haider acknowledged that all parties were involved in land grabbing*: Interview with Taj Haider, March 2010.

194 *"Gutter Baghicha is one place"*: Ibid.

194 *"the government's coalition partners" . . . "this is the largest land scam"*: "Chief Justice Save Karachi from Lawlessness and Land Grabbers—Nisar Baloch," *Daily Awam*, November 7, 2009.

195 *"They're going to take me now"*: Interview with Madiha Baloch, March 2010.

195 *He wanted to find what had been written about his press conference*: Ahmed Baloch statement to police, First Information Report (FIR), November 7, 2009.

195 *"I received information that Nisar faced an accident"*: Ibid.

195 *"Who will be next on the list?"*: Ardeshir Cowasjee, "Death of a Social Activist," *Dawn*, November 15, 2009.

195 *"Importantly, Nisar Baloch had criticized"*: "Another Activist Falls," *Daily Times*, November 10, 2009.

196 *"the right of the lesser mortals"*: Ibid.

196 *"I am sure Kamal was a good man"*: Interview with Amber Alibhai, March 2010.

196 *"In front of my eyes"*: Interview with Mustafa Kamal, March 2010.

196 *"I don't know"*: Interview with Nasreen Jalil, July 2010.

197 *And on this day, Nader Baloch was also killed:* "9 More Die as Karachi Bleeds," *The Nation*, January 8, 2010.

CHAPTER 13: PREMIER LIFESTYLES

199 *gunmen opened fire on a radical Sunni Muslim cleric . . . killed three other Sunni clerics:* "Three Sunni Muslim Clerics Killed in Pakistan," Reuters, March 12, 2010.

200–202 *Jabir Hussain Dada:* All quotes from interview, March 2010.

203–4 *Nadeem Riaz:* All quotes from interview, March 2010.

204 *Provincial environmental officials challenged the beachfront project:* **Dawn**, September 18, 2009.

205 *In 2008 the Malaysian developers said:* "CDGK to Fund $200m IT Tower Project," *Dawn*, October 5, 2008.

205 *"You're going to enter Southern California right now"*: Interview with Steve McCartt, May 2008. "Builders See Profit, Promise Along Karachi Coast," NPR News, June 6, 2008.

205 *"And where are you in the world?"*: Ibid.

206 *They were actually building an entire satellite city:* Philip Reeves, "Growing Pains in the Land of Bollywood," NPR News, July 16, 2008.

206 *a man-made island; an American firm was leading the project:* "New Songdo City: Atlantis of the Far East," *Independent*, June 22, 2009.

206 *Chinese officials brought in a Chilean planner:* Douglas Gray, "Pop-Up Cities: China Builds a Bright Green Metropolis," *Wired*, April 24, 2007.

206 *The rumor said that Karachi was about to become the new Hong Kong:* Laurent Gayer, "A Divided City: 'Ethnic' and 'Religious' Conflicts in Karachi, Pakistan," May 2003. http://www.ceri-sciencespo.com/archive/mai03/artlg.pdf.

207 *He believed that it was in response to his broadcasts:* Interview and e-mails with Baseer Naweed, November–December 2009.

208 *"Over here, basically, for failures, they want to hush it up"*: Interview with Adnan Asdar, May 2008.

209 *"6-star facilities"*: www.creekmarina.com.

210 *"They have night golf"*: Interview with Tariq Alexander Qaiser, May 2008.

210 *Ayesha Siddiqa had published a book:* Ayesha Siddiqa, *Military Inc.* (London and Ann Arbor, MI: Pluto Press, 2007).

211 *"Kids, bring the generator out"*: Interview with Adnan Asdar and Mahboob Khan, May 2008.

212 *"very idealistic," . . . "break even is fine"*: Interview with Zia-ul Islam, May 2010.

212 *"Whenever you give these as gifts"*: Interview with Adnan Asdar, May 2010.

214 *"When I came here three months ago, none of the walls were here"*: Ibid.

217 *"It was a wonderful design"*: Interview with Mumtaz Ahmed, May 2010.

CHAPTER 14: DREAMWORLD

219 *"I forced them"*: Interview with Afridi, March 2010.

220 *The ride cost about fourteen dollars:* Interview with Ali Akbar, bus company manager, March 2010.

221 *Waitresses and factory workers reluctantly returned:* Louisa Lim, "Unemployment Swells in China," NPR News, April 16, 2009.

222 *"What else can I do?"*: Interview with Mohammad Nader, March 2010.

224 *"The next generation will not be like this":* All quotes from interview with Abdul Sattar Edhi and Bilquis Edhi, March 2010.

228 *"Welcome to Dreamworld":* http://www.dreamworld.pk/.

229 *"When I came":* Interview, July 2010.

229 *a one-time lifetime membership fee . . . monthly maintenance fees:* Source: Michael Shahzad, manager, July 2010.

229 *Michael Shahzad:* Interview, July 2010.

231 *"I really love Karachi":* Interview with Azeira Channa, July 2010.

CHAPTER 15: BIRDS

235 *"America":* Interview with Mustafa Hussain Zaidi and Iqbal Zaidi, May 2010.

236 *Exactly two policemen were guarding the four terror suspects:* "Jundallah Frees Ashura Accused from Court," *Dawn,* June 20, 2010.

236–37 *managed to free all four:* Ibid.

237 *"if we find anyone guilty of negligence":* Ibid.

237 *By July he was fully restocked:* Visit to shop of Khalid Rashid, July 2010.

237 *money came from the U.S. Agency for International Development:* "U.S. Relief for Bolton Market Traders: $10 Million in Grants Assist Recovery of Riot," USAID press release, February 16, 2010. www.usaid.gov.

237 *and from the American Business Council:* Interview with Ikram Sehgal, security consultant for ABC disbursements, July 2010.

238 *"it doesn't matter" . . . "Every MQM activist will now be looking":* "Pakistan Violence: Sparked by Karachi's 300th Assassination This Year," *Christian Science Monitor,* August 3, 2010.

238 *"We have received 10 bodies with gunshot wounds":* "Karachi Burns in Wave of Violence," onepakistan.com, reprinting news agency reports, August 3, 2010.

239 *"Big changes are in the offing":* E-mail exchange with Arif Hasan, September 2010.

239 *The United Nations estimated Karachi's 2010 population at 13.1 million:* United Nations Population Division, *World Urbanization Prospects: The 2009 Revision Population Database,* http://esa .un.org/wup2009/unup/index.asp?panel=2.

239 *would grow to 16.7 million in 2020, and 18.7 million in 2025:* Ibid.

239 *encompassing around 36 million people:* Ibid.

239 *These smaller cities will encompass most of the world's urban growth:* UN-HABITAT, *The Challenge of Slums: Case Studies for the Global Report on Human Settlements* (London and Sterling, VA: Earthscan, 2003), 3.

242 *The program had to be put on hold:* "Anti-encroachment Drive Leaves Two Dead," *Dawn,* July 16, 2010.

242 *"suspended, demoted or transferred":* "Anti-encroachment Drive: 3 Police Officers Allegedly 'Punished' for Being Incorrupt," *Express Tribune,* December 29, 2010.

BIBLIOGRAPHY

BOOKS

Advani, L. K. *My Country, My Life.* Kolkata: Rupa & Co., 2008.

Ahmed, Akbar S. *Jinnah, Pakistan and Islamic Identity: The Search for Saladin.* London and New York: Routledge, 1997.

Ansari, Sarah. *Life After Partition: Migration, Community and Strife in Sindh, 1947–1962.* New York: Oxford University Press, 2005.

Asdar Ali, Kamran, and Martina Rieker, eds. *Comparing Cities: The Middle East and South Asia.* New York: Oxford University Press, 2009.

Baden-Powell, Robert. *Scouting for Boys.* Republished as *Scouting for Boys: The Original 1908 Edition.* New York: Oxford University Press, 2004.

Chandler, Tertius. *Four Thousand Years of Urban Growth: An Historical Census.* Dyfed, Wales: Mellen House, 1987.

Cohen, Adam, and Elizabeth Taylor. *American Pharaoh: Mayor Richard J. Daley: His Battle for Chicago and the Nation.* New York: Warner, 2000.

Cohen, Stephen Philip. *The Idea of Pakistan.* Washington, D.C.: Brookings Institution Press, 2004.

Davis, Mike. *Planet of Slums.* London and New York: Verso, 2006.

Doxiadis, Constantinos. *Between Dystopia and Utopia.* Hartford, CT: Trinity College Press, 1966.

Edhi, Abdul Sattar, and Tehmina Durrani. *A Mirror to the Blind.* Karachi: Edhi Foundation, 1996.

Garratt, G. T. *The Legacy of India.* Oxford: Oxford University Press, 1937.

Glaeser, Edward. *Triumph of the City: How Our Greatest Invention Makes Us Richer, Smarter, Greener, Healthier, and Happier.* New York: Penguin, 2011.

Gottmann, Jean. *Megalopolis: The Urbanized Northeastern Seaboard of the United States.* Cambridge, MA: MIT Press, 1961.

Guha, Ramachandra. *India After Gandhi: The History of the World's Largest Democracy.* New York: HarperCollins, 2007.

Gunaratna, Rohan, and Iqbal Khuram. *Pakistan: Terrorism Ground Zero.* London: Reaktion, 2011.

Hasan, Arif. *Understanding Karachi.* Karachi: City Press, 1999.

———. *The Unplanned Revolution.* New York: Oxford University Press, 2009.

Herman, Arthur. *Gandhi and Churchill: The Epic Rivalry That Destroyed an Empire and Forged Our Age.* New York: Bantam, 2008.

Husain, Rumana. *Karachiwala: A Subcontinent Within a City.* Karachi: Jaal, 2010.

Ispahani, M. A. H. *Qaid-e Azam As I Knew Him.* Karachi: Forward Publications, 1966.

Jacobs, Jane. *The Economy of Cities.* New York: Random House, 1969.

Khan, Akhtar Hameed. *Orangi Pilot Project: Reminiscences and Reflections.* Karachi: Oxford University Press, 1996.

Khan, Nichola. *Mohajir Militancy in Pakistan: Violence and Transformation in the Karachi Conflict.* London and New York: Routledge, 2010.

Khan, Roedad. *Pakistan: A Dream Gone Sour.* New York: Oxford University Press, 1997.

Khan, Yasmin. *The Great Partition: The Making of India and Pakistan.* New Haven, CT: Yale University Press, 2007.

Khuhro, Hamida, and Anwer Mooraj. *Karachi: Megacity of Our Times.* Karachi: Oxford University Press, 1997.

Kibel, Paul Stanton, ed. *Rivertown: Rethinking Urban Rivers.* Cambridge, MA, and London: MIT Press, 2007.

Kotkin, Joel. *The City: A Global History.* New York: Modern Library, 2006.

Kux, Dennis. *The United States and Pakistan, 1947–2000: Disenchanted Allies.* Washington, DC: Woodrow Wilson Center Press / Baltimore: John Hopkins University Press, 2001.

Lamb, Christina. *Waiting for Allah: Benazir Bhutto and Pakistan.* London and New York: Penguin, 1992.

Lari, Suhail Zaheer. *An Illustrated History of Sindh.* Karachi: Heritage Foundation, 2002.

Lari, Yasmeen, and Mihail S. Lari. *The Dual City: Karachi During the Raj.* Karachi: Oxford University Press, 2001.

Menon, Ritu, and Kamla Bhasin. *Borders and Boundaries: Women in India's Partition.* New Brunswick, NJ: Rutgers University Press, 1998.

Merchant, Liaquat, and Sharif Mujahid. *The Jinnah Anthology.* Oxford University Press, Karachi, 1999.

Nadeem, Azhar Hassan. *Pakistan: The Political Economy of Lawlessness.* New York: Oxford University Press, 2002.

Nasr, Vali. *The Shia Revival: How Conflicts Within Islam Will Shape the Future.* New York: W. W. Norton, 2006.

———. *The Vanguard of the Islamic Revolution: The Jama'at-I Islami of Pakistan.* Berkeley: University of California Press, 1994.

Neuwirth, Robert. *Shadow Cities: A Billion Squatters, a New Urban World.* New York: Routledge, 2006.

Orangi Pilot Project–Research and Training Institute. *Katchi Abadis of Karachi,* vol. III. Karachi: OPP-RTI, 2009.

Owen, David. *Green Metropolis: Why Living Smaller, Living Closer, and Driving Less are Keys to Sustainability.* New York: Riverhead, 2009.

Raman, T. A. *Report on India.* New York: Oxford University Press, 1943.

Richter, Linda K. *The Politics of Tourism in Asia.* Honolulu: University of Hawaii Press, 1989.

Royko, Mike. *Boss: Richard J. Daley of Chicago.* New York: Penguin, 1971.

Schmidle, Nicholas. *To Live or to Perish Forever: Two Tumultuous Years in Pakistan.* New York: Henry Holt, 2009.

Sharma, M. S. M. *Peeps into Pakistan.* Patna: Pustak Bhandar, 1954.

Siddiqa, Ayesha. *Military Inc.: Inside Pakistan's Military Economy.* London and Ann Arbor, MI: Pluto Press, 2007.

Smith, Donald E., ed. *South Asian Politics and Religion.* Princeton, NJ: Princeton University Press, 1966.

Sorensen, Andrei. *The Making of Urban Japan: Cities and Planning from Edo to the Twenty-first Century.* New York: Routledge, 2002.

Sperling, Daniel, and Deborah Gordon. *Two Billion Cars: Driving Toward Sustainability.* New York: Oxford University Press, 2009.

Tsang, Steve. *A Modern History of Hong Kong.* London: I. B. Tauris, 2004.

Verkaaik, Oskar. *People of Migrants: Ethnicity, State and Religion in Karachi.* Nashville: Vanderbilt University Press, 1994.

Wolpert, Stanley. *Jinnah of Pakistan.* New York: Oxford University Press, 1984.

———. *Zulfi Bhutto of Pakistan: His Life and Times.* New York: Oxford University Press, 1993.

REPORTS, SPEECHES, AND SCHOLARSHIP

Ahmed, Lt. Col. N. "Report on Urban Construction Survey in Karachi 1963," 1964. Library of Congress, Washington, DC.

Ahmed, Moinuddin, Nazir. "Report in Compliance of Court's Order." High Court of Sindh at Karachi, Suit No. 1484 of 2008, Ardeshir Cowasjee and 5 Others, Plaintiffs, C.D.G.K. and 4 Others, Defendants, September 2009.

Ali Budhani, Azmat Haris Gazdar, Sobia Ahmad Kaker, and Hussain Bux Mallah. "The Open City: Social Networks and Violence in Karachi." Collective for Social Science Research, 2010.

Amnesty International. "Pakistan: Human Rights Crisis in Karachi." February 1, 1996. http://www.amnesty.org/en/library/info/ASA33/001/1996.

City District Government of Karachi. "History of Court Cases Against KMC Officers' Co-operative Housing Society, Karachi, C.D.G.K., Govt of Sindh & Others."

Daechsel, Markus. "Sovereignty, Governmentality and Development in Ayub's Pakistan: The Case of Korangi Township." *Modern Asian Studies* 45 (2011): 131–57.

Deshpande, S. R. "Report on an Enquiry into the Family Budgets of Industrial Workers in Karachi." Rawalpindi: Government of India, 1946.

Doxiadis Associates. "Confidential: Greater Karachi Resettlement Programme, Weaknesses and Problems," 1961. Ford Foundation archives.

———. "Islamabad the Capital of Pakistan," undated.

Ford Foundation. "Design for Pakistan: A Report on Assistance to the Pakistan Planning Commission by the Ford Foundation and Harvard University." New York: Ford Foundation, February 1965.

Gayer, Laurent. "A Divided City: 'Ethnic' and 'Religious' Conflicts in Karachi, Pakistan." Sciences Po, Paris, May 2003. http://www.ceri-sciencespo.com/archive/mai03/artlg.pdf.

Government of Pakistan. "White Paper on the Performance of the Bhutto Regime, Vol. I." Islamabad: Government of Pakistan, 1979.

Green, Leslie, and Vincent Malone. "Urbanization in Nigeria: A Planning Commentary." *International Urban Survey*. New York: Ford Foundation, 1972 or 1973 (date unclear).

Hasan, Arif. *Understanding Karachi*. Karachi: City Press, 1999.

Hasan, Arif, and Masooma Mohib. "The Case of Karachi, Pakistan," p. 3, from UN-HABITAT, *The Challenge of Slums: Case Studies for the Global Report on Human Settlements 2003*. London and Sterling, VA: Earthscan, 2003. http://www.ucl.ac.uk/dpu-projects/Global_Report/pdfs/Karachi.pdf.

Human Rights Commission of Pakistan. "Karachi—Brief Report on Aushora Incident on 28th December 2009." Karachi, January 9, 2010.

Investment Advisory Centre of Pakistan. "Socio-economic Survey of Karachi, Part I." Karachi-Dacca, August 1971.

Khan, Ghulam Farid, "Identification of Attitudes of Juggi-Dwellers Living in Jacob Lines Towards Korangi Township." Thesis, Graduate School of Ekistics, Karachi, October 1970.

Khan, Nichola. "Violence, Anti-Convention and Desires for Transformation Amongst Pakistan's Mohajirs in Karachi." *Cultural Dynamics* 22, no. 3 (November 2010): 225–45.

Masud, Mohammad O. "IDS Working Paper 172: Co-producing Citizen Security: The Citizen-Police Liaison Committee in Karachi." Brighton, Sussex, England: Institute of Development Studies, 2002.

Maududi, Abul A'La. "Jihad in Islam," 1939 speech reprinted by International Islamic Federation of Student Organizations, Salimiah, Kuwait.

———. "System of Government Under the Holy Prophet (with discussion of the method of implementing it in Pakistan today)." Lahore: Islamic Publications, 1978.

Morrison, Peter. "Migration from Distressed Areas: Its Meaning for Regional Policy." New York: Ford Foundation, 1973.

Salimullah, Chaudry. "A Study of the Various House Types Constructed for the Low Income People at Korangi." Thesis, Graduate School of Ekistics, Karachi, 1962.

UN-HABITAT. *The Challenge of Slums: Global Report on Human Settlements 2003*. London and Sterling, VA: Earthscan, 2003.

———. *State of the World's Cities 2010/2011: Bridging the Urban Divide*. London and Sterling, VA: Earthscan, 2008.

United Nations Development Program. "Pakistan National Human Development Report, 2003." http://www.un.org.pk/nhdr/htm_pages/cp_1.htm.

United Nations Population Division. *World Urbanization Prospects: The 2009 Revision Population Database.* http://esa.un.org/wup2009/unup/index.asp?panel=2.

Urban Resource Centre. "Total no. of vehicles in Karachi up to 2007." www.urckarachi.org.

Wiktorowicz, Quentin. "A Genealogy of Radical Islam." *Studies in Conflict and Terrorism* 28 (2005): 75–97.

Winthrop, Rebecca, and Corinne Graf. "Beyond Madrasas: Assessing the Links Between Education and Militancy in Pakistan." Washington, DC: Center for Universal Education, Brookings Institution, 2010.

ARCHIVED MATERIALS

Archives of Constantinos Doxiadis, Doxiadis Associates, Athens, Greece.

Daily Gazette (Karachi), 1944–1949. Library of Congress, Washington, DC.

Dawn, 1947–present. Library of Congress, Washington, DC.

Disclosure reports collected by the Charity Commission (UK), www.charitycommission.gov.uk.

Disclosure reports collected by the New York State office of the Attorney General, www.charitiesnys.com.

Edward Durell Stone Papers, University of Arkansas Libraries, Fayetteville, AK.

Ford Foundation Archives, New York, NY.

Foreign Relations of the United States, 1955–57, vol. VIII, *South Asia.* Washington, DC: U.S. Government Printing Office, 1987. Also online: http://digicoll.library.wisc.edu/FRUS/Search.html.

———. *1958–60,* vol. XV, *South and Southeast Asia.* Washington, DC: U.S. Government Printing Office, 1992. Also online: http://digicoll.library.wisc.edu/FRUS/Search.html.

NPR News Archives, www.npr.org.

Sind Observer, 1944–1950. Library of Congress, Washington, DC.

Times of Karachi, 1955–1959. Library of Congress, Washington, DC.

CURRENT PAKISTANI NEWSPAPERS FREQUENTLY CITED

Daily Awam
Daily Times
Dawn
Express Tribune
The Nation
The News International/Jang

INDEX

Page numbers in *italics* refer to photo captions.